AIR POWER 21
CHALLENGES FOR THE NEW CENTURY

Edited by
Peter W Gray

Defence Studies (Royal Air Force)
Directorate Air Staff
Ministry of Defence
Whitehall
LONDON
SW1A 2HB

LONDON: THE STATIONERY OFFICE

© Crown Copyright 2000
Published with the permission of the
Ministry of Defence on behalf of the
Controller of Her Majesty's Stationery Office

Applications for reproduction should be made in writing to The Copyright Unit, Her Majesty's Stationery Office, St. Clements House, 2-16 Colegate, Norwich NR3 1BQ

ISBN 0 11 772960 4

Published by The Stationery Office and available from:

The Stationery Office
(mail, telephone and fax orders only)
PO Box 29, Norwich NR3 1GN
Telephone orders/General enquiries 0870 600 5522
Fax orders 0870 600 5533

www.thestationeryoffice.com

The Stationery Office Bookshops
123 Kingsway, London WC2B 6PQ 020 7242 6393 Fax 020 7242 6412
68-69 Bull Street, Birmingham B4 6AD 0121 236 9696 Fax 0121 236 9699
33 Wine Street, Bristol BS1 2BQ 0117 926 4306 Fax 0117 929 4515
9-21 Princess Street, Manchester M60 8AS 0161 834 7201 Fax 0161 833 0634
16 Arthur Street, Belfast BT1 4GD 028 9023 8451 Fax 028 9023 5471
The Stationery Office Oriel Bookshop 18-19 High Street, Cardiff CF1 2BZ
029 2039 5548 Fax 029 2038 4347
71 Lothian Road, Edinburgh EH3 9AZ 0870 606 5566 Fax 0870 606 5588

The Stationery Office's Accredited Agents
(see Yellow Pages)
and through good booksellers

FOREWORD

By the Chief of the Air Staff
Air Chief Marshal Sir Peter Squire
KCB DFC AFC ADC FRAeS RAF

With the heritage of less than a century's worth of powered flight, air power has progressed from the canvas and wire aircraft of *Sagittarius Rising* to the very limits of space and beyond, with characteristics that make it the force of first choice. I have little doubt that the next century will be even more demanding in terms of the rate of progress facing this and the next generation of airmen and air power thinkers. This book *Air Power 21: Challenges for the New Century* contributes to the debate that will be absolutely essential if we are to manage successfully the pace of change. It is the most recent product of a series of air power workshops that have been running since 1994. Its predecessors, *The Dynamics of Air Power* and *Perspectives on Air Power* represented significant contributions to our thinking on contemporary air power. I believe that this volume is a worthy successor.

The scope of the book ranges from the thorny issues of political limitations on military intervention to a re-evaluation of air power in the so-called Revolution in Military Affairs. All of the chapters are both topical and relevant to the tasks facing us in the new century. I am most grateful to the academics, analysts and military officers who have freely given their spare (and not so spare) time to the completion of this book. I would not expect everyone to agree with all of their sentiments or with the views expressed. Nor should the opinions be taken as representing the views of the Ministry of Defence or Royal Air Force policy.

One of the primary aims of the Workshop and its product is to stimulate healthy debate among air power theorists, practitioners and commentators. I also commend it to all involved in Joint and Combined operations and to those who contribute to the wider arena of policy formulation.

CONTENTS

Title	Page
Foreword	iii
Contents	v
Glossary	vii
Acknowledgements	ix
Introduction	xi

Chapter 1	Air Power and Military Intervention: The Political Limitations *Professor Michael Clarke*	1
Chapter 2	Air Power: The Instrument of Choice? *Doctor David Gates*	23
Chapter 3	Air Power and the Revolution in Military Affairs *Wing Commander David Caddick*	41
Chapter 4	Air Strategy and the Underdog *Professor Philip Sabin*	69
Chapter 5	European Air Power *Sir Timothy Garden*	99
Chapter 6	The Airmen's Dilemma: To Command or to Control? *Air Commodore Stuart Peach*	123
Chapter 7	The Land/Air Interface: An Historical Perspective *Brigadier Mungo Melvin*	153
Chapter 8	Air Power and Expeditionary Warfare *Doctor Christina Goulter*	183
Chapter 9	Rethinking the Conceptual Framework *Professor Tony Mason*	209
Biographies		237

GLOSSARY

AAA	Anti-Aircraft Artillery
AASF	Advanced Air Striking Force
AEF	Aerospace Expeditionary Force
ASUW	Anti-Surface Warfare
ASW	Anti-Submarine Warfare
ATAF	Allied Tactical Air Force
ATO	Air Tasking Order
AWACS	Airborne Warning and Control System
BDA	Battle Damage Assessment
CAOC	Combined Air Operations Centre
CID	Committee for Imperial Defence
COMAO	Composite Air Operations
COTS	Commercial Off-The-Shelf
CSAR	Combat Search and Rescue
C4ISR	Command, Control, Communications, Computers, Intelligence, Surveillance and Reconnaissance
DCA	Defensive Counter Air
DCI	Defence Capabilities Initiative
EU	European Union
FRY	Federal Republic of Yugoslavia
GDP	Gross Domestic Product
GPS	Global Positing System
HUMINT	Human Intelligence
JFACC	Joint Force Air Component Commander
JFC	Joint Force Commander
JSTARS	Joint Surveillance and Target Attack Radar System
KLA	Kosovo Liberation Army
MOD	Ministry of Defence
MPA	Maritime Patrol Aircraft
MTR	Military Technical Revolution
NATO	North Atlantic Treaty Organisation
NGO	Non Governmental Organisation
OSCE	Organisation for Security and Cooperation in Europe
PGM	Precision Guided Munition
PSO	Peace Support Operation
RMA	Revolution in Military Affairs
ROE	Rules of Engagement

SACEUR	Supreme Allied Commander Europe
SAM	Surface to Air Missile
SDR	Strategic Defence Review
SEAD	Suppression of Enemy Air Defences
SSN	Nuclear-powered Attack Submarine
TBM	Theatre Ballistic Missile
UAV	Uninhabited Aerial Vehicle or Unmanned Aerial Vehicle
UN	United Nations
USAAF	United States Army Air Force
WEU	Western European Union
WMD	Weapons of Mass Destruction

ACKNOWLEDGEMENTS

First and foremost, I would like to thank not only each of the authors for taking time from their pressing schedules and other duties to contribute their essays but also for engaging fully in the workshop process of developing ideas and stimulating debate. My thanks go also to Air Commodore Stu Peach who, as the previous Director of Defence Studies (RAF), started the series of Air Power Workshops which culminated with this publication. I also wish to thank Wing Commander Philip Greville for assisting in the editing process and for acting as the project manager. Many thanks also to Squadron Leader Alan Riches for carrying out the duties of Secretary to the Air Power Workshops and for undertaking the arduous task of final proof-reading. I am most grateful for help and support in providing many of the photographs to the Ministry of Defence, Air Historical Branch (RAF), Defence Intelligence Photography Department of the Defence Intelligence Staff and to the Directorate of Corporate Communications (RAF). Thanks also to Sue Hutchinson for her efficiency in dealing with the countless day-to-day tasks in support of this project. Production of the book would not have been possible without the assistance of Mr Mike Skinner and his team in Media Services, Training Group Defence Agency at RAF Innsworth. The cover photograph was provided by the Photographic Section, BAE Systems, Warton Aerodrome.

INTRODUCTION
By Group Captain Peter W Gray, Director of Defence Studies (Royal Air Force)

Air Power 21 - Challenges for the new Century is the product of the Chief of the Air Staff's Air Power Workshop; this consists of an ad hoc collection of leading academics and senior military officers. The chapters represent the leading edge of air power thinking in the United Kingdom based on detailed research and enhanced by considerable operational experience. The authors have shown how air power thinking has developed over the last decade in particular, but have not fallen into the 'comfort zone' of pretending that history only started in 1990 after the fall of the Berlin Wall and just before the Gulf War. Many of the lessons of history, even over the relatively short span of air warfare, remain valid and germane; we ignore the voices from the past at our peril as we will only have to relearn their message painfully. Where lessons have been drawn from history, these have been carefully selected to be relevant especially where the writings of strategists have been cited - just because Clausewitz said 'X' or Sun Tzu said 'Y', they were neither necessarily right, nor need their aphorisms be pertinent to modern warfare. At the other end of the spectrum, lessons emerging from the aftermath of the air operations over Kosovo and continuing fighting in Chechnya have been incorporated.

Beyond the self-evident theme of air power, several factors are common through this book. The first of these is the significant changes brought about by the collapse of communism and the concomitant demise of the Warsaw Pact. This removal of the threat brought with it the inevitable calls for so-called 'peace dividends' which, in many cases, were little more than treasury-inspired demolitions of national military capabilities. Only in a very few cases were cuts based on serious analytical work. Had such an examination taken place, it would almost certainly have indicated a need for caution somewhat akin to allowing steam to escape gradually from a pressure cooker. As the constraints imposed on world order by the ever-present risk of superpower confrontation were loosened it was inevitable that conflict would flare and that elements of the international community would have less hesitation than hitherto in responding with force. It is axiomatic that military forces that had spent two generations configured for war against a monolithic threat would take a finite period of time to adapt their structures to the new world order. In such an era of change, the flexibility and versatility of air power ensured that it would inevitably take its place in the vanguard of any action.

The Gulf War and subsequent operations over northern and southern Iraq have ensured that air power - at least for the United States and Britain - has been in constant operational use rather than just constant readiness. The political appetite for intervention as a force for good in the world has meant that readiness to respond has had to be maintained at high levels in those countries that have a desire for expeditionary operations. There is an immediate tension, however, between the competing resource demands on maintaining forces in operation theatres, having units at high readiness to deploy and having the assets with which to move them. Rather than a peace dividend there is arguably a case for a surcharge!

The financial pressures have inevitably been exacerbated by the rate of change of technology over the last decade - the so-called revolution in military affairs (RMA). This important area is another common theme through the book and is the subject of a chapter in its own right. The other side of this particular coin is the dilemma facing every nation that purports to have a role on the world stage - how much of the 'revolution' can we afford to join? To complicate matters this applies as much, if not more, to the non-state actors who could and do have a major impact on international affairs. The days of a relatively finely balanced arms race between two superpower-dominated alliances seem balmy in comparison with the proliferation of weapons of mass destruction and the risk of asymmetric warfare. This again is both a common theme and one that has generated its own chapter.

The role of the media in society at large, in the conduct of international affairs in general and in the trouble spots of the world has always generated debate and controversy. We would be wrong to suppose that concern over media influence and involvement is a new phenomenon. Investigative reporters roamed the battlefields of Balaclava to the chagrin of many. During World War I, The Times newspaper reported that a lack of shells was 'a fatal bar to success'. The ensuing uproar resulted in the formation of a Ministry of Munitions. A generation later, Beaverbrook's campaign for a second front did little to help Churchill's equanimity.

It is also a truism worth stating that political sensitivity to public opinion is not new either. The manifestations may vary, but the importance of these factors is so great that the Commander ignores, or mishandles, them at his peril. The issue of open and informed debate is important; when conflict is enjoined in the direct defence of the nation, scope for debate is limited. Conversely, the less tangible the national interests that are at stake, the more the actions of the government are open to question. This can be done through the democratic process in Parliament or Congress. Or the debate can be conducted through the media - whether this is the printed press or TV/radio.

During the Gulf War, there was considerable debate within the American press as to the likely scale of US casualties in the event of a ground war meeting serious opposition. The media was also used as the debating ground between the exponents of the land war versus the air war[1]. A similar theme developed at an early stage of the Kosovo air

---

1. See Dr Richard P Hallion, *Storm over Iraq; Air Power and the Gulf War* (Smithsonian, 1992) page 145 etc. See also the graphic cartoons on this debate in the plates to Hallion's book.

operations involving numerous pundits and retired senior officers. How much influence these debates had either on the public or, more importantly, on the decision-makers is inevitably hard to quantify. There can, however, be little doubt that all arms of the media occasionally descend into a self-feeding frenzy where the generation of column-inches and audience ratings is of more concern than the dispute at hand. Sensationalism becomes the norm with accuracy, balance and debate the first casualties. Or at least this is how the majority of military audiences see the media. The verisimilitude of this viewpoint is, however, barely relevant. What actually counts is the real power of the media to change the direction of events. This again is impossible to quantify, leaving us with arguably the key question of influence. This can be exercised through editorial comment; inclusion or removal of a topic from the agenda; opinion polling or just the 'spin' that a given organ of the press gives to a story. What really counts is the sensitivity of the political/military leadership to what is being said and to a lesser extent by whom.

The supposed glamour of air power has always had its special appeal for the press, not least because of its photogenic nature. Professor Michael Clarke covers this in his chapter on *Air Power and Military Intervention: The Political Limitations*. In terms of the political context within which decisions are made, Professor Clarke highlights the difference between what a computer or a planning team would advise versus the intuitive judgements of the political (or military) leadership. These judgements, particularly of what is at stake, will be based on instincts, values and culture. No matter what the frustrations, those charged with the conduct of military operations must accept the reality that perceptions are all-important and that they can change rapidly. [Churchill's 'before and after' attitudes to the bombing of Dresden are an excellent example from history of this scope for change of attitudes.] As if coping with changing perceptions was not difficult enough, having to do so in times of rapid inherent change is all the more difficult. As Professor Clarke admits in his conclusion, air power analysts may be forgiven for feeling victimised by the contradictions of the current era.

Parallel contradictions are immediately evident in Dr David Gates's chapter on *Air Power: The Instrument of Choice*? Dr Gates highlights the dangers of the advocates of air power achieving their nirvana - the state of bliss in which air power can achieve political goals without the involvement of land or maritime forces. The risk, of course, is that they are called upon to do so in circumstances that require the synergy of joint forces acting together. Dr Gates goes on to discuss the risk of the United States' technological supremacy resulting in potential opponents seeking asymmetric responses including the proliferation of missile technology.

The place of air power in an age of rapid technological change is addressed by Wing Commander David Caddick in his chapter entitled *Air Power and the Revolution in Military Affairs*. Wing Commander Caddick enters the lists with a valuable debate on the definition of RMA with particular emphasis on the revolutionary aspects of the change. He situates the RMA within its contemporary and United States settings before going on to look at the role of air power as an essential component thereof. The American aspect of this debate is critical - not least because much of the academic output on the subject hails from there. Wing Commander Caddick leaves us to ponder the unponderable: does the so-called revolution exist, or is it merely wishful thinking?

The huge lead, particularly in air power capabilities, that the United States has developed will inevitably increase the risk of asymmetric response. Not only is asymmetry a serious problem per se, but it is exacerbated by the extra resources that could be diverted should no attempt be made to develop even a token response. Professor Philip Sabin's chapter, *Air Strategy and the Underdog*, looks at the options open for those who are potentially on the receiving end of air dominance. These range from limiting vulnerability through fostering restraint to generating the ability to strike back. Professor Sabin also describes the difficulty facing all sides in cobbling together advantages into some form of coherent strategy.

The issue of US dominance also applies amongst allies. In *European Air Power*, Air Marshal Sir Timothy Garden highlights the comparative wealth of the European Union which is out of proportion to the military capabilities that the member states are prepared to deploy. Air Marshal Garden points out the force structure implications of numbers of ground forces versus other arms; he also looks at the imbalance of air defence fighters over offensive aircraft and highlights the shortfalls in combat support aircraft. He goes on to argue that this latter area has the most potential for early co-operation with an airlift capability as a prime contender. Combat Search and Rescue and air-to-air refuelling could then follow before the more problematic areas of offensive aircraft were addressed.

It is, however, not sufficient to purchase or lease specific capabilities. Allowance has to be made for how the assets will be deployed and by whom they will be commanded and controlled. In his chapter entitled *The Airmen's Dilemma: To Command or to Control*, Air Commodore Stuart Peach has provided a stark reminder that the theory of both command and control may be far removed from the practical aspects. Air Commodore Peach draws on examples from the advent of air power in the First World War onwards. His comments on more recent operations strip away much of the gloss with valuable assessments on air operations over former Yugoslavia.

The value of the historical perspective is carried on by Brigadier Mungo Melvin whose chapter *The Land/Air Interface: An Historical Perspective* 'looks forward from the past and its lessons'. The theme of command and control is moved on from air operations into the joint arena with an emphasis on where the scope for friction in the joint battlespace of the future can be eradicated. Brigadier Melvin highlights the role of people in reducing this friction. This may seem obvious, but history is littered with examples of well-equipped forces whose training and doctrine have matched their operational needs, only to be let down by unseemly squabbles at the highest levels.

The joint arena is completed with a chapter from Dr Christina Goulter on *Air Power and Expeditionary Warfare*. She reaffirms that air power must never be so tightly defined as to omit naval aviation whether carrier borne or otherwise. The advent of Joint Force Harrier and the decision to order two new carriers is testimony to UK commitment in this area. Dr Goulter adds to the debate on the future potential of this force. Among the threats posed to a Joint Task Force, Dr Goulter highlights the dangers from diesel submarines - especially in the littoral and en route to the area of operations.

In the final chapter, *Rethinking the Conceptual Framework*, Air Vice-Marshal Professor Tony Mason looks at the inheritance of air power and how air power thinking has had to evolve over the last decade to cope with the multiplicity of potential conflicts. He stresses that doctrine and conceptual thinking must escape from the realms of dogma if it is to reach its full potential in the new century. This is indeed a challenge worthy of the name.

CHAPTER 1

AIR POWER AND MILITARY INTERVENTION: THE POLITICAL LIMITATIONS
Professor Michael Clarke

IN THE LAST DECADE AIR POWER has enjoyed an increasingly upbeat image which appeared to reach its zenith in the Kosovo operation of March - June 1999. John Warden's analysis in *The Air Campaign*, published in 1988, appears to have been confirmed by practice, in a growing trend described in 1999 as the 'High Noon of Air Power'.[1] The turn of the century seems to have ushered in the mature age of military air power as the high-tech air forces, primarily of the Western allies, have enjoyed the relative political freedom of the post-Cold War world to demonstrate their strengths. But such relative political freedom comes at a price, and after a decade of impressive air operations we are in a better position now to analyse the general political constraints under which modern - particularly high-tech - air power operates.

A PATTERN OF DOMINANCE

The benefits to be derived from such evident air superiority as the Western Allies and, to an extent, Russia have enjoyed since the end of the Cold War have been well demonstrated throughout the 1990s in a succession of varied military operations (See Figure 1.1). In the Kuwait case - the Gulf War of 1990-91 - a massive and co-ordinated multinational air campaign quickly and effectively suppressed the air force of what was claimed by the Pentagon to be the fourth largest military power in the world.[2] In Somalia from 1992-1995 and in Haiti in 1994 the dominance of US air power was a critical element in the military equation, notwithstanding the losses in the Somalia operations which did so much to turn US opinion against continued involvement[3]. During the prolonged Bosnian Crisis from 1991-1995, Bosnian Serb and Yugoslav air forces were

---

1. John A Warden III, *The Air Campaign* (London: Brassey's, 1989). Alan Stephens, 'High Noon of Air Power', *Air Power Review* 2 (2), Summer 1999, p. 1-23.
2. This was not quite true, but Iraqi military capabilities were nevertheless genuinely 'substantial'. See L Freedman and E Karsh, *The Gulf Conflict 1990-1991* (London: Faber, 1993) p. 279.
3. See Karin von Hippel, *Democracy By Force: US Military Intervention in the Post-Cold War World*(Cambridge: Cambridge University Press, 2000).

AIR POWER AND MILITARY INTERVENTION: THE POLITICAL LIMITATIONS

effectively contained to the point that the Western Allies had complete dominance of the relevant airspace in support of their evolving military objectives, and since the adoption of a more muscular approach by the Western powers towards driving and maintaining a political settlement in Bosnia after February 1995, air power has been used in that country in a wide variety of roles, from outright coercion to the delivery of humanitarian aid.[4] Russian military operations against Chechen secessionists from December 1999 also demonstrated the stark importance of controlling the airspace above any military operation, whether it be all-out war, counter-insurgency or other forms of military operations short of war. The Russian air operation in the Chechen war of 1994-96 was critical and its lack of success was one of the keys to the military failures of that campaign in general.[5] In 1999 Russian planners appeared to have learned many of the technical air power lessons of their earlier campaign, if not the political ones. The Russian ground offensive of December 1999 was preceded by a week-long air bombardment, and then continued with a series of air-to-ground attacks that appeared to be designed both to offer tactical air support as well as performing a brutal coercive role against civilians, given that it was used so indiscriminately.[6]

Above all, the Kosovo crisis of 1999 seemed to demonstrate the capabilities of air power at their most mature. Some 38,000 sorties where flown during the period 24 March - 10 June (30% of which were strike sorties), around 700 Yugoslav SAMs were launched - or locked onto - Allied aircraft, and no Allied pilots became casualties, despite the loss of 2 aircraft.[7] The eventual acquiescence on the part of Slobodan Milosevic to NATO's demands after a 78-day aerial campaign appeared to offer the supreme example of air power as a safe, high-tech and successful military instrument in its own right. Allied air forces had conducted both a coercive air campaign against the Serbian leadership and a campaign of denial from the air against Yugoslav Army and Special Forces in Kosovo. Given that Allied leaders considered the campaign to be strategically successful, the use of air power in this crisis might be regarded not just as a prerequisite to a victorious ground force campaign, but in fact as a substitute for it.[8] This air campaign allowed a 'permissive' entry of ground forces into Kosovo in what might otherwise have been an extremely hostile environment. If air power in the Gulf War had achieved much in 'preparing the battlefield' for ground forces, then air power in Kosovo seemed to have

---

4. See Part II Essays 'Air Power in Peace Support Operations', in A Lambert and A Williamson, eds, *The Dynamics of Air Power* (Bracknell: RAF Staff College, 1996).
5. Timothy L Thomas, 'Air Operations in Low Intensity Conflict: The Case of Chechnya', *Air Power Journal*, Winter 1997.
6. 'War in the Caucasus' *Strategic Comments*, 5(10), December 1999.
7. General John Jumper, 'Kosovo Victory - A Commander's Perspective', *Air Power Review* 2(4), Winter 1999, p. 5, 8.
8. Shaun Clarke, *Strategy, Air Strike and Small Nations*, Fairbairn Australia, Air Power Studies Centre, p. 63.

gone a step further where it removed the need to confront a ground battlefield so that Allied ground forces were, in the event, unopposed. Of course, the realities of both the Gulf and Kosovo operations were far more mixed than these simplistic assertions would suggest. The use of air power in both cases was also controversial, at the time and in post-mortem debates about them. Nevertheless, the fact remains that military victory was achieved in both cases at small or no human cost to the Allies. Assertive statements were made on behalf of air power in general and US air power in particular at the end of the Kosovo crisis which suggests a degree of euphoria, rather than cool analysis, in the assessment of air power's current utility. Henceforth, it was said, dictators all around the world would have to be aware that they could be reached by US air power - with or without the use of foreign bases - and pressured into political acquiescence by the sheer precision of bombing and the progressive dismantling of their military machines or apparatus of dictatorship. To some, it appeared that the Revolution in Military Affairs on the basis of undisputed American technical superiority had started to become a tangible reality.

An RAF Chinook deploys British paratroops into Kosovo, June 1999.
Operation Allied Force allowed a permissive entry of ground forces into Kosovo in what might otherwise have been an extremely hostile environment.

The failings and limitations of the use of air power in all of these cases - failings that included casualties, collateral damage, the unavailability of sufficient numbers of precision munitions, inability to overcome local weather conditions or the limitations on interoperability between different Allied airforces - were regarded essentially as

AIR POWER AND MILITARY INTERVENTION: THE POLITICAL LIMITATIONS

technical failings and limitations rather than reservations about the essence of air power applied to such scenarios. If the technology were to be properly developed, if munitions stockpiles were maintained, if more progress were to be made on interoperability and so on, and so on, then there would be no reason in principle why all should not be well.

Given the superiority of the major military powers since the end of the Cold War, and the 10 or more operations in which they have been engaged - for the most part successfully - in that time, it is not surprising that the promise of air power should appear to be so great. From the American-led invasion of Panama in 1989 to the Australian-led UN intervention in East Timor in 1999, air power can be seen to have played crucial roles in several respects in these cases. Two particular effects can be noted from this range of instances.

Panama	1989	US intervention
Kuwait	1990-1991	Allied operation
Iraq	1992-2000	Allied air enforcement
Somalia	1992-1995	US-led intervention
Rwanda	1994	French intervention
Haiti	1994	US intervention
Chechnya	1994-1996	Russian domestic conflict
Bosnia	1995	US-led operations
Albania	1997	Italian-led intervention
Kosovo	1999	US-led intervention
East Timor	1999-2000	Australian-led intervention
Chechnya	1999-2000	Russian domestic conflict

Cases of Military Intervention After the Cold War
Figure 1.1

Firstly, Western air power, in particular, has embarked on a stage of what can confidently be described as 'technical maturity' at the turn of this century in its proven ability to integrate its different elements - manned, unmanned, space-based, command, support, transport, ordnance delivery etc - with the information and communications revolutions. That is to say, the ability to deploy efficiently a full range of aerial techniques and vehicles on the basis of a real-time, accurate picture of the operational area in all its myriad dimensions is close to being an air power reality. This may be regarded as a 'maturing' of the promise inherent in military air power from its operational debut in the First World War.

Secondly, such technical maturity can have a critical effect on military cost/benefit calculations. As a cost/benefit calculation, the use of western air power in international military interventions in most of the cases in Figure 1.1 would appear to be self-evidently favourable, even where the full potential of western air power's maturity is not yet realised. Not only do these cases suggest that costs are potentially low and benefits potentially high for air power assets themselves, but also that they can dramatically improve the calculation for other military and diplomatic instruments. Ground and maritime operations, international humanitarian interventions and diplomatic initiatives to establish stability in a dangerous situation can all gain from the judicious use of air power supremacy to increase their anticipated benefits while reducing their anticipated costs. The fact that air power is regarded as such a critical determinant in the overall success of an intervention operation - a necessary though not a sufficient condition - is evidence of its anticipated effect in keeping the cost/benefit calculation favourable for other instruments of policy.

Nevertheless, if technical maturity and a favourable cost/benefit ratio appear to exist for the air power of the major military forces in most likely scenarios in the present era, we should not automatically assume that this will be complemented at the political level, where, in certain circumstances, air power constraints may be just as great as air power opportunities. It is important, therefore, to set air power - as any other military instrument - in the particular political context of its use.

THE POLITICAL CONTEXT OF THE USE OF AIR POWER

The political context in which air power, like all military instruments, is employed will be dominated by the decisions of politico-military leaders. It is not relevant to this discussion which politico-military leaders wear uniforms and which do not. The fact is that decisions to employ a military instrument in pursuit of policy objectives are fundamentally political decisions, whoever actually makes them, or however anonymously they are arrived at by a policy machine. As such, political decisions are subject to two overwhelmingly important conditions: firstly, they are taken on the basis of leaders' perceptions rather than any somehow 'more objective' reality; secondly, such perceptions will, in themselves, be subject to change as a given situation develops. Neither of these points is remarkable, but they both take on added significance in the present era, particularly in the case of air power, since they are both subject to greater variation than existed during the Cold War.

AIR POWER AND MILITARY INTERVENTION: THE POLITICAL LIMITATIONS

Political Decisions Are Perceptual

As politico-military leaders contemplate the prospects of using military instrumentalities to achieve their objectives, they will be weighing in their minds the calculation of benefits and costs likely to apply in the case before them. This calculation will be fundamentally on the basis of the leadership's political judgement of what is at stake: the chances of military success, the losses, the acceptability of losses, ethical limits on the use of force, the economic and opportunity costs of operations, the anticipated political effects on the adversary, and so on. Such calculations are likely to be more instinctive than analytical, however, given that leaders have to make them whilst also making any number of other such calculations on quite separate issues. It is not that political and/or military leaders are unaware of all the necessary parts of their calculation; rather that they will conflate them in their own minds without thinking each one through to some logical point of conclusion. Their instincts will filter out much of the calculation that a computer or a planning team would work through; and though they may be presented with the evidence provided by computers or planning teams as they make their actual decisions, a leader's sense of what is a 'rational', or at least an 'analytical', decision will be heavily - perhaps overwhelmingly - determined by their instincts, culture and values.

Only Some Cost/Benefit Calculations Will Be Carefully Made

The spectrum of cost/benefit calculations (see Figure 1.2) in terms of how leaders perceive their national interests, can be expressed as a cross-section between very direct national interests at one end, to very indirect national interests at the other. Both ends of the spectrum should be seen as extremes, in one where national survival itself might be at stake, in the other where a commitment to a highly abstract and contestable proposition such as 'world order' might be at stake. Yet these ends of the spectrum are not synonymous with levels of violence or high or low intensities of warfare. Rather, the spectrum indicates that nearer the extremes, grand political imperatives will operate more powerfully; nearer the middle, careful cost/benefit calculations will be more relevant.

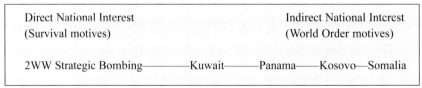

Spectrum of national interests in cost-benefit calculations
Figure 1.2

AIR POWER AND MILITARY INTERVENTION: THE POLITICAL LIMITATIONS

In extreme cases, the cost/benefit calculation may be reduced to a series of relatively simple choices. During 1940-41 the use of allied strategic air power for offensive bombing operations against Nazi Germany, with all its failings, its high casualties, its unachieved strategic objectives etc, had one overwhelming argument in its favour; namely, that it was virtually the only way, at the time, the Allies could hit back at the enemy, when so little else was available to them.[9] Even in 1943, with operational effectiveness somewhat higher, the spectacular raid on the Ruhr Dams was given the go-ahead by Churchill, Portal and Harris more because a military success was needed for political reasons than for the intrinsic calculation of risks and benefits involved in a 'strategic raid' itself. Harris, in particular, was scathing about the prospects and utility of the raid from the very beginning, declaring that 'the weapon is balmy',[10] but in this case the judgement of the chiefs that there was a political need for a 'spectacular' - not least in the eyes of the US - was decisive.[11] In both examples high risks were accepted for the sake of the grand strategy involved and aircrew losses in both were correspondingly high.

The Mohne Dam, 17 May 1943. The Dams Raid was undertaken more because a military success was needed for political reasons than as a result of a calculation of the risks and benefits involved in a strategic raid.

---

9. Peter Calvocoressi and Guy Wint, *Total War* (London: Penguin Books, 1972) p. 495.
10. John Sweetman, *The Dambusters Raid* (London: Cassell, 1999) p. 82.
11. Ibid., p. 42, 84-86.

At the other end of the spectrum where national interests may appear highly indirect - as in the cases of the Somalia and Kosovo operations - the detailed choices appear more complex but the overall priorities are nevertheless simplified by the extreme nature of the case. For the United States, the operation in Somalia in 1992 or the Kosovo crisis in 1999 were both extremes insofar as they were highly indirect interests from a US point of view and certainly not worth appreciable losses among allied service personnel. In Somalia this overwhelming fact led to the effective failure of the operation. In October 1993 18 US Rangers died and 77 were wounded in a major fire fight with local forces in what was the bloodiest single confrontation in any UN operation, and the US 'began a policy shift that had it out of the country by the following March',[12] its strategic objectives confused and unfulfilled. In the Kosovo case the failure of the air campaign to dismantle completely the Serbian air defence system at the beginning posed a continuing threat to aircrews throughout the 78-day campaign, and the policy of keeping most operations above 15,000 feet, constantly re-adjusting the target set to meet individual Allied sensibilities, was clearly a political imperative driven by the overwhelming need to avoid losses and thereby maintain domestic and coalition support for the operation. Other military trade-offs and calculations were subsumed by the fact that this was an offensive air operation, out of area, in a situation of extreme political delicacy, operating, in the words of the NATO Air Commander, 'with the omnipresent mandate of no collateral and no allied loss of life.'[13] In situations of such extreme political delicacy the use of air power, no less than in situations of total warfare, is likely to be dominated by instinctive political imperatives that render other carefully calibrated cost/benefit projections essentially irrelevant.

A less extreme example from the list of interventions in Figure 1.1 provides an illustrative contrast which points up the paradox that Somalia and Kosovo are near the extreme end of the spectrum. The Panama operation of 1989 was not a case of such extreme political delicacy either within the US or in the need to maintain an allied coalition. In fact, 23 US personnel were killed in the course of the invasion. There was no domestic uproar in the US at the losses nor any significant deflection in the objectives or ultimate success of the operation, for Panama did seem to embody an important and legitimate interest to the US and was presumably worth both risks and losses.[14] Equally, the Kuwait case - the Gulf War of 1990-91 - can be placed squarely in the middle of this spectrum. National interests were highly engaged for the US and most of its allies,

---

12. Robert C Owen, 'Aerospace and Land Power in Peace Operations: Towards a New Basis for Synergy', *Air Power Review*, 2(4) Winter 1999, p.35.
13. General John Jumper, 'Kosovo Victory - A Commander's Perspective', *Air Power Review* 2(4), Winter 1999, p. 5.
14. See Karin von Hippel, *Democracy By Force: US Military Intervention in the Post-Cold War World* (Cambridge: Cambridge University Press, 2000) p. 27-54.

AIR POWER AND MILITARY INTERVENTION: THE POLITICAL LIMITATIONS

somewhat short of 'national survival', but clearly more than an indirect sense of the need to preserve international principles or aid victims of aggression. As such, the operation as a whole involved intensely sensitive and finely-balanced calculations of the appropriate military force to use and the political costs and benefits of doing so. In this, the success of the air campaign was absolutely critical to the calculation of what was acceptable, designed as it was both to communicate to Baghdad allied willingness to use force as well as to prepare for the ground offensive by attacking tactical and deep targets simultaneously.

Political Commitment is More Volatile in the Present Era

This calculation of costs and benefits, measured against a scale of the perception of national interests at stake, is intrinsic to political decision-making and would apply in any historical era. In the present case, however, it is not merely a more complex process than during the Cold War period. It is also subject to greater volatility, both in the judgements leaders will make and in the pressures they find themselves under. Firstly, the *values* for which military force is now used - certainly by the Western powers in the cases outlined in Figure 1.1 - are by no means obvious. Defending 'interests' is not as clear cut as defending oneself, even where the interests are perceived in stark terms as in the Kuwait case. Defending 'international' or 'world order' interests is even less certain, and defending 'humanitarianism' by resort to arms automatically raises the question of whether the cure becomes worse than the disease. The 'militarisation of international aid' is a major political dilemma that hardly arose during the Cold War since force was seldom used in tandem with international aid operations. Secondly, the *cases* in which most Western force has been used are distinguished generally by the fact that they arise from the weakness of states and governments rather than their strengths. Far from opposing a strong alliance (the Warsaw Pact) centred around a superpower, Western forces now find themselves opposing small countries, local leaders or regional dictators, warlords, domestic instabilities, and so on. The rationale of collective defence against a powerful external threat, which was the bedrock of all else Western forces prepared for in the Cold War, has not been replaced by anything so persuasive in the last decade. Thirdly, the *readiness to use force* by Western powers is now a subject of critical uncertainty. During the Cold War any resort to military force - anywhere in the world - carried ominous implications for the central balance between the two great alliances and their superpowers. Except in very specific counter-insurgency operations, the use of force tended to be regarded either as a last resort, or else a serious international threshold to cross. But in operations closer to peace support and policing it could be argued that the calculated resort to force early in a crisis may represent - as in domestic policing - the most judicious use of the military for good. There can be no hard and fast rule, but the cases listed here

AIR POWER AND MILITARY INTERVENTION: THE POLITICAL LIMITATIONS

demonstrate a pattern of great uncertainty on the part of Western leaders: reluctance to use force in the early stages of a crisis, followed often by an imperative to use it more extensively in later stages when the situation is worse and the options more unpalatable.

This becomes particularly relevant to air power studies in the present era. For air power may appear to offer leaders some attractive options to escape from many of these dilemmas. If force can be employed through air power in a way that is highly discriminating against targets, low risk to the user and can be turned on and off quickly and flexibly as operations can be escalated, suspended, restarted, without leaving forces on the ground during pauses in the action etc, then leaders will be tempted to feel that they can steer their way through the political problems posed by indeterminate cases, ambiguous values or doubts about the resort to arms. Faced with so many uncertainties and yet driven also by the 'Do something!' effect, the instincts of leaders will incline them towards the use of air power where they feel that force is necessary.[15]

On the other hand, these virtues of air power are only available to leaders when it performs at its best, and even then, the inevitable risks associated with the use of air power are magnified by the symbolism that it carries. Any aircraft losses - through any cause - become a political victory for opposing forces on the ground. Aircraft losses in the Gulf War, Somalia and Chechnya all had major effects on the respective morale of very unequal forces. And the use of air power in conditions of overwhelming superiority can create images of 'Goliaths', 'bullies', 'cowards', 'colonialists' etc., so that operations of enforcement, such as those over Iraq for eight years after 1992, tend to lose international support if they persist. Even operations with wholly or largely humanitarian purposes have become difficult to defend both internationally and domestically where the imagery of air power has seemed to symbolise the imposition of political power. This happened to varying extents in the Somalia, Rwanda, Bosnia and Kosovo cases. In short, there is at least as much chance that the instinctive leader will misapply air power as a military instrument, as use it most appropriately.

Allied to the instinctive temptation to reach for air power to apply force in modern Western interventions is the fact that political perceptions are subject to greater volatility than in the previous era. It is tempting to say that the 'Do something!' effect is rapidly followed by the 'Why do we have to be the ones to do it?' effect. But the volatility of political perceptions is far less simple than this and does not always work in the direction of disengagement. In both Bosnia and Kosovo, commitment to military action hardened in crises that were of only indirect interest to Western powers, once it was felt that NATO's credibility was at stake and was in danger of being undermined by the actions of much weaker but ruthless opponents. In the Department of Defense's Report to the US

---

15. See Karin von Hippel and Michael Clarke, 'Something Must be Done', *The World Today*, 55(3),1999, p. 4-7.

AIR POWER AND MILITARY INTERVENTION: THE POLITICAL LIMITATIONS

Congress on Kosovo, 'ensuring NATO's credibility' was set out as one of the three 'primary interests' embodied in the operation, although this was hardly intended to be a primary interest in October 1998 when the threat of force was first explicitly made against President Milosevic over the behaviour of Serbian forces in the Kosovo province.[16]

The fact is that in a world where the conditions of international crises are as volatile as they now are - where the *values*, *cases*, and *resort to force* are so much more ambiguous than they were prior to 1990 - the political responses of the major military powers are similarly volatile. This is not something that can merely be ascribed to the irresolute politico-military leaders, but more accurately to the pressures they are under. In democracies leaders must carry their publics with them, and run the risks of unpopularity at any military reverses or excessive military costs incurred in any action. More importantly, the politico-military leadership of Western Powers in the crises we are discussing will almost invariably be highly multi-national and multi-institutional. As Figure 1.3 demonstrates, the number of participating countries in contemporary peace keeping or intervention operations, in all parts of the world and involving different organisations, is generally high enough to pose considerable political problems, even where one of the participants is clearly taking the lead.

BOSNIA	SFOR/NATO OP	33
KOSOVO	KFOR/NATO OP	34
HAITI	UN OP	34
HAITI	US/UN OP	12
ANGOLA	UNAVEM 3	36
CYPRUS	UN OP	8
GUATEMALA	UN OP	9
BURUNDI	OAU OP	6
LIBERIA	ECOMOG OP	8
TAJIKISTAN	CIS OP	4
GEORGIA	CIS OP	1

Number of participating countries in recent International/Peace Support Operations
Figure 1.3

Not least, the involvement in such operations of major international organisations - generally the United Nations - as the source of political authority, to say nothing of the role of host country governments for stationed forces, civilian contributors, major Non

---

16. Department of Defense, *Report to Congress: Kosovo/Operation Allied Force After Action Report*, 31 January 2000, p. 1.

AIR POWER AND MILITARY INTERVENTION: THE POLITICAL LIMITATIONS

Governmental Organisations and the political authorities in the countries subject to intervention, all ensure that the political context will be of the utmost delicacy. The 30,000 International NGOs and over 2 million domestic NGOs are now estimated to dispense more money internationally than the World Bank.[17] Collectively, they have become major players in world politics, and form a global marketplace of their own that is at least as powerful as the network of formal international institutions. They are influenced but not controlled by governments. It is not surprising, therefore, that under conditions of such complexity political perceptions of what is at stake in a crisis and how the cost/benefit ratio should be interpreted at any given moment, is likely to change. Though the military are right to press for clear political mandates and operational orders in their missions, it is unlikely that they will get them and even where they do, mandates are unlikely to remain unchanged. This is one of the new realities of the use of military force after the Cold War.

A good example of this phenomenon is the Bosnia case in the period after February 1995. In 1992 the nature of the UN military operation was strictly limited to facilitating the delivery of humanitarian aid. But UN forces were failing to cope not merely with the warring parties in the conflict, but also with the ever more complex international political arena of the operation: UN civilian organisations, over 200 NGOs operating independently in theatre, irregular foreign forces, private mercenary and advisor companies, multinational companies with facilities to protect, organised criminal activities, and a proliferation of political forums to try to co-ordinate the political and military approaches from intervening governments. The mere protection of humanitarian aid deliveries became impossible without active military involvement in the politics of the crisis itself. By mid-1995 the mission had effectively expanded out of all proportion to the original design and far more was by then at stake - not least the political credibility of the western allies in the Contact Group. Both risks and losses were contemplated and it was clear during May 1995 that though the UN favoured a scaling down of its operations, in response to the worsening situation on the ground, the US and its European allies now felt that there was too much at risk to back away from Bosnian Serb military offensives forcibly to partition the country. At the end of August the allies launched Operation Deliberate Force - steeped in costs, human and political risks - which flew some 100,000 sorties over Bosnia in the next four months - the largest air operation in NATO history.[18]

---

17. *The Economist*, 29 January 2000, p. 25.
18. Tim Ripley, *Operation Deliberate Force: The UN and NATO Campaign in Bosnia 1995* (Lancaster: Centre for Defence and International Security Studies, 1999).

AIR POWER AND MILITARY INTERVENTION: THE POLITICAL LIMITATIONS

The protection of humanitarian aid deliveries to Bosnia eventually became impossible without active military involvement in the politics of the crisis itself.

AIR POWER AND GREATER POLITICAL VOLATILITY

A number of factors contribute to the general volatility in the political circumstances in which contemporary air power is employed. Three developments relevant to air power are particularly worthy of further analysis, only one of which is normally associated with the phenomenon of political volatility.

Coercive Air Power as a Peace Enforcer

The western powers who have been so involved in providing military force to UN or other multinational operations have become increasingly aware of the scale of the tasks they undertake. Major peace support operations in Somalia, Rwanda, Bosnia, Albania, Kosovo and East Timor have proved to be protracted, expensive, dangerous to those on the ground and politically frustrating as the intervening forces find themselves having to 'enforce' as much as 'support' a political framework or agreed settlement. They have looked for short cuts to achieve their political objectives and have reawakened an interest in trying to use coercive tactics at key moments in the 'politics of enforcement', whether in a PSO or in support of a broader UN or other international resolution. Whereas aerial coercion was generally thought about chiefly in the nuclear context during the Cold War, now there is a trend to try to use it at the tactical level in situations far short of war, precisely *because of* - not despite - the fact that national interests are only indirectly engaged. The promise of modern air power appears to make it an ideal instrument for the discriminating and safe use of both strategic and tactical coercion.

If the promise is tempting, however, the practice of coercion suggests that the political limits are also severe. During 1994-1995 the Western powers operating in Bosnia attempted to use air power to enforce political agreements in this way. The case reflects an indecisive outcome. Attempts to enforce agreements on the ground through the use of air-to-ground operations were frustrated by the failure of the UN to authorise the use of air power in time or with the flexibility that would have been required to make a difference.[19] Linked to this were constant weather problems that made accurate target identification difficult and, eventually, a reported reluctance on the part of CINCSOUTH in Naples to run the continued risks of losses inherent in tactical-level operations. According to Michael Rose's account, CINCSOUTH - as commander of air operations in the region - decided on 15 April 1995 that henceforth 'he would only accept strategic-level targets.'[20] It is impossible to determine whether more effective tactical coercion was technically possible in this situation, and if it was, whether it might have headed off greater confrontations later, or merely made a volatile situation on the ground even worse. Both interpretations are plausible. Following the confusions of Spring 1995, however, aerial coercion was then used on a much bigger and more strategic scale against the Serbs in Pale after August 1995, and then in Operation Deliberate Force, where it certainly contributed - along with other major political turnarounds - to pressurising the Bosnian Serb leadership towards the agreements that were eventually enshrined in the Dayton peace talks of November and December.

Similar tactics have been used in the continuing air operations against Iraq from 1992 to the present, where they have been part of an attempt to enforce UN policy over the no-fly zones in Northern and Southern Iraq and over Iraq's lack of co-operation with the UNSCOM team charged with supervising the elimination of its weapons of mass destruction. In this case, degrees of tactical coercion were attempted in attacking those SAM batteries and associated air defence systems which locked onto allied aircraft enforcing the no-fly zone. This was extended to a more strategic coercive approach in Operation Desert Fox in December 1998 where an attempt was made in an intensive four day campaign to enforce Saddam Hussein's compliance with UNSCOM by showing him how his military machine could be efficiently dismantled through the use of stand-off and direct air power. This approach was then scaled down again in 1999 to the

---

19. General Sir Michael Rose, *Fighting for Peace* (London: The Harvill Press, 1998) p. 85-6, 106-108, 112.
20. Ibid, p. 114.

continuation of tactical coercion in response to the regular - virtually daily - incidents over the no-fly zones. Since Desert Fox there have been some 225 Iraqi aircraft violations, 640 lock-ons or firings against US and UK aircraft, and over 150 retaliatory attacks as a result.[21] The allies claim that Iraqi power has been 'contained' by these tactics, pending the removal of Saddam Hussein by internal opposition. Critics point out the lack of useful options open to the allies as a result of such indeterminate - and long term - coercive actions, and the diplomatic price paid in relations with Turkey, Saudi Arabia, Russia and France who were all one time supporters of the policy and who have gradually distanced themselves from it. Again, the case must be regarded as indecisive in judging air power in the tactical coercion role. But it illuminates very clearly both the political temptation to use it in this way and the inherent limitations on the way it must operate in a situation where national interests are only engaged indirectly.

Operation Desert Fox, December 1998: an RAF Tornado GR1 takes off from its base in Kuwait. In air operations against Iraq since 1992, both tactical and strategic coercion has been used to enforce Saddam Hussein's compliance with UN policy.

The case of aerial coercion as an enforcer of the Rambouillet agreement on the future of Kosovo provides a more clear-cut instance since it began with an overt commitment to strategic coercion only. It was expected at the beginning of the air campaign in March 1999 that a few days of cruise missile and aircraft attacks against the Serbian air defence system would have the desired psychological effects on the Milosevic leadership. NATO air forces were not initially configured for anything much more extensive. It palpably failed to have the desired effect, however, and an ever-expanding mixed strategy of

---

21. *Jane's Defence Weekly*, 33(15), 12 April 2000, p. 22

strategic coercion in Serbia and aerial denial in Kosovo was forced on the NATO allies over the next two months. In the end, the campaign was brought to a conclusion by a number of factors, of which the continued air attacks were clearly one. But what had begun as a largely one-dimensional military enforcement operation had rapidly become a wider crisis in its own right - and a considerable test of Allied political resolve - that created a new political situation in the region. Milosevic eventually bowed to NATO requirements, but by then the role of NATO countries in the region as a whole had taken on new dimensions. If by June 1999 the campaign was a military success it must be judged, at best, to have been a diplomatic draw.

The cases available over the last decade suggest that despite the pattern of aerial dominance enjoyed by the major powers and the political attractions of trying to achieve military objectives by the efficient use of coercive force, neither the theory nor practice of aerial coercion have been vindicated by events to date. The apparent stability of Cold War theories of nuclear deterrence - which by definition remained empirically untestable - have created a presumption of understanding and control in a different era where both theory and practice are being all too frequently tested. In the context of the military operations under discussion here, modern 'strategic coercion' - where force must be used discriminatingly, quickly and with minimum risk - requires very careful understanding of the target at which it is directed, *as well as the extra options which these modern self-limitations give to the target.* By the same token, aerial coercion at the tactical level magnifies to a considerable extent both the requirements of the self-limiting conditions, as well as the room for political and military manoeuvre on the part of any adversaries.

Where it works, coercion represents the most efficient and cost-effective use of force. That is why it currently appears such an attractive option. Where it fails, it represents one of the most inefficient and dangerously unpredictable uses of force. And the difference in performance between success and failure can be fine indeed. At the very least, coercive air power should be seen as a likely part of packages of political, economic, diplomatic and other military measures, and attention should be directed to the synergies, or contradictions, likely to arise within the packages when air power is employed in this way.

The Promise of the RMA in Air Power

The Revolution in Military Affairs is a second major trend that bears on the increasingly volatile political commitments that are likely to underpin military operations. Specialists on both sides of the Atlantic have expressed concerns that the RMA may be more apparent than real. But there is little doubt that western politicians and their publics instinctively believe in it. Air power may find itself having to live up to the levels to which it has been talked up by some commentators in the crises listed here.

Technological progress has moved in the direction of precision-guided weapons and strategic and tactical communication. In the Kuwait operation in 1991 only some 8% of aerial munitions delivered were precision weapons; in Operation Deliberate Force in Bosnia during 1995 the figure had jumped to 90%. In Operation Allied Force in Kosovo in 1999 the level was something over 35%.[22] Meanwhile, communication, in its broadest sense, is pursued through the increasing digitisation of the whole battlespace, with all the advantages and new vulnerabilities that implies.[23] Such developments are logical and undoubtedly promise steep changes in military effectiveness across a broad spectrum of capabilities. The problem, however, is that technological development in these directions does not automatically relate to the particular challenges embodied in the range of operations of the last decade. As the US Air Force has begun to realise, Operation Allied Force in 1999 revealed - as it was bound to do - not only some of the technical limitations of 'revolutionary air power', but more surprisingly some of the difficulties of applying it even in a situation that cried out for a highly discriminating approach. Any real operation is bound to reveal 'a series of shortfalls in key weapons platforms;' in this case, for example, JSTARS, AWACS, Joint Direct Attack Munitions, and some critical shortages in technical personnel.[24] Of more long term significance, however, are the organisational problems and limitations on flexibility revealed by USAF operations in Kosovo. Inflexibilities of the deployment constrained political choices throughout the operation and contributed greatly to the increased pressures both on its effectiveness and the allied consensus underlying it.

As a result, the USAF has moved to restructure itself around the concept of more flexible Aerospace Expeditionary Forces (AEFs), at least for operations below the level of 'major theatre wars'.[25] The AEF is an attempt to provide a complete package of aerospace assets using all relevant arms of the forces for rapid, flexible and sustainable deployment anywhere in the world. To be successful, AEFs will have to embody many of the features of the RMA in the support and logistical areas, and not least in the efficient interoperability of a diverse range of assets operating in a smaller, devolved command structure. RMA effort, however, currently tends to go into air power lethality rather than into deployment, sustainability, flexibility and application. This will be a major challenge for the future.

---

22. Department of Defense, *Report to Congress: Kosovo/Operation Allied Force After Action Report*, p. 88-93: S Clarke, *Strategy, Air Strike and Small Nations*, Fairbairn Australia, Air Power Studies Centre, p. 63.
23. Nigel Vinson, 'SDR Unsung Sound-byte: Digitisation of the Battlespace', *World Defence Systems* (London: Royal United Services Institute, 1999) p. 102-104.
24. 'USAF: The Strategic Vision', *Jane's Defence Weekly*, 32(10), 8 September 1999, p.33.
25. 'The New Air Force Line-up - Lighter, Leaner and More Lethal', *Jane's Defence Weekly*, 32(10), 8 September 1999, p. 34-35.

The importance of these challenges in terms of political commitments to operations is in the fact that all RMA technologies are expensive and have to be justified by practice. There is inevitably an ambiguous response to the need to devote high-tech resources to less glamorous and longer-term improvements in mobility, sustainability, flexibility, the interface between different types of military unit in the aerospace sector and so on, as opposed to investment in 'the teeth' of forces as political leaders would understand them. If modern forces appear incapable of getting properly to grips with the operations they are called upon to perform, there will be a decline in the political commitment to modernise them and take advantage of new technologies. On the other hand, some of the cases reviewed here indicate that high-tech forces still have real problems in responding fully to the indeterminate and shifting nature of the political mandates under which they are asked to operate. The 'promise of the RMA', at least in the way it is put in the public arena, coupled with the increased frequency with which military forces are now called upon, may put all military forces, but especially air power, in a no-win political situation.[26]

Air Power, Intervention, and Public Opinion

A final factor making for political volatility is the reaction of domestic public opinion to the use of air power in operations for less than manifestly national interests. Military planners have long since accepted the critical importance of understanding the dynamics of the media as they plan and conduct modern campaigns. The air power element of the Gulf War and Operation Deliberate Force in Bosnia in 1995 have been noted as media successes for air power in that they were over reasonably quickly and appeared demonstrably effective, maintaining high levels of domestic support within key allied countries for the action.[27] These two cases, however, should not automatically be regarded as typical. The air operations over Northern and Southern Iraq since 1992, in Somalia for three years to 1995, in Kosovo during 1999 and Russian air operations in Chechnya 1999-2000, are as likely to become the norm. In these cases air power can be seen to prevail - but not quickly or completely, without casualties, collateral damage, or civilian deaths. The more indeterminate nature of these cases suggest that there may be an interesting trade-off for military planners between the media advantages and disadvantages of using air power in pursuit of more indirect national interests.

---

26. The USAF is estimated, for example, to be flying now on 400% more operations than during the Cold War.
27. M Bratby, 'Air Power and the Role of the Media', in A Lambert and A Williamson, eds, *The Dynamics of Air Power* (Bracknell: RAF Staff College, 1996) p. 97-100.

AIR POWER AND MILITARY INTERVENTION: THE POLITICAL LIMITATIONS

The media occupies a critical interface with domestic political opinion, and hence domestic support, for military operations. Though debate continues over how far the media can *shape* public opinion - the consensus is that in the longer term it is less powerful than many of its critics normally contend - there is little doubt that the western media is a major channel of short term communication between government and popular opinion, in both directions.[28] During the Kosovo operation some important and heated debates took place in the media itself about the role of news management and its effect on public support for military action.[29] At the extreme, Kosovo has been characterised as a new breed of 'virtual war' in western perceptions, risk-free and high-tech, driven by the realities of the media rather than events in the theatre of operations. For others, this is to mistake the style for the substance.[30] There is little doubt, however, that the media and public attitudes to an international crisis feed off each other and the combination of opinion polling during crises and wars, and the media reporting of the results, creates broad 'trends of opinion' to which politicians and military planners have to be sensitive.

Opinion polling in the US and Europe on recent cases of military intervention is fraught with problems of comparison between different surveys and the reliability of general interpretations based on specific questions. Certain generalisations appear to be confirmed with reasonable consistency, however.[31] One is that the public is more likely to be supportive of air 'enforcement actions' where there is a clear adversary, where national interests are perceived to be greater, and where the action - if not over quickly - at least has a logical endpoint.[32] The air war in the Gulf in 1990-91 conformed to all these criteria. The operation in Somalia palpably did not. Operation Desert Fox over Iraq in December 1998 represents a middle case. It maintained high levels of public support in the US, since it was possible to distance it from the ongoing air operations against Iraq since 1992. To the US public it appeared to be a one-off discrete action, justified as a UN enforcement and directed at a palpable adversary. Though this was a highly simplified version of the truth, it was sufficient to maintain around 80% public support for it, and the action was over quickly.[33] On the other hand, even small losses or a longer span of operations might have provoked the volatility of public support that has characterised US opinion on relations with Iraq since the end of the Gulf War.

---

28. See the excellent book by Philip M Taylor, *War and the Media* (Manchester: Manchester University Press, 1998).
29. See, for example, John Pilger, 'Acts of Murder', *The Guardian*, 18 May 1999, and Ian Black, 'Bad News', *The Guardian*, 19 May 1999.
30. See, for example, Michael Ignatieff, *Virtual War: Kosovo and Beyond* (London: Chatto and Windus, 2000): Mark Mazower, 'War Seen on Television Still Sheds Blood', *The Times*, 6 Apr. 2000, p.17
31. Paul Dixon, 'Britain's "Vietnam Syndrome"?', Public Opinion and British Military Intervention from Palestine to Yugoslavia', *Review of International Studies*, 26(1), January 2000, p. 99-121.
32. Ibid, p. 115.
33. *Gallup Political Index*, December 1998.

It is also clear that the public makes quite carefully graduated judgements of its own - judgements clearly affected by media images - as to the national interests at stake in any given crisis and the losses and economic costs that are justified by it. The Kosovo air operation revealed almost from the beginning that a large majority of the public in Britain (70%) did not expect the air action to succeed on its own, that a ground operation would sooner or later have to be mounted, and believed that there was a significant danger it would lead to a more generalised conflict in the Balkans. On these wider implications of the operation, there remained a majority (52%) in favour of pressing ahead in any case, though opposition to doing so reached levels of around 40%.[34] As in the case of the Bosnia operation, the British public displayed graduated shades of opinion which was not averse to domestic casualties at any cost, but which was also subject to some rapid fluctuations since there was never an overwhelming sense that the interests at stake were more than indirect or humanitarian.[35]

A tentative conclusion on the role of the media and public opinion in relation to air operations in the present era would suggest that air power offers planners the potential advantages of photogenic images, high-tech equipment, and a persona of military superiority with which to gain public support for short, sharp and effective enforcement of international norms and rules. But not even the most potent air power images can compensate for an unfavourable reality. The effects on public opinion are likely to be debilitating of operations that appear open-ended, to have a weak rationale, an indeterminate adversary, or which seem to be failing to get to grips with the locus of the military power they oppose, or else which appear disproportionate to the problem itself. The 'Vietnam syndrome', in other words, must justifiably hover over any operations where the reality was as unfavourable as it was in Vietnam. The use of air power evokes powerful public emotions, both positively and negatively. Its employment increases the domestic political stakes in an operation and may be regarded, in itself, as one of the drivers of the public's volatility of opinion over post-Cold War military interventions.

---

34. The Gallup Organization, *Poll Releases*, 30 March 1999.
35. Paul Dixon, 'Britain's "Vietnam Syndrome"?', Public Opinion and British Military Intervention from Palestine to Yugoslavia', *Review of International Studies*, 26(1), January 2000, p. 119-120. On the specific reactions, and volatility, with regard to casualties in Bosnia, see *Gallup Political Index*, June 1995.

AIR POWER AND MILITARY INTERVENTION: THE POLITICAL LIMITATIONS

CONCLUSION

Political constraints on military action come in all shapes and sizes and few trends in world politics ever go in one direction only. Nevertheless, air power analysts could be forgiven for feeling particularly victimised by the contradictions of the present era. Technical dominance of the major air power nations has been assured in the operations of the last decade. They can operate with low levels of risk, at high levels of military effectiveness, almost anywhere in the world. The twentieth century promises of air power are being, or are on the verge of being, realised at the start of the twenty-first. Yet the difficulties of applying air power - as with other military instruments - to political purpose are multiplying all the time. This is not only because the agents of government find themselves in uniquely complex circumstances, having always to tailor their commitment to military action to the contradictory pressures they are under. It is also because governments - and the competition between them - no longer provide the only political framework in which effective force is exercised. Political limitations are now also driven by public opinion, local actors behaving 'asymmetrically', the world's media, international and non-governmental organisations, major economic interests, and so on.

A world in which political power is diffused and fragmented in this way is, of course, nothing new. There are many historical counterparts for it prior to the twentieth century. But air power happened to be born in the twentieth century and 'grew up' only in the second part of it when the Second World War and then the Cold War created unique historical conditions that are not likely soon to be repeated. The fact is that the diffused political circumstances of the present era may turn out to be more the historical norm than that in which air power actually developed. In this case, air power theorists will be challenged to throw away a number of their teenage perceptions as they enter middle age.

AIR POWER AND MILITARY INTERVENTION: THE POLITICAL LIMITATIONS

CHAPTER 2

AIR POWER: THE INSTRUMENT OF CHOICE?
Doctor David Gates

THE 1990s WITNESSED THREE major aerial offensives which, if only at first glance, appeared to be as revolutionary as they were successful. In the case of the Gulf War, Western aerospace power took the lead in rendering the Iraqi occupation of Kuwait untenable. In Bosnia in 1995, an aerial bombardment by NATO forces seemed to be instrumental in imposing peace - of a kind at least - on the warring factions. Most recently, eleven weeks of air strikes appear to have been the single most important factor in compelling the government of the Federal Republic of Yugoslavia to come to terms with the transatlantic alliance regarding the crisis in Kosovo.[1] Indeed, aerospace power has emerged from all of this as, it would seem, the supreme form of military muscle, the obvious instrument of choice. But is this really so and can things remain that way? Should the West strive to consolidate and indeed extend its dominance of the skies and space? Can that advantage be preserved at a time of declining defence expenditure, of 'globalisation'[2] and of rapid technological change? If so, should it be at the cost of neglecting other military capabilities? Can modern aerospace power truly be a panacea, or, for all its technical sophistication, are there insurmountable contextual constraints on its applicability?

---

1. It is worth noting that the terms eventually agreed to by the Yugoslavian authorities were not identical to those that the West originally sought to impose on them at the Rambouillet Conference. Two demands in particular made hostilities with NATO virtually impossible to avoid. Yet, neither of these conditions was actually included in the subsequent cease-fire settlement: the Yugoslavian government neither granted NATO military personnel the right to move freely throughout the Federal Republic, nor did they accept anything that might compromise the future retention of Kosovo by that polity. The latter issue will ineluctably prove a troublesome one in the future.
2. There are various definitions of the phenomenon known as 'globalisation'. For the purposes of this piece, it is best summarised as the erosion of the distinctions between foreign and domestic affairs as a result of the declining influence of bodies, most notably governments, that have traditionally mediated in the relationships between individual citizens and the wider world. The opportunities offered by the world-wide web, the spiralling intrusion of international law into a state's internal affairs and the growth of non-governmental agencies and multi-national corporations are among the many symptoms of 'globalisation'.

AIR POWER: THE INSTRUMENT OF CHOICE?

The success of the Allies' great aerial offensive during the Gulf War, Operation Instant Thunder, was such that, at the beginning of the 1990s, many commentators were already arguing that air power had 'come of age'; after centuries of being dominated by land and maritime forces, warfare seemed to be entering a new epoch, the aerospace era. Thanks to night-vision devices and highly accurate navigational aids, at this juncture advanced combat aircraft could operate in virtually any weather conditions and on a round-the-clock basis. Integrated, sophisticated intelligence-gathering and dissemination systems furnished them with an unparalleled amount of information regarding the battle space. The availability of precision-guided munitions, including a new generation of aerodynamic missiles, also gave them an unprecedented capacity for striking at discrete targets, while the inherent flexibility of air power - which enables it to be switched from one assignment to another with comparative ease and alacrity - had been enhanced through the development of multi-role platforms equipped with versatile, and often interchangeable, systems. In other respects, too, modern airforces were better able to make use of the advantages that had always flowed from a capability to exploit the freedom of the skies, not least the ability to venture almost anywhere; whereas the majority of the Earth's surface is covered by sea, with just a third made up of dry land, and all of it is enshrouded by the atmosphere. Their reach extended through in-flight refuelling, aircraft - always relatively swift - could now also attain speeds that greatly exceeded those of even the fastest surface forces.

The ubiquity, perspective and reach of aerospace platforms liberate them from the obligation to engage in sequential patterns of operations. Whereas ground forces have to achieve tactical breakthroughs in order to fulfil operational objectives which in turn leads to progress at the strategic level of war, in theory at least air power can undertake missions on all three levels from the very outset of a conflict. Furthermore, not only has the accuracy and lethality of modern weaponry endowed aerospace forces with unprecedented scope in terms of the spectrum of targets they can engage with a good prospect of success, but also such forces remain, for the time being at least, less vulnerable to destruction by terrestrial ones than the other way round.

All of this suggests that, in certain circumstances at least, air forces can project power relatively swiftly and with fewer risks than would attend the employment of other types of military units. In fact, some analysts have come to see air and aerospace power as being at the very heart of warfare in the post-industrial, information age. They subscribe to the belief, or hope, that the vision of the early air power theorists can now be fulfilled and that conflicts can be decided without the need for potentially protracted, gory and expensive terrestrial operations; requiring little, if any, assistance from surface forces, air power is the obvious instrument of choice.

Indubitably, Operations Deliberate Force over Bosnia in 1995 and Allied Force against the Federal Republic of Yugoslavia in 1999 offered further persuasive evidence in support of this view. Indeed, experience in the Gulf and the Balkans suggests that,

AIR POWER: THE INSTRUMENT OF CHOICE?

today, armed conflicts can be concluded quickly and decisively at an affordable, essentially monetary, price. Whereas, in the case of the Gulf War, an offensive by ground forces which lasted just four days and incurred minimal Allied losses was all that was needed to complete the rout of an Iraqi army that had been profoundly weakened by weeks of bombardment from the skies, in Bosnia and Kosovo air power's contribution to the coercion of the enemy appeared to be of paramount importance. Here, protracted aerial attacks evidently exerted sufficient pressure to obviate the need for Western troops to take the offensive at all. Formerly hostile territory could be occupied after having been rendered untenable through the direct and indirect application of aerospace power.

THE TRANSFORMATION OF THE CONTEXT OF INTERNATIONAL AFFAIRS

All of these instances of the employment of military power and force occurred within a geostrategic environment that had been transformed by, among other things, the end of the Cold War. For the overwhelming majority of that contest, neither superpower had had cause to regard its position at the peak of the international hierarchy as ephemeral. Rather, each had had good grounds for believing that time was on its side. A significant change in the *status quo* might have been achievable by military means, but it would have called for a general war in which both sides stood to lose far more than they were likely to gain. They preferred instead to maintain a shared position at the top, albeit an uneasy and highly competitive one, by seeking to avoid anything that might precipitate real change. Indeed, for a time during the late 1980s especially, alongside the established concept of deterrence, theories concerning the disutility of war *per se* abounded.

However, as the Cold War's deadening hand withered, many states found themselves enjoying very much more discretion with regard to the use of military force. Its revival as a useful instrument of foreign policy was coincident with and influenced by the advent of 'globalisation' and by the supersession of mechanical by electrical technology and of the industrial by the information age. In many respects, the maturation of air power was symbolic of the last of these wider processes, which has been depicted by many, if mostly American, analysts as a revolution in military affairs. As Lawrence Freedman has observed, this concept:

> *'fits in with the assumption that, for the moment at least, Western countries can choose their enemies and are not obliged to fight on anybody else's terms. Invitations to war need only be accepted on certain conditions: public opinion must be supportive; the result must be pre-ordained; and the conflict must be structured as a contest between highly professional conventional forces. Military commanders must devise strategies that not only keep their own casualty levels low, but also*

> *respect the expectation - bordering on moral presumption - that fire will be directed with precision and only against targets of evident military value'.*[3]

This perceived revolution in military affairs (RMA) is not a universal phenomenon, however. In fact, it is essentially an American notion, rooted in views, values and circumstances that pertain almost exclusively to the USA. Whilst all major states in the northern hemisphere have adjusted their foreign policies and defence expenditure in the light of the end of the Cold War, the radical and rapid technological change that is the principal hallmark of the RMA is affecting the USA's armed forces - above all, the USAF - much more profoundly than those of other leading powers. The concept of choice is inextricably bound up with capability. Yet, owing to technological and financial constraints, no other single state can realistically aspire to acquire and maintain a balanced air force comparable to that of the USA. By any qualitative or quantitative measurement, the USAF is now well ahead of its counterparts in other countries, including those in other leading NATO states. Not only an air but also a space force, its very sophistication is posing problems for its allies and potential foes alike. If some developed countries now regard air power as the instrument of first resort, for some others and for many less developed ones it is at best such an indiscriminative and unwieldy weapon as to be of very limited use indeed, if they possess it at all. Moreover, as Freedman concludes, the basic assumptions underpinning the notion of an RMA and the manner in which it will shape the future of warfare are essentially applicable to 'political entities that are not fearful, desperate, vengeful or angry and that can maintain a sense of proportion over the interests at stake and the humanity of the opponent. They are not necessarily the views of those whom Western states might confront in combat.'[4]

---

3. L Freedman, 'The Revolution in Strategic Affairs', *Adelphi Paper* 318 (Oxford, 1998) p. 77.
4. Ibid.

AIR POWER: THE INSTRUMENT OF CHOICE?

A line-up of F117 Nighthawks. Owing to technological and financial constraints, no other single state can realistically aspire to acquire and maintain a balanced air force comparable to that of the USA.

Indeed, the very success of Western, particularly American, air power is bound to accelerate the search for possible countermeasures to it. If we proceed from the assumption that no single state can even hope to duplicate the aerospace power of the USA, then other instruments will have to be relied upon to a proportionately greater degree. This suggests that, in the event of conflict, escalation could be initiated either vertically or horizontally and that it could include the selective use of some form of air power.

AEROSPACE POWER AND EUROPEAN DEFENCE CAPABILITIES

This last point is as true of many affluent, developed states as it is of lesser ones. After all, without the active participation of the USAF and other American units, operations of the scale and complexity of Instant Thunder, Deliberate Force and Allied Force would have been utterly impracticable.[5] This fact raises numerous questions, not least about the

---

5. Indeed, it is doubtful whether, without the active support of the USA, the European powers would have intervened in the fashion that they did in any of the conflicts of which these operations formed a part.

reality of the perceived RMA and about the details of any purely European security and defence 'identity'. The European powers' principal contribution to all of these aerial offensives - which are widely depicted as the harbinger of a new type of warfare - was political, not military. Air power's reach and speed make it an obvious rapid-reaction instrument which can, with comparative ease, be committed to a coalition as a way of demonstrating solidarity. Unfortunately, the very technological sophistication of modern aerial operations means that, more often than not, such apparent accessions of strength can be of little practical utility. As a result, even some NATO air forces might yet conclude that role-specialisation constitutes the only way out of the dilemma of trying to keep abreast of their putative partners.

However, even this approach would not be without its drawbacks. From a national perspective, such a policy would ineluctably involve narrowing the spectrum of competencies and might well heighten inter-service rivalries. Moreover, occupying a particular, perhaps pivotal, niche within a permanent alliance can be burdensome, too. Preserving a first-class capability and genuine interoperability can still prove expensive and difficult, not least because it calls for ongoing research and development work to cope with changing conditions. States that adopt role-specialisation also suffer a further diminution in their political autonomy and, with it, lose much if not all of their scope for exercising discretion. Without unanimity, the alliance's martial machine might not be able to function at all. Yet, as we saw in Operations Deliberate Force and Allied Force, there may well be circumstances in which some members of the coalition might prefer to play a purely nominal role in any military operations, or might even decline to take part in them altogether. In fact, there have been instances where, in seeking to develop certain types of military power, governments have encountered domestic resistance on the grounds that they might find the active use of the new capabilities all too tempting, or that putative foes might interpret their very acquisition as a clear signal of intent. The debate within NATO about the substitution of 'Flexible Response' for a posture founded on massive retaliation is a good case in point. At the heart of the former doctrine was the notion of choice. Some critics, however, argued that this would send the wrong message to the Warsaw Pact, while others feared that an enhanced capacity for conventional warfare, particularly bigger and better ground forces, could only lead to the USA dabbling in peripheral conflicts, notably that in Vietnam.

If it is difficult to see how, in the light of current trends, the core air forces of the transatlantic alliance can preserve their scope for genuine interoperability, it is still harder to envisage a way for new or non-NATO units to function alongside them. At a time when the USAF is diverting resources into capabilities that will allow it to counter ballistic missiles and generally make ever more use of the ultimate high ground, space, the RAF, for instance, has more in common with Saudi Arabia's air force than with that of, say, Poland. Indeed, in terms of technological incompatibility, the gap between the RAF and the USAF appears somewhat narrower than that which separates the Polish and

AIR POWER: THE INSTRUMENT OF CHOICE?

British air forces. Neither should the difficulties encountered in the sharing of information, as opposed to equipment, be underestimated. Too much intelligence is too sensitive for it to be extended to every member of even quite close and proven partnerships like NATO. The Greeks, for instance, would be wary of allowing certain details of their military capabilities and dispositions to pass into the hands of the Turks. For the same reason, the reverse is also true. Likewise, the Americans have been very selective in granting their allies access to both intelligence and technological innovations. Again, this sort of consideration is frequently overlooked in discussions about a European security and defence 'identity', with the result that political ambitions all too often exceed that which is practicable.

Furthermore, if air power has reached maturity, it has done so at a time when emphasis is being placed increasingly on joint operations. Air forces have to collaborate more intimately with surface ones, not least because they have lost their monopoly on the exploitation of air power.[6] Particularly through the acquisition of helicopters and missile systems of varying descriptions, navies and armies are seeking to replicate capabilities that were once the preserve of air forces. It is unsurprising that, rather than stressing roles, missions and discrete organisations and structures, the latest doctrinal thinking concerning the employment of aerospace power stresses generic capabilities and competencies, such as power projection, air and space control, precision engagement and the exploitation of information. Just as communication systems and other core technologies need to be genuinely interoperable, if air power assets nominally owned by different services are to make the optimal contribution to joint endeavours, the doctrine underpinning their use needs to be harmonised, too.

MISSILES: THE BEST ALTERNATIVE?

A solution to the problems of commonality might yet be found within NATO's integrated military structure. Since they are unlikely to be part of a permanent alliance framework, putative foes, by contrast, will have to choose one or two systems from among those discrete forms of air power that are affordable and attainable on a purely national basis; and, of these, those that offer the most flexibility, operationally speaking, are likely to be favoured. It is highly probable that missiles, particularly modern, aerodynamic versions, and their cousins, uninhabited aerial vehicles (UAVs), will be seized upon as a cost-effective alternative to a balanced air force. Whilst missiles and UAVs alone cannot match the range of capabilities inherent in such a force, even those states that, traditionally, have

---

6. For a discussion of the land-air interface, for example, see Mungo Melvin's chapter, below.

regarded fleets of fixed- or rotary-wing aircraft as otiose or beyond their technical and financial means are likely to be tempted by the prospect of enjoying many of the advantages offered by air power without having to shoulder its wider costs.[7]

Royal Navy Tomahawk cruise missile. It is highly probable that missiles will be seized upon as a cost-effective alternative to a balanced air force.

Missiles not only continue to undergo refinement but also, despite the restraints imposed by the Missile Technology Control Regime, carry on proliferating. Ballistic models - once the only alternative to planes - have already spread far and wide, but these lack the flexibility afforded by aerodynamic versions, which possess many of the qualities and yet do not suffer from some of the disadvantages of crewed aircraft. Functioning in accordance with the same principles as planes, cruise missiles remain aloft through aerodynamic lift and, steered by organic computer or remote control, are powered and guided throughout their flight. Whilst this enables them to imitate inhabited aircraft to a degree at least, it also liberates them from the constraints that the presence of aircrew ineluctably entails. Unlike people, cruise missiles and UAVs neither tire, nor 'grey out', nor become bored. This permits them to achieve levels of endurance and agility that inhabited aircraft cannot. As they do not get frightened either, they have no qualms about approaching well-defended targets. In any event, they are that much more expendable than valuable aircrew.

In contrast to ballistic models, which are best suited to delivering indiscriminate blows against suitably large targets, advanced aerodynamic missiles are, furthermore, accurate to within a few metres, making them ideal for surgical strikes with conventional warheads. Their precision, variable flight-paths and comparatively low velocity, make them excellent platforms for the dispersal of biological or chemical agents as well.

---

7. For a wider, more far-reaching discussion of air strategy and the underdog, see Philip Sabin's chapter, below.

AIR POWER: THE INSTRUMENT OF CHOICE?

Moreover, being relatively compact, such missiles can be transported and stored in protective canisters and, as they do not need to be stabilised before use and require relatively little logistical support, can be unleashed from a wide variety of platforms. These characteristics render them that much more elusive, complicating any hostile counterforce operations. However, the principal merits of the modern aerodynamic missile are the ease with which it can be replicated and its intelligence. The latter depends upon software that can be copied endlessly and relatively cheaply, as can the airframe. Particularly in the larger, modular-design versions, refinements can be incorporated into the missile without too much difficulty, be they to its payload, reach or 'smartness'.

Accurate information is the key to the use of any precision weaponry, and a lack of integrated intelligence-gathering or dependable navigational systems can prove impediments to the optimal exploitation of such armaments. Nevertheless, even where they can only be employed against targets that are easily discernible, aerodynamic missiles and UAVs offer a satisfying degree of operational flexibility for a fraction of the cost of crewed aircraft, not least because they do not need the infrastructure, highly skilled workforces and advanced supporting industries associated with the maintenance and operation of fleets of sophisticated combat planes. They are likely to be identified by inferior powers as the best available instruments for offsetting the West's current dominance of the skies.

Indeed, the USA's intense and growing fascination with missile defence is surely testimony to this.[8] Although, during the Gulf War, the Iraqis proved wholly incapable of challenging the qualitatively and quantitatively superior airforces of the Allies with their own combat aircraft, they were able to cause appreciable political and, in some respects at least, military problems through their use of crude Scud rockets. Since then, the USA has invested a great deal of effort and resources in trying to develop a range of active defence systems to counter the threat posed by ballistic and, to a lesser extent, aerodynamic missiles. It has also forged collaborative programmes with those of its client states that are seen as being particularly at risk, such as Taiwan and Israel. At the same time, it has made ever more use of cruise missiles in its own operations following their debut in the Gulf War. Whilst one might debate whether there is a RMA or not, the sight of these weapons darting through the streets of Baghdad to attack discrete buildings did appear to be something revolutionary. Certainly, they have since been employed to great effect against important, fixed targets, such as command, control, surveillance, target-acquisition and communication centres, weapons laboratories and munition and supply dumps, many of which were so heavily protected as to make attacking them with

---

8. For a more detailed discussion of this and some comparison with European attitudes, see D Gates, 'Transatlantic Perspectives on Extended Integrated Air Defense', *Comparative Strategy*, Vol. 18, 1999, p. 59-85.

crewed aircraft an unpalatable alternative. Indeed, asymmetries in vulnerability as well as in power play a part in determining the outcome of a conflict; and, just as cruise missiles have been employed to cripple opposing air-defence networks from the outset of an attack, they have also been used in missions where any loss of aircrew could have proved politically disastrous. A good case in point occurred in 1996 when, just eight weeks before the US presidential election, President Clinton authorised punitive action against Iraq following her occupation of the Kurdish 'safe haven' of Sulaymaniyah. The attacks comprised, not raids by crewed planes, but salvos of cruise missiles directed at targets in southern Iraq. Regardless of how effective these actually proved in terms of the material and psychological damage they inflicted on the Iraqi military machine, the strikes seem to have been successful in fulfilling their principal goal of helping to rescue the president from a political dilemma.

During the Kosovo campaign, US forces launched no fewer than 220 cruise missiles. Apart from the Americans, only the British Royal Navy possessed such weapons and the concomitant capability to mount precise attacks on targets that lay out of sight. Even this was largely dependent upon navigational data supplied by the USA, however. Nearly a third of the UK's entire stock of Tomahawk Land Attack Missiles was consumed in the course of Operation Allied Force. Similarly, the contribution made by UAVs to the aerial offensive against the Federal Republic of Yugoslavia is noteworthy. Although its endurance is at most 30 minutes and its maximum operating altitude is just 600 metres, French and German forces found the CL-289, with its infrared and video scanners, which provide almost real-time information, quite useful. The Americans also fielded Predator and Hunter UAVs. The former, which had already seen extensive service over Bosnia between 1995 and 1998, is capable of attaining an altitude of nearly 8,000 metres and can stay aloft for up to 24 hours. Equipped with an assortment of sensors, including synthetic aperture radars, which can penetrate cloud cover, and advanced data links that can be integrated into a wider intelligence network, it is representative of a new, sophisticated generation of uninhabited platforms that seems destined to play an ever greater role in military operations.

WAR AND THE RELATIONSHIP BETWEEN PEOPLE AND TECHNOLOGY

The replacement of people by machines, be they 'smart' missiles or UAVs, is, however, a controversial matter. No man-made reconnaissance device can match the human brain and eye, nor can computers replicate much of humankind's complex sense of discretion or political consciousness. The spectre of a brave, new world in which we have lost control is an alarming one at the best of times. Today, however, we face a paradoxical situation. The very availability of, above all, precision weaponry has created not so much the hope as the assumption that war - which is an activity unique to *homo sapiens* - can be conducted to a standard of perfection that is seldom expected, still less found, in any other sphere of human endeavour. War is and always was a profoundly intractable business that is all about inflicting death and suffering for political purposes. Yet the belief that it can be successfully prosecuted with few, if any, casualties is proving too appealing for a public that has been seduced into applying peacetime standards to armed conflicts through, ironically, the calculated use of such anodyne terminology as 'peace support operations' and 'collateral damage'; that has been encouraged to equate sophistication with infallibility; and that glimpses the possibilities of modern warfare without understanding the problems inherent in it. Again, it is misconceptions such as these that make the RMA dream so alluring. In the final analysis, however, any technology is only as good as the people operating it. This makes morale the single most important factor in war, which is essentially a psychological process, not an exact science.

From its earliest days as a military instrument, air power was portrayed by many of its advocates as the revolutionary weapon that would banish the need for protracted and gory surface combat by deciding conflicts quickly, cheaply and relatively cleanly. In the aftermath of the bloody trench warfare of 1914-18 and the economic, social and political collapse that it engendered, this was a particularly appealing vision, even if it was to fade in the light of actual experience over the next few decades. Now, some theorists maintain, thanks essentially to information-age technology, that promise can not only be fulfilled but even surpassed; armed conflicts can be successfully waged by aerospace forces at the cost of very few, if any, casualties to themselves and only minimal losses among non-combatants.

THE POLITICAL CONTEXT OF AEROSPACE OPERATIONS

Again, however, reality would seem to be more complex than the theory suggests. War is a political activity that takes place within a cultural, technical, economic and social framework that varies in time and space, making historical experience unique. After all, technology is just one feature of a given environment and has been known to form an island of constancy in a sea of political and social upheaval.[9] As armed forces tend to

---

9. A good illustration of this phenomenon is the technological consistency experienced in warfare in Europe between the early 1700s and the mid 1800s. This seduced many military intellectuals, notably Antione-henri de Jomini, into arguing that the basic nature of war could not alter. Certainly, the campaigns of Napoleon were waged with essentially the same technology that Malborough had employed a hundred years earlier. Indeed, it was not until the Crimean War that this stability was revealed to be in any jeopardy. Even then, theorists like Jomini and Colonel William Napier insisted that any changes were marginal, not revolutionary. During the same period of 150 years, however, the Eurocentric world went through a period of tremendous political and social turbulence, not least because of the incidence of major wars.

reflect the societies that spawn them, it is improbable that a significant change in one will not lead to alterations to the other. Any discussion of a revolution, or a process of lesser change, in military affairs has to be seen in this context. Operation Provide Comfort, which sought to give displaced Kurds humanitarian aid; the air exclusion zones over Southern and Northern Iraq; the destruction of facilities suspected of being connected with Iraqi WMD programmes: all of these are illustrations of how air power has offered at least partial solutions to a variety of recent problems. Nevertheless, if the 'information age' opens up new possibilities for armed forces, particularly air forces, it also creates new difficulties.

Not the least of these are two interrelated phenomena: popular access to information about military operations and the sheer intrusiveness of the international news media, which function on a global basis and seize upon the anecdotal rather than the statistical. Ever since the Crimean War, when, thanks to the electric telegraph and the latest printing techniques, the reporting of events as or very soon after they occurred was first shown to be feasible, professional war correspondents have been locked in a somewhat ambivalent relationship with the political and military classes of their and other states.[10] Nowadays, the public in general and in the West in particular are more politically conscious, if not informed, than ever before, and sensitivities about the use of military force are commensurably acute. In the great aerial campaigns of the 1990s, the focus of media concern has oscillated between, on the one hand, the infliction of collateral damage and, on the other, the loss of planes and crews. Public opinion - or the vociferous element of it at least - has followed these shifts, influencing targeting strategy and even tactics. The early losses of RAF Tornado aircraft and the capture of crewmen in the Gulf War only increased the emphasis placed on the safety of attacking units; Allied aircraft were habitually kept above a certain altitude so as to minimise the threat posed by Iraqi defences. Indeed, it was largely owing to the fact that aircrew losses were kept extraordinarily low that public and political support for the protracted air offensive was forthcoming. There were moments when it wavered, however, notably when the Al Firdos bunker was bombed and most of its occupants - some of whom at least turned out to be civilians - were incinerated.

Although engaging targets from a safe height helps avoid casualties among attacking units, it also increases the scope for mishaps, as several incidents during the Kosovo campaign illustrated; civilian traffic was mistakenly perceived to be hostile and bombed accordingly. Incidences of collateral damage like these call into question the very assumptions upon which information-age warfare is supposedly founded. They also underscore the fact that information *per se* is of little value; it needs to be interpreted by

---

10. See, for instance, T Royle, *Crimea: The Great Crimean War*, 1854-56 (London, 1999) p. 178-9.

AIR POWER: THE INSTRUMENT OF CHOICE?

people and put to good use.[11] However, the very speed and sophistication of modern command and control mechanisms has greatly increased the scope for 'reach down', active interference in the minutiae of combat by higher commanders and politicians. This is particularly true of air operations, which, throughout the radio age, have generally been subject to an appreciable degree of centralised, remote regulation. Winston Churchill's tribute to the 'few', the RAF fighter pilots who fought the Battle of Britain, is as revealing in this regard as it is famous: only a tiny proportion of an air force's personnel actually engage in combat. If only because of that fact, aircrew have customarily been regarded as the elite of their service and have enjoyed a pre-eminent role in decision-making at every level. Today, however, the very complexity of aerial warfare is making this state of affairs appear anachronistic. Whilst aircrew must still face the physical dangers inherent in combat, the temptation to seek to control their every move is one that senior officers and politicians can find irresistible. At the very least, this compounds the ethical strains imposed on the lower ranks and leads to them engaging in 'reach back', whereby they seek sufficient clarification of their superiors' instructions to create an audit trail should anything go awry.

Particularly in circumstances where every bomb dropped has the potential to cause a political as well as a physical explosion, the search for such safeguards is only to be expected. Furthermore, as Thomas Keaney and Eliot Cohen have suggested, air power's principal merit is that it offers the prospect of gratification without demanding much in the way of commitment.[12] It is surely revealing that, with the launching of Operation Deliberate Force in August 1995, for instance, it was not so much to the UN's reinforced terrestrial forces as to NATO's air power that the task of imposing peace on the Balkans' warring factions was entrusted. Similarly, whilst enjoining them to achieve success without incurring *any* casualties, it was to aerospace forces that the West's leaders turned in their search for a solution to the Kosovo conundrum. This feat was achieved; just two combat aircraft were lost in the course of over 38,000 missions, while no aircrew were killed or taken prisoner. Nevertheless, Western politicians were evidently that much more willing to risk the death or capture of a relative handful of their military personnel than they were to sanction the employment of ground forces.[13] These would not only have had to be of very appreciable dimensions indeed but, once committed, would also have been comparatively vulnerable and far harder to extricate, as subsequent events have proved.

---

11. As Stuart Peach highlights in his chapter below, the sheer volume of information flowing into a modern headquarters and demanding interpretation can all too easily exacerbate, rather than ease, the problems of command and control.
12. T A Keaney and E A Cohen, *Revolution in Warfare? Air Power in The Persian Gulf* (Annapolis, Maryland, 1995) p. 321.
13. This point was repeatedly made by officials and politicians involved in the crisis, not least in the television documentary *War in Europe* that was broadcast on Britain's Channel 4 in January and February, 2000.

AIR POWER: THE INSTRUMENT OF CHOICE?

On the other hand, whilst aircrew might be regarded as relatively expendable, in absolute terms, they are not. Just as cavalrymen have always looked down figuratively and literally on 'poor foot sloggers', today's air force pilots especially are modern knights mounted on high-technology steeds and, in contrast to naval and army aviators, who are widely seen as mere adjuncts to the reach and perspective of their warships and regiments, respectively, tend to be regarded, if only within their own service, as an elite. In any case, precisely because air power is such a symbol of technological supremacy, the downing of a single aircraft can all too easily be depicted by an adversary as a political and moral victory, particularly when the platform involved is a state-of-the-art stealth aircraft, as happened during Operation Allied Force. But whereas technology can usually be replaced, individual people cannot; and the death or capture - the latter all too easily triggering ongoing media interest - of aircrew can prove commensurably disconcerting to politicians and the public alike. Certainly, reaction to such an eventuality can be vigorous. The priority attached to the search for and rescue of Allied aircrew shot down over the Balkans - notably Captain Scott O'Grady and the pilot of the stealth aircraft mentioned above - is revealing in this respect. Likewise, the apparent unwillingness to actually employ Apache attack helicopters over Kosovo was politically embarrassing, not least because their movement to the Balkans had been accompanied by a blaze of publicity. Intended to terrify the Serbs into submission, these platforms seem to have had more of an impact on America's political leaders; though stalwarts of the Gulf War and lauded for their firepower and sophistication, they were, it was feared, too vulnerable to destruction by low-level air defences.

Air power is widely perceived as a coercive instrument, even when it is not being utilised coercively. When it is, the fact that its very use can be seen as escalatory makes any employment of air power difficult to reconcile with the notion of a limited war, particularly one that is presented as a peace enforcement or support operation. The whole objective of the latter is to prevent any kind of escalation. Yet the methodical 'degrading' of an opponent's military capabilities inevitably takes time and, particularly when conducted under media and public scrutiny, can all too easily lead to the belligerents experiencing a growing sense of frustration. This is likely to lead to the expansion of target sets in any aerial offensive. Indeed, during the Kosovo campaign, the Yugoslavian electricity grid, chemical plants and even a television station were portrayed as legitimate targets by NATO in a war that was supposedly directed against a regime, not its people. Here, as with the bombing of facilities thought to be connected with Iraq's WMD programme, for all its sophistication air power proved a rather crude instrument when set against the flexibility that the use of ground forces offers; ideal for destroying things, it is less adept at controlling events and terrain. Although at least one eminent commentator on military affairs had the candour and nobility to admit that his predictions about the efficacy of Operation Allied Force had been flawed.[14] That a 52,000-strong occupation force has had to be stationed in Kosovo to maintain what is at best a semblance of peace surely confirms that air power cannot do everything.

In fact, the success of the great aerial offensives of the 1990s owes much to the contribution made by ground forces, even if this often only took the form of a passive threat to intervene. This point is too frequently overlooked or understated by air power's more ardent advocates. If, for example, Operation Deliberate Force can claim to have been at least a qualified success, its precursor - the pinprick, aerial attacks on mostly Serbian terrestrial forces threatening the integrity of the UN's 'safe havens' - was largely ineffectual. In this thoroughly maladroit attempt to manage a war as if it were a chemical process, not only were the Serbs not coerced but also their opponents were encouraged to go on resisting by the expectation that the great powers in general and the West in particular would, sooner or later, be compelled to resort to intervention of a more decisive nature, if only to salvage their own credibility. As acrimonious disagreements over policy regarding Bosnia emerged between both the Americans and the European members of NATO and between the Russian Federation and the West, this surmise proved correct. With the reputation and cohesion of the transatlantic alliance in jeopardy, the USA initiated a policy that was to effectively subordinate the UN's role in Bosnia to that of NATO.

THE GROUND-AIR INTERFACE

That, prior to the commencement of Operation Deliberate Force, actual or threatened air strikes failed to yield the desired results can for the most part be attributed to the restrictions imposed by the UN on NATO's use of violence against the warring parties. Perhaps the most glaring illustration of this can be seen in the reluctance of General Janvier and the UN authorities to even try to use air power to save the enclave of Srebrnica, a town that had been misleadingly - and, as things turned out, fatally - decreed a 'safe haven' by an organisation that, if only because it was endeavouring to remain an impartial, humanitarian agency in the midst of a civil war, manifestly lacked the military capabilities and political will to make it one. However, once the transatlantic alliance effectively supplanted the UN and these 'dual key' arrangements were removed, it was possible to articulate a less convoluted mission statement and fulfil it by means of a more liberal application of military muscle. Whilst this took the form of an aerial bombardment of Serbian troops and positions, it should not be forgotten that Operation Deliberate Force supplemented the operations mounted against the Serbs by their adversaries on the ground.

---

14. See John Keegan's remarks in the [London] *Daily Telegraph*, 4 and 6 June, 1999.

AIR POWER: THE INSTRUMENT OF CHOICE?

   Similarly, the activities of hostile ground forces also complicated matters for the Serbian units operating within Kosovo and should be taken into consideration in any evaluation of Operation Allied Force. Although the precision weapon systems at their disposal had undergone at least incremental improvements since the time of the Gulf War, many attacking aircraft were constrained by, firstly, orders to venture no lower than an altitude of 5,000 metres so as to minimise the danger posed by enemy air defences and, secondly, by poor visibility, which resulted from adverse weather and smoke. Since all the armaments utilised by the RAF, for example, employ line-of-sight guidance mechanisms - namely, laser, infrared or television - which can be thwarted by low cloud, mist or smoke, poor visibility was a limitation that the Yugoslav forces could capitalise on and often did, particularly during the first three weeks of the campaign when the weather conditions were frequently so unfavourable as to make bombing too hazardous an undertaking for many NATO aircraft to risk. By contrast, though not susceptible to the vagaries of the atmosphere, weapons that rely upon inertial navigation - notably the Tomahawk cruise missile and the air-delivered Joint Direct Attack Munition - were suited only to the attack of static targets. Whilst these can often be identified before hostilities commence and cannot evade attack, mobile assets are a different matter entirely. Certainly, whenever they were not obliged to concentrate so as to be able to engage KLA guerrillas or, if necessary, invading NATO troops, the Yugoslav forces could disperse and take cover, denying the enemy worthwhile targets and reducing the impact of any aerial bombardment appreciably. When, on the other hand, they were caught in the open or in cohesive formations, they invariably sustained serious losses.

   Indeed, it would be interesting to speculate just how effective NATO's air power would have proved had it been called upon to deal with a nebulous threat like the KLA rather than with the more viable target presented by the armed forces of the Federal Republic of Yugoslavia. Certainly, in their struggle with the rebels in Chechnya during the winter of 1999-2000, the Russian armed forces found that heavy, remote bombardment by aircraft and artillery might help reduce casualties among attacking troops, but is only an imperfect solution to this kind of problem, not least because of the high degree of 'collateral damage' it can result in. The Russian government, however, proved adept at shrugging off any international or domestic criticism of its armed forces' actions in a conflict that was evidently seen as, at worst, regrettable but necessary by the majority of the Russian people.

CONCLUSION

There are moments when the peaceful competition that normally prevails between human beings has the potential to degenerate into violence. After all, war is - or should be, at least - the continuation of policy by other, namely violent, means. Every armed conflict is unique and waging one at all is essentially an act of choice; it is the degree of choice involved that varies from case to case. If, in the eyes of some states, aerospace forces have become the instrument of first resort, it is also true that not just the availability of air power but also the achievement of air superiority, if not supremacy, are now prerequisites for the launching of many types of terrestrial operation. Indeed, today, it is almost inconceivable that, for all the strength of its surface forces, the world's sole remaining superpower, the USA, would embark on *any* military venture without enjoying control of the skies over the region concerned. Securing this at a price that the public and their elected politicians are prepared to pay could, however, prove increasingly difficult to achieve. Employing violence as precisely as conditions and technology permitted, in Operations Instant Thunder, Deliberate Force and Allied Force, aerospace power enabled coalitions to achieve success within the parameters laid down by their dominant political authorities, not the least of whose stipulations was that casualties among their servicemen and women and among non-combatants should be kept to a minimum. The very extent to which that particular goal was fulfilled sets a precedent that can only prove immensely difficult to maintain. The exact circumstances that prevailed in the Gulf and in the Balkan campaigns cannot and will not be replicated. Any 'lessons' drawn from these conflicts have to be seen in this context.

AIR POWER: THE INSTRUMENT OF CHOICE?

CHAPTER 3

AIR POWER AND THE REVOLUTION IN MILITARY AFFAIRS
Wing Commander David Caddick

INTRODUCTION

THE END OF THE COLD WAR and the seemingly effortless victory of the US-led coalition in the 1990/91 Gulf War saw the emergence of a new school of thought that professed there was a technology driven 'Revolution in Military Affairs' (RMA) taking place. Not only was it perceived that an RMA was underway, but also it was claimed that air power was a leading force in this new epoch. The concept of an RMA quickly gained momentum, but the term RMA, like all popular terms, has lost much of its meaning through over use. Therefore, the aim of this paper is to critically expose the thinking behind the RMA and offer some thoughts as to the role that air power may play in such a concept. It will examine the RMA concept from a historical perspective and examine the evidence that suggests an RMA is occurring. It will then explore how air power is seen as a central tenet of the RMA before highlighting some problems that the RMA may bring.

DEFINING THE RMA

We use words because they have a meaning. So what then do we mean by the term RMA? This is our first problem. The term RMA has no agreed definition, and it is precisely how one defines an RMA which will in turn decide the relationship between an RMA and air power. At first glance the concept of an RMA suggests profound change; after all, that is what revolutions are all about, but how do we judge if that change has been revolutionary? Here we fall into our first problem, that of self interest. The term, like so many others, is often used without definition[1] to describe or justify many different aspects of contemporary military affairs. Professor Lawrence Freedman

---

1. Like the current vogue for using the term 'international community'. No one has yet defined to the author's satisfaction who or what makes up the international community and, more importantly, who is not considered to be part of this community.

points out that the term RMA has advantages as a 'marketing device' which dramatises issues by linking them to a sense of profound change, and thus giving them more credibility than perhaps they merit[2]. Similarly Professor Colin Gray claims:

> 'The point is not that the historians at issue are foolish or wrong; far from it. Rather is the point that everyone has an RMA story to tell, a cause to advance. The general point of relevance is that scholars armed with grand, high and elusive concepts assuredly will find that for which they search.'[3]

Our second problem is our perception of a revolution. The term suggests a rapid transformation, but is the RMA rapid? Over what period of time does change need to take place in order for it to be revolutionary? Indeed can a series of small incremental evolutionary changes cumulatively provide such synergy (the whole being greater than the sum of the parts) that it becomes revolutionary? Remaining with the problem of perception, can we judge an RMA from the viewpoint of the present or can it only be with hindsight that a revolution can be discerned? Freedman sums the situation up thus:

> 'Revolution involves more than change, and certainly more than simply change of an incremental variety. It represents a moment of transformation. Such moments may not be appreciated until later historians study them; occasionally, they may be imagined in advance. With the RMA, as with most revolutions, there is confusion over whether it represents a stage in the historical process, or a vision that cannot be realised unless the visionaries seize the initiative.'[4]

It is, therefore, not merely enough to have some form of change to constitute an RMA. After all change abounds wherever one looks in military affairs; it is rather that an RMA must also involve some form of conceptual change in the way in which military affairs are conducted. Thus for an RMA to be truly 'revolutionary' it must encompass the wider aspects of conflict. An RMA cannot be formulated simply by platforms, munitions, information systems and hardware. These necessary preconditions must be

---

2. L Freedman, 'The Revolution in Strategic Affairs', International Institute for Strategic Studies, *Adelphi Paper* 318 (Oxford: Oxford University Press, 1998) p. 7.
3. C S Gray, 'The American Revolution in Military Affairs: An Interim Assessment', *The Strategic and Combat Studies Institute Occasional Paper*, No 28, 1997, p. 11-12.
4. L Freedman, Op Cit, p. 7-8.

supported by an important set of intangibles that have determined the outcome of war since its inception, namely, clarity of purpose backed by proficiency of execution.[5] Therefore, the recognition of the potential effects of change upon military affairs and subsequent adaptation of concepts and organisations, concerned with the whole spectrum of military affairs, are required to constitute an RMA.

AN HISTORICAL PERSPECTIVE

Historically the term RMA was first coined as a result of the historical debates over the major changes in warfare that occurred in the 16th and 17th centuries. However, despite this wealth of historical debate over previous RMAs, the precise definition and agreement over what constitutes an RMA is no more clear than the current debate. The essential elements appear to be some form of change, be it technological, economic, political or social, which results in step changes in the conduct of military affairs with subsequent impact upon the operation of the international political system. Viewing RMAs historically, Ritcheson identifies three common features to military revolutions. First, and most importantly, new technologies must be complemented by doctrinal and organisational adaptations as it is the synergy among these three elements that fundamentally alters the conduct of warfare. Second, the magnitude of change compared to the previous state of military affairs must be great. This can be manifested in decisive military results, relatively low casualty rates and a disproportionate destruction of enemy forces. The third feature of an RMA is the blending or blurring of the strategic, operational and tactical levels. Increased battlefield manoeuvrability and communications have been a key feature, particularly in this century, of the merging of these three levels.[6]

Tilford claims that from an historical perspective, technology does not necessarily always drive an RMA and whilst it can be a part, indeed a major part, of an RMA, it does not necessarily lead to an RMA. Indeed the effects of improved technology or new discoveries are not always felt immediately. The possession of a technological advantage means little if there is no impetus to use it conceptually and strategically:

---

5. B S Lambeth, 'The Technology Revolution in Air Warfare', *Survival*, Vol 39, No 1, Spring 1997, p. 75.
6. P L Ritcheson, 'The Future of Military Affairs: Revolution or Evolution?', *Strategic Review* Vol 24, No 2, Spring 1996, p. 31-40. See also D Jablonsky, 'US Military Doctrine and the Revolution in Military Affairs', *Parameters*, Vol 24, No 3, Autumn 1994, p. 18-36 for a detailed examination of the RMA and the blurring or mixing of the strategic, operational and tactical levels of war.

AIR POWER AND THE REVOLUTION IN MILITARY AFFAIRS

> *'RMAs and rapid advances in technology are not always related. The armies of Napoleon, for instance, were part of a revolution in military affairs that derived from the social and political upheavals of the French Revolution. While the armies of the French Revolution coincided with the beginnings of the Industrial Revolution, the incorporation of the people into the war effort through the levee en masse was more important than anything issuing from the Industrial Revolution. Furthermore, the weapons used by the armies of 1815 were basically the same as those available in 1789 or, for that matter, in 1715. Conversely, the military-technical revolution that issued from the maturing Industrial Revolution at the beginning of the 20th century did not translate into a true RMA until after the First World War, although all the technological elements were available during the war: the railroad, machine guns, tanks, long-range and rifled artillery, rapid-fire rifles, electronic means of communication, and airplanes.'* [7]

Tilford's point is well made; the use of technology to achieve decisive changes in warfare relies as much on the conceptual and consequent doctrinal vision of how to harness the new technologies. Thus the potential impact of machine guns, barbed wire, entrenched fortifications and heavy artillery at a tactical level was evident in the late 19th and early 20th centuries during the American Civil War, the Boer War and the Sino-Japanese Wars, but military and strategic thinkers in Europe were unable to grasp their significance to future European wars.[8] Similarly, the strategic potential of economic warfare, submarine warfare and the mobilisation of the whole nation's resources as demonstrated in the American Civil War were lost on the political and strategic thinkers of the time. Thus are those actually involved in embryonic RMAs, whether as direct participants or observers, really able to recognise and judge the significance of developments which lead to an RMA? Indeed given their conceptual framework, which is largely based upon past experience and knowledge, is it reasonable to assume that an RMA can be perceived by those actually involved, or is it only with hindsight and the view of the historian that RMAs can be discerned? Indeed is an RMA really a construct of the historian? As Gray points out, there are many examples of transformations of warfare but only a certain few have been selected as RMAs:

---

7. E H Tilford, 'The Revolution in Military Affairs: Prospects and Cautions', *US Army War College Strategic Studies Institute Paper,* June 23 1995, Pt 1, p. 1.
8. For a detailed historical background and analysis of the inertia in adopting the machine by European armies prior to WWI see J Ellis, *A Social History of the Machine Gun* (London: Croom Helm,1975).

AIR POWER AND THE REVOLUTION IN MILITARY AFFAIRS

'The historical point is that candidate RMAs, arguable transformations of war, or just plain old significant-seeming changes in the terms and conditions of war, abound wherever one looks.'[9]

There is no doubt, however, that the First World War did see a transformation of warfare as new technologies and concepts of their employment were applied to the conduct of the war. Indeed it is possible to argue that the RMA of the First World War did not cease with the signing of the Armistice in 1918 but continued through the inter-war years with the work of Liddel-Hart, Fuller, Douhet and other military strategists who continued to develop the conceptual use of new technologies and new ways of waging war.

Although somewhat neglected in discussions of RMAs, the advent of nuclear weapons must also be classed as an RMA. Although, thankfully, they have never been used, the threat of nuclear weapons during the Cold War was a major influence on the conduct of war during that period, resulting in the development and articulation of various nuclear doctrines such as Assured Destruction, Tripwire, Mutually Assured Destruction and Graduated Response. Whilst these strategies now seem relegated to the annals of history, it must be remembered that the Cold War, with its ever present threat of nuclear war, was a major influence on the development of military capabilities and strategic and doctrinal thought, and although a nuclear war was never fought, the impact of nuclear weapons on military affairs must surely qualify this period as an RMA.[10] Indeed thinkers such as Bernard Brodie argued that after 1945 the nature of military affairs had changed fundamentally in so much as the task of the military was to prevent wars, not to fight them.[11]

---

9. C S Gray, 'The American Revolution in Military Affairs: An Interim Assessment', *The Strategic and Combat Studies Institute Occasional Paper*, No 28, 1997, p. 11.
10. For a detailed history of nuclear strategy see L Freedman, *The Evolution of Nuclear Strategy* (2^{nd}Ed) (Basingstoke: MacMillan Press Ltd, 1989). Chapters 1 and 2 in particular deal with the impact of nuclear weapons on conventional military doctrine in the late 1940s.
11. See B Brodie, *Strategy in the Missile Age* (Princeton New Jersey: Princeton University Press, 1965), in particular Chapter 8 'The Anatomy of Deterrence'.

AIR POWER AND THE REVOLUTION IN MILITARY AFFAIRS

The advent of nuclear weapons must be regarded as an RMA owing to
their impact on military doctrine since the Second World War.

In more recent times, and somewhat ahead of their Western counterparts, writers in the Soviet Union coined the phrase 'Military Technical Revolution' or MTR in the early 1980s when discussing the impact of the West's, primarily the United States', military technological lead over the Soviet Union and its impact on superpower relations.[12] The Soviets recognised that although their doctrinal ability would be able to exploit new technologies, their economic and technical abilities would not be able to exploit the MTR. This highlights the need for the marrying up of technical advances and the conceptual ability to exploit those advances in ways that will offer transformations in warfare.

History then gives us no clearer definition of what constitutes an RMA and if anything emphasises that an RMA is not a precise phenomenon which has a clearly identifiable start and end, or indeed that its impact can be recognised without the benefit of historical analysis. However, the common elements of an RMA appear to require some form of change to take place, be it technological, economic, political or social, combined with the recognition of the potential effects of that change upon military affairs, and subsequent adaptation of concepts and organisations concerned with the whole spectrum of military affairs.

---

12. See D Gourd, 'Is There a Military-Technical Revolution in Americaís Future?', *The Washington Quarterly*, Vol 16, No 4, Autumn 1993, p. 176-179.

AIR POWER AND THE REVOLUTION IN MILITARY AFFAIRS

A CONTEMPORARY RMA?

The catalyst for the debate over whether there is a current RMA was undoubtedly the spectacular success of air power in the Gulf War of 1990/91.[13] In this conflict the technological superiority of the coalition forces, led and dominated in numbers, organisation and doctrine by the United States, shattered the Iraqi army, driving it from its occupation of Kuwait, so that in the space of a few months the Iraqi army fell from being the fourth largest army in the world to being the second largest army in Iraq. However, the seeds of the technological victory of the coalition in the Gulf had been sown back in the 1960s and 1970s when satellites, computers and laser guidance had all been developed and to some extent tested in the lesser conflicts of the Cold War. However, the Gulf War can be seen as the culminating point of all these developments. The victory of the coalition was not due solely to its technological edge. It was the first opportunity that the United States had to put into practice its doctrinal Air/Land Battle concept which it had developed as an antithesis to its perceived failing in the Vietnam war.[14] Thus its manoeuvrist approach to the conflict was as much a factor in its victory as its possession of advanced superior military technology, in particular air power:

> 'The 1991 Gulf War is commonly viewed as the first real 'electronic war'. The sight of cruise missiles and smart bombs roaming to their destination with pin-point accuracy has created a widespread impression of an uneven match between a high-tech superpower and a hapless, ill-equipped, and backward Third World army. Yet much as it is common, this popular perception is largely misconceived. The key to allied success lay not in overwhelming technological superiority - for the Iraqi Army was a far cry from the technologically backward force portrayed by many accounts of the war. Rather, the allies' astounding victory represents the triumph of an advanced manoeuvre-oriented operational doctrine over an archaic attrition-oriented one.'[15]

---

13. For a review of the impact of technology and information war on the conduct of the 1990/91 Gulf War see E Mann, 'Desert Storm: The First Information War?', *Airpower Journal*, Vol 8, No 4, Winter 1994, p. 4-14. See also S Biddle, 'Victory Misunderstood. What the Gulf War Tells Us about the Future of Conflict', *International Security*, Vol 21, No 2, Fall 1996, p.139-179; E Karsh, 'Reflections on the 1990-91 Gulf Conflict', *The Journal of Strategic Studies*, Vol 19, No 3, September 1996, p. 303-320; and T G Mabuken and B D Watts, 'What the Gulf War Can (and Cannot) Tell Us about the Future of Warfare', *International Security*, Vol 22, No 2, Fall 1997, p. 151-162, for a debate over whether technology was the deciding factor in the outcome of the conflict.
14. The Air/Land Battle doctrine was published in 1986 as US FM 100-5. See D Jablonsky, 'US Military Doctrine and the Revolution in Military Affairs', *Parameters*, Vol 24, No 3, Autumn 1994, p. 21-22.
15. E Karsh, 'Reflections on the 1990-91 Gulf Conflict', *The Journal of Strategic Studies*, Vol 19, No 3, September 1996, p. 313.

The Basra Road 'Highway of Death'. The spectacular success of air power in the Gulf War has stimulated the debate about whether a technological RMA is in progress.

    Thus the fusing together of incremental technological advances (together with the recognition of the potential effects of those changes upon military affairs) with a subsequent adaptation of doctrine suggests that the Gulf War was indeed an identifiable point at which it could be concluded that an RMA was in progress. Aside from the merely technical advances which were employed to great effect, the Gulf War seemed to once and for all lay the ghosts of the American experience of Vietnam. In many circles military power, and air power in particular, was now seen to be an appropriate instrument to use in international affairs, and more importantly the cost in human terms, particularly American human terms, was seen to be low. War fighting, through the medium of air power, was now swift, decisive and affordable. Additionally, the end of the Cold War reduced or indeed removed the threat of regional conflicts escalating into nuclear Armageddon between the superpowers. This perhaps is one of the key changes in military affairs since the end of the Cold War. The military instrument has gained a new utility and acceptability in the psyche of the western nations. However, the Gulf War was exceptional in many respects and the unique geographical, political and climatic conditions which overwhelmingly favoured the United States and its technological advantages over Iraq, are often conveniently forgotten when analysing the effects of the Gulf War. Nonetheless there has been a distinct shift in thinking concerning the utility of the military instrument.

AIR POWER AND THE REVOLUTION IN MILITARY AFFAIRS

In these changes in both technology and attitudes towards military affairs three distinct but inter-related areas of development can be identified. These are: the development of information war, the development of a 'system of systems' and conceptual and doctrinal changes; all of which are underpinned by United States dominance of these three activities and the subsequent peculiarly American approach to military affairs.

Information war is not a new phenomenon; it is as old as warfare itself, as epitomised in Sun Tzu's dictum of "knowing the enemy and oneself, one will be invincible"[16] In simple terms it involves degrading an opponent's information system whilst enhancing one's own information system. The US Air Force have a much more detailed definition: 'Actions taken to achieve information superiority by affecting adversary information, information-based processes, information systems, and computer-based networks while leveraging and defending one's own information, information-based processes, information systems, and computer-based networks.'[17] In the past information warfare has been limited by the ability of opposing sides to collect, interrupt and disseminate information. Advances in technology have so increased this capacity that some writers argue that the realm of information or 'cyberspace' can be counted as one of the main arenas in any future conflict.[18] Information war may indeed replace conventional armed force as the main military instrument and information war should be seen as a war winner in its own right and not merely an adjunct to the traditional use of force:

'It would be a strategic mistake of historical proportions to focus narrowly on the technologies; force the technologies of information warfare to fit familiar, internally defined models like speed, precision, and lethality; and miss the vision and opportunity for a genuine military revolution. Information warfare is real warfare; it is about using information to create such a mismatch between us and an opponent that, as Sun Tzu would argue, the opponent's strategy is defeated before his first forces can be deployed or his first shots fired.'[19]

---

16. General Tao Hanzhang, *Sun Tzu The Art of War* (Wordsworth Editions: Herts, 1993).
17. *Air Force Doctrine Document 1* (Maxwell AEB: Alabama, Headquarters Air Force Doctrine Center, September 1977).
18. For detailed discussions about cyberspace operations see M Libbiki, 'The Emerging Primacy of Information', *Orbis*, Vol 40, No 2, Spring 1996, p. 261-276, and 'Defending Cyberspace and Other Metaphors', *National Defence University*, Washington DC, February 1997.
19. G J Stein, 'Information Warfare', *Air Power Supplement*, Air Clues, London 1997, p.21 (Unpublished RAF Journal).

AIR POWER AND THE REVOLUTION IN MILITARY AFFAIRS

Returning to the Gulf War, it is noticeable that the United States and its allies went to the battlefield with a total dominance of satellite Earth orbits, and marshalled unprecedented space-dependent military capabilities to help it achieve decisive victory. The Iraqi leadership, conversely, approached war in such a conventional fashion that it did not even exploit the space-based information potentially available to it. Thus this unchallenged advantage in space has persuaded American military analysts that such global hegemony, in terms of surveillance, may be taken for granted, or indeed is a key to future victories.[20]

If the developments in information warfare are indeed linked together with more conventional military force then a new system of war fighting is possible, as the British Ministry of Defence foresee:

> *'The biggest change in the conduct of future military operations is likely to come not from weapons alone but from the application of information technology to military command and control. There is a growing body of opinion, particularly in the US, that we are approaching a 'Revolution in Military Affairs' in which we will see a step change in military capabilities resulting from the synergistic combination of long-range precision weapons with networks of advanced sensors and data processors. Radically improved capabilities in the field of information processing and communications systems will increase situational awareness (knowing where hostile and friendly forces are, and where they are not) by combining information from all available sources and rapidly distributing it to those who need it, thus permitting more effective and efficient use of our forces. Smart long-range precision weapons will enable us to attack targets accurately from distance, thereby reducing our own and civilian casualties.'*[21]

---

20. Lambakis, 'Space Control in Desert Storm and Beyond', *Orbis*, Vol 39, No 3, Summer 1995, p. 418.
21. Ministry of Defence (UK), *Strategic Defence Review Supporting Essays* (London: The Stationery Office, 1998), p. 32.

However, this application of technology hardly represents an RMA, rather it is the enhancement of existing ways of doing business. If these technological advances are to be fully exploited to produce a true 'revolution', they must be used to fundamentally alter the way in which military affairs are conducted. One visionary of this is Admiral W A Owens of the United States Navy who conceptualises a 'system of systems' in which all the military capabilities of a nation (in this case the US), including information warfare capabilities and conventional war fighting capabilities, would be drawn together to create an integrated higher order military instrument capable of utilising and exploiting all spectrums of activity relevant to the conduct of military affairs. He asserts that it requires a joint perspective that frees individual services with vested interests from sterile debates about individual service requirements and focuses on far more important issues such as the character of armed forces in total, and the manner in which they can work synergistically to increase their overall military capability. In short, the system of systems is fundamentally a joint military entity, and only the co-ordinated interactions of all the services can produce it.[22] However, the ability to integrate all the elements of military affairs in a system of systems requires fundamental changes to conceptual and doctrinal thinking. Admiral Owens claims that the underlying forces behind the new military capabilities are the rapid advances in computer technology and communications, and the rapidly declining cost of both. These phenomena have already fundamentally changed civilian corporate organisations in ways not seen since the creation of the mass bureaucracy in the nineteenth century. If these developments are to be incorporated into the conduct of military affairs, then changes of comparable magnitude will have to occur. The most fundamental notions of hierarchy, span of control, response time and centralisation must be re-evaluated, and it likely that dramatic transformations seen in commercial organisations will produce a similarly dramatic impact in the military sphere.[23] However it is not apparent that these changes are being made or indeed contemplated by those organisations involved. Restructuring of the military affairs organisation or 'process redesign' is required in the whole of the defence establishment, not just in those areas or forces which actually engage in combat. Until there is a recognition that new technologies may require new concepts about how military affairs are conducted then there cannot be revolutionary advancement:

---

22. W A Owens, 'The Emerging System of Systems', *US Naval Institute Proceedings*, Vol 121, No 5, May 1995, p. 38.
23. P Bracken , 'The Military After Next', *The Washington Quarterly*, Vol 16, No 4, Autumn 1993, p. 162.

> *'Technology alone, however, does not constitute an RMA. A fully exploited RMA requires that technology be effectively fleshed out by doctrine and organisation. Elements of the US military have begun to do this. But the military, civilian policymakers, and legislators need to expand their thinking about how the nation plans for, organizes and wages future high-technology warfare and what the implications are for deterrence and the use of forces. Attaining the full benefits of a potential RMA will be a challenge in the current environment.'* [24]

Tilford argues that barring an unforeseen technological leap of fantastic dimensions, no single technological advance is likely to foster an RMA, at least not by itself. Rather it is the integration of capabilities, those that exist along with new ones, that makes for an RMA. The masters of the art of war in the 21st century will be those individuals who can put capabilities together in innovative ways to achieve tactical, operational and strategic objectives.[25] Bracken argues that this potential to fuse together new technologies with changes in conceptual and doctrinal thinking really does constitute a classic RMA:

> *'In the military sphere it is likely that changes in the nature of warfare brought on by the enabling power of new technologies combined with fundamental changes in doctrine, employment concepts, and force structures will alter the character of warfare to a degree witnessed only in periods of military revolution. That is, military potential may be about to vault from one technical era to the next, as it did between the Napoleonic era and the Franco-Prussian War, or between the two world wars.'* [26]

---

24. P L Ritcheson, 'The Future of Military Affairs: Revolution or Evolution?', *Strategic Review* Vol 24, No 2, Spring 1996, p. 38.
25. E H Tilford, 'The Revolution in Military Affairs: Prospects and Cautions', *US Army War College Strategic Studies Institute Paper,* June 23 1995, Pt 2, p.2.
26. P Bracken, 'The Military After Next', *The Washington Quarterly*, Vol 16, No 4, Autumn 1993, p. 161.

AIR POWER AND THE REVOLUTION IN MILITARY AFFAIRS

A US REVOLUTION?

All the developments which might suggest that there is indeed an RMA are almost totally dominated by the United States. As the only world superpower it enjoys an unprecedented technological and economic lead over its rivals. Thus the development of an RMA is so far a peculiarly American phenomenon. This American-led revolution stems from advances in several technologies and, more important, from the ability to tie these developments together and build the doctrines, strategies, and tactics that take advantage of their technical potential, something of which perhaps only the United States is capable.[27]

Thus if there is an RMA occurring then it is an American-led RMA, and based upon American concepts of how and why military affairs are conducted. This peculiar American view of the RMA is shaped by the unchallenged hegemony in the international system of the United States and the lack of any challengers to this sole superpower position for the next 20 to 30 years. The 'American Way of War' is also influenced by its own historical experience, its societal and cultural perceptions and the experiences of its current military and political leaders. Thus the perception, and indeed the desire, that war should be, and can be, swift, decisive and affordable is a key factor in the development of the RMA. As Caldwell states:

> 'In short, the American vision is to win quickly, decisively, with overwhelming force: send our troops in with massive quantities of high-tech firepower and maximum logistical support to defeat the opposition quickly while simultaneously minimizing casualties through exploitation of our technological superiority. Near bloodless conflict - neat, clean and fast.'[28]

This American perception relies upon unchallenged American technological superiority, and the American historical reliance upon technology as a solution to its problems. For example the manufacturing processes of component standardisation and mass production were technological solutions to the problem of a shortage of labour, in particular skilled labour, in 19th century America. In the purely military sphere the development of the machine gun as a mechanised way, and therefore more efficient way, of killing was a peculiarly American concept until its utility was brutally brought home

---

27. J S Nye and W A Owens, 'Americaís Information Edge', *Foreign Affairs*, Vol 75, No 2, March/April 1996, p. 23.
28. W Caldwell, 'Promises, Promises', *US Naval Institute Proceedings,* Vol 122/1/1, 115, January 1996, p. 55.

AIR POWER AND THE REVOLUTION IN MILITARY AFFAIRS

to the European armies in the First World War. It is of no coincidence that Gattling, Maxim, Browning, Lewis and Thompson were all American designers and engineers.[29] Is the RMA therefore only applicable to situations where the United States choose to become involved, and what are the implications for those conflicts that do not involve the US?

AIR POWER - AN ESSENTIAL COMPONENT OF THE RMA

From the very beginning of manned flight air power was essentially an activity at the cutting edge of technology. The frail machines of wood, wire and canvas that we now look upon with a sense of curiosity and wonderment were, in their time, pushing at the very boundaries of scientific and technological knowledge. The point is not so much that aviation is glamorous or romantic but that it has always been, and is likely to continue to be, an essentially technological business. Therefore if a technological RMA is occurring then it is most likely to become apparent in the realms of air power. But first we must define air power. The UK definition of air power is:

> 'The ability to project military force in air or space by or from a platform or missile operating above the surface of the earth. Air platforms are defined as any aircraft, helicopter or unmanned air vehicle.'[30]

The technological and conceptual development of air power has usually occurred most rapidly during time of war. During the First World War air power was developed initially as an adjunct to land and maritime operations and latterly, on the Allied side, as an independent military arm in its own right.[31] During the inter-war years the proponents of air power advocated its potential to conclude wars through strategic bombing without the apocalyptic land and sea battles that many foresaw. This swift conclusion to conflict was not to be, but the strategic bombing campaigns of the Second World War nonetheless attempted to bring about a faster end to the war. This theme of air power providing a panacea to the problems of war has continued. The bombing campaigns conducted in Korea, Vietnam, Egypt (1967), Iraq and Kosovo all have one thing in common, namely the vision that air power can provide a swift solution to the military and political problems in hand. The current RMA seems to promise the same, through the medium of

---

29. For a detailed historical background and analysis of the inertia in adopting the machine by European armies prior to WWI see J Ellis, *A Social History of the Machine Gun* (London: Croom Helm, 1975).
30. British Air Power Doctrine, AP 3000 (London: TSO, 1999) p.1.2.1.
31. See Andrew Boyle, *Trenchard* (London: Collins, 1962).

air power, a high-tech, clean, easy and risk-free application of military force. It can be argued that the RMA represents the maturity of air power. Whereas before the promises of air power could not be met due to technical limitations, now it seems they can.

> *It's not your father's air force. I don't care how old you are; it's not your father's air force. It's a different world out there. We really have moved from an old era of attrition warfare - which was an era of very low probability warfare with individual bombs unlikely to hit anything - into an era of precision where things are significantly more predictable than they have ever been in the past.* [32]

HAS AIR POWER REACHED MATURITY?

In the West air power is seen to be an efficient way of delivering the military instrument. Within the current state of technological capability air power can deliver an effect against a target at ranges greater than any that can achieved by land or maritime forces. It can be argued that the weight of effect delivered on a target by air power, in proportion to the platform used, is considerably greater than any that could be achieved by land or maritime forces, and yet the numbers of personnel placed in direct danger from enemy action in the course of delivering that effect are a mere handful. Compared to the numbers of personnel in a ship's company or an army battlegroup, aircrews represent a very small risk. Admittedly it takes the efforts of many tens of personnel to produce one sortie by a combat aircraft, but these personnel can now be located outside the danger area as the range and payload of modern air systems can be increased through the use of air-to-air refuelling. The use of UK-based USAF B52 bombers in the Gulf War and Germany-based RAF Tornados in the Kosovo campaign are but two examples of this. To risk losing even half a dozen modern attack aircraft risks the loss of only a dozen or so aircrew, aircrew who are volunteers, who have been selected by a rigorous training system and who willingly, in the eyes of the public, have chosen to place themselves in danger. To place even a small warship in the situation where it could be sunk potentially risks over 100 lives. Similarly, to place land forces into action against even relatively weaker opposition has the potential for casualty figures in the hundreds. Therefore in terms of our own potential casualties air power is cheap. Thus air power can be seen as a key factor in an RMA that exploits technology to provide almost bloodless war.

---

32. John Warden, 'Planning to Win', *Air Power Studies Centre*, Paper No 66, July 1988, p. 23.

AIR POWER AND THE REVOLUTION IN MILITARY AFFAIRS

But air power is also efficient in terms of damage to the opposition. Increasingly the western states are concerned about enemy casualties, particularly non-combatant casualties, and unnecessary damage to 'enemy' infrastructure. This is all the more so when national survival is not threatened and liberal democracies may have the luxury of indulging in casualty sensitivity. Air power offers the ability to strike at specific targets without the need for costly ground campaigns or maritime battles. Video images of Precision Guided Munitions (PGMs) hurtling into their targets and new footage of individual buildings destroyed whilst those around them are relatively unscathed epitomise the vision of the RMA.[33]

Video images of PGMs destroying individual buildings while those around remain unscathed epitomise the vision of air power as the key to a technological RMA.

Air power also reduces the need for commitment. The application of air power is, by its very essence, temporary. It does not require the stationing of troops in hostile territory. It can come and go in seemingly effortless style. It offers no basis for long standing commitments or entanglements. The US reluctance to even discuss the requirement to station ground forces in Kosovo did not prevent the use of air power as an instrument of coercion. In keeping with a technology driven RMA air power can provide a rapid response to the requirement for military action. The mere presence of military forces sends a signal of intent to the opposition. Such signals of intent may lose their effect if it takes a week for the ship to steam into view or months for heavy ground equipment to arrive. However, the presence of combat aircraft in an area of operations, or the arrival of cruise missiles on target within hours, or even minutes, of a political statement reinforces the message. Air power is therefore perceived as rapid in keeping with the RMA. So does the RMA herald the final maturity of air power?

---

33. See Charles J Dunlap Jnr, 'Technology: Recomplicating life for the Nationís Defenders', *Parameters*, Vol XXIX, No 3, Autumn 1999, p. 24-53 for an interesting debate on the use of PGM in modern conflict.

AIR POWER AND THE REVOLUTION IN MILITARY AFFAIRS

THE PROBLEM WITH RMAs

It seems then that an RMA manifested in the maturity of air power has indeed arrived, but things are not always as straightforward as they may seem.

The American Dream?

It appears to be generally accepted that the main driver of change in the current supposed RMA is that of technology. As air power is essentially a technologically dependent activity, it is reasonable to assume that a technology-driven RMA will enhance the utility of air power and, in its turn, air power may drive a technology-based RMA. However, there is concern in many circles about a blind faith in the ability of technology to radically alter the conduct of military affairs. The technical solution and consequent substitution of advanced technology for conventional military capabilities reflect a peculiarly American faith in science's ability to engineer simple solutions to complex human problems. The possession of such technical supremacy could not prevent Holland's defeat in Indonesia, France's defeats in Indochina and Algeria, America's defeat in Vietnam, the Soviet Union's defeat in Afghanistan, or Russia's first defeat in Chechnya. This historical experience demonstrates that technological superiority does not automatically guarantee victory and that technological innovation alone does not fundamentally alter the conduct of military affairs.[34] Unlike other activities, war and the application of air power is such a complex business that even the technology of the late 20th century is unable to bring order to the confusion of the conduct of operations. General Rose, speaking of air operations in Bosnia, was not convinced air power had reached its zenith:

> 'The UN was beginning to be rather sceptical about the capabilities of NATO aircraft. They could not engage our targets in cloud, in rain, at night, or with the sun in their eyes. They were beginning to sound very like British Rail.'[35]

---

34. P Van Ripper and R H Scales, 'Preparing for War in the 21st Century', *Parameters*, Autumn 1997, p. 1.
35. Sir Michael Rose, *Fighting For Peace* (London: Harvill Press 1998) p. 177.

History demonstrates that ambiguity, miscalculation, incompetence, and above all chance will continue to dominate the conduct of war. In the end, the incalculables of determination, morale, fighting skill and leadership far more than technology will determine who wins and who loses.[36]

> *'For those placing unbridled faith in technology, war is a predictable, if disorderly, phenomenon, defeat is a matter of simple cost/benefit analysis, and the effectiveness of any military capability a finite calculus of targets destroyed and casualties inflicted. History paints a very different picture. Real war is an inherently uncertain enterprise in which change, friction, and the limitations of the human mind under stress profoundly limit our ability to predict outcomes; in which defeat to have any meaning must be inflicted above all in the minds of the defeated; and in which the ultimate purpose of military power is to assure that a trial at arms, should it occur, delivers an unambiguous political verdict.'*[37]

An RMA for All Seasons?

What the proponents of the RMA do not fully address is the applicability of the RMA to the lesser levels of conflict other than interstate military-to-military limited war and to those actors who are fighting what Freedman identifies as 'wars of necessity' rather than 'wars of choice'. He defines these as:

> *'Wars of necessity are prompted by direct threats to the survival of the state. With wars of choice there are no direct threats to primary, truly 'vital' interests: secondary interests may be at stake, and life may be more difficult if they are not secured, but the state will survive if no action is taken'*[38]

Thus the RMA seems to be developing around only the wars of choice concept, whereby information-age forces, composed of a professional all-volunteer military which is relatively isolated from the remainder of society, will only fight the wars which they choose. Freedman summarises it thus:

---

36. P Van Ripper and R H Scales, 'Preparing for War in the 21st Century', *Parameters*, Autumn 1997, p. 5.
37. Ibid, p. 2.
38. L Freedman, *The Future of Military Strategy*, Brassey's Defence Yearbook 1996 (London: Brassey's, 1996) p. 7.

AIR POWER AND THE REVOLUTION IN MILITARY AFFAIRS

'It fits in with the assumption that, for the moment at least, Western countries can choose their enemies and are not obliged to fight on anybody else's terms. Invitations to war need only be accepted on certain conditions: public opinion must be supportive; the result must be pre-ordained; and the conflict must be structured as a contest between highly professional conventional forces. Military commanders must devise strategies that not only keep their own casualty levels low, but also respect the expectation - bordering on moral presumption - that fire will be directed with precision and only against targets of evident military value. Such views are suitable for political entities that are not fearful, desperate, vengeful or angry and that can maintain a sense of proportion over the interests at stake and the humanity of the opponent. They are not necessarily the views of those whom Western states might confront in combat.'[39]

The RMA may therefore only be applicable in certain well-defined situations. That is not, however, to confine the advances in military capability which an RMA promises simply to the situations described above. In any level of conflict the gathering and processing of data to provide intelligence is a key element to the successful conduct of operations, be it anti-drugs operations, counter-insurgency or limited conventional war. Air power also has a role to play in these types of operations but may only improve the existing way of doing things, not change the fundamental way of doing things. Therefore the application of new technologies will have benefits at all levels of the spectrum of conflict, but it will not necessarily revolutionise military affairs at all levels.

Keeping Ahead

The use of air power in the Gulf War and more recently in Kosovo suggests that rather than a revolution through information dominance and precision strike, an RMA will come about through the ability to exploit the mistakes of the other side through technological superiority. This, however, requires the recognition and implementation of this superiority. If new technology offers the potential for tremendous military power, through the medium of air power, to any who acquire the new systems (and reforms their military doctrine to exploit it), this implies a powerful incentive for radical change.

---

39. L Freedman, 'The Revolution in Strategic Affairs', International Institute for Strategic Studies, *Adelphi Paper* 318. (Oxford: Oxford University Press, 1998) p. 77.

AIR POWER AND THE REVOLUTION IN MILITARY AFFAIRS

Those who realise the full potential of the new era will enjoy enhanced security and influence, while those who do not do so will risk being left behind.[40] This highlights the problems faced by the US. In order to maintain qualitative superiority the United States must commit itself to an ever increasing process of transformation of all the elements involved in the conduct of military affairs, including society itself:

> *'Our quest for qualitative superiority is an ever elusive one whose pursuit entails costs whose implications are only dimly perceived. Thus we have also bound ourselves over to a process that demands continuous organisational transformation, if not revolution, if we are to stay ahead technically. To master the necessary organisational transformations requires much more fidelity to coalition warfare; new, more flexible force packages; dependence on foreign suppliers, organisation and co-ordination of multi dimensional warfare; information gathering and dissemination; constant readiness to project power, etc. This in turn requires the constant transformation of our military and political structure, defence industrial base, and overall economy and society.'*[41]

One of the great failings of the proponents of the RMA is to assume that only the West will benefit from an RMA. What is constantly overlooked is the inevitability that technology will transfer, and an opponent need not have the full spectrum of the latest technological capabilities to counter an information-age force.[42] Technical RMA advocates often display a misplaced confidence in the ability of technology to overcome fundamental problems that increasingly are manifest in the post-bipolar environment. They suggest that the United States will be virtually unchallenged in its ability to control precisely every aspect of conflict, to achieve battlefield dominance through full exploitation of the electronic spectrum and unimpeded use of space-based sensors, communications and intelligence networks, stealth drones and precision guided weaponry:

---

40. S Biddle, 'Victory Misunderstood. What the Gulf War Tells Us about the Future of Conflict', *International Security*, Vol 21, No 2, Fall 1996, p. 176.
41. S J Blank, 'Preparing for the Next War: Reflections on the Revolution in Military Affairs', *Strategic Review*, Vol 24, No 2, Spring 1996, p. 24.
42. See Lambakis, 'Space Control in Desert Storm and Beyond', *Orbis*, Vol 39, No 3, Summer 1995, p. 417-433 for a review of how the outcome of the 1990/91 Gulf War could have been different had Iraq used some existing technology to modify its weapons and procedure (P 417) and how future opponents of the use maybe able to counter the technological lead of the US. See also S Biddle and R Zirkle, 'Technology, Civil-Military Relations, and Warfare in the Developing World', *The Journal Strategic Studies*, Vol 19, No 2, June 1999, p. 171-212 for a detailed review of the potential importance of civil-military relations upon the effectiveness of advanced weapon technology in the developing world.

AIR POWER AND THE REVOLUTION IN MILITARY AFFAIRS

'In short, Operation Desert Storm replayed - only bigger and with more microchips - will be the way all future wars will be conducted'.[43]

However, the inevitability of technology transfer to other states is vividly described by Stein:

'It's a smaller world, and our potential opponents can observe our technologies and operational innovations and copy ours without them having to invent new ones for themselves. Remember, the biggest centre for developing new computer software is not Silicon Valley but Madras, India. What will they sell and to whom? Finally, and to return to an earlier point, if the US military approaches information warfare merely as a force multiplier and adapts bits and pieces of technology to just do our current way of warfare a bit better - if we "digitise the battlefield" for an endless rerun of mechanised desert warfare - the real danger will be that someone else will refuse to play the game our way.'[44]

Air power is no exception. History shows that every advantage that technology offers will soon be countered by corresponding developments to negate that advantage:

'While the most radical of the tank theorists of the inter-war period were wide of the mark, the more radical advocates of strategic bombing - the Douhets, Trenchards and Mitchells - were even more so. The two groups had some sources of error in common. It is all too easy for the advocates of a particular type of military instrument to assume that the general trend of future technical development will enhance its power. In reality future developments may just as easily work against it.'[45]

It is not only technology transfer which can counter the RMA. The ability of other states to develop their own technologies or indeed employ existing technologies in totally new conceptual ways is also a possibility. Bracken argues that with the growing economic capacity of many countries, there is a danger that a large, wealthy (in terms of gross national product [GNP]) state could convert 10 to 20 percent of their GNP into

---

43. W Caldwell, 'Promises, Promises', *US Naval Institute Proceedings,* Vol 122/1/1, 115, January 1996, p. 54.
44. G J Stein, 'Information Warfare', *Air Power Supplement,* Air Clues, London 1997, p. 25.
45. P Harris, 'Radicalism in Military Thought' in M Melvin, ed, 'The Nature of Future Conflict: Implications for Force Development', *Strategic and Combat Studies Institute Occasional Paper,* No 36, September 1998, p. 40.

modern forces that will use strategic concepts never used before. Should a state with such capabilities emerge, then dealing with such competitors cannot be based on existing US operational doctrines.[46] Similarly, Lambakis points out the vulnerability of relying on space-based satellites to perform military functions. A future anti-satellite, or ASAT, wielding adversary of the United States might be capable of leveraging a victory out of otherwise hopeless military circumstances. By striking down, disrupting or neutralising US imagery satellites, the enemy could blind critical intelligence sensors. By denying US forces segments of the GPS constellation, the enemy could make troop movements and logistics more difficult, particularly when troops loose the ability to navigate without GPS through lack of practice, and may render weapons that rely on mid-course guidance useless or unreliable. Although the United States is not likely to encounter an enemy skilled in counter-space operations for the remainder of this century (unless the enemy is Russia), space is rapidly becoming America's Achilles' heel.[47] Braken may, however, be too optimistic in his assessment of the potential threat. It is not just satellites which are vulnerable but the whole system of down-link from satellite to earth and up-link from earth to satellite which can be attacked with simple weapons. Similarly, the technology to jam satellite information is already commercially available. Aviaconversia, a Russian company, displayed a prototype jammer at the 1997 Moscow Air Show, capable of disrupting GPS over a 120 mile radius and priced at US$ 4,000 (£2500).[48]

Space - America's Achilles' heel?

---

46. P Bracken, 'The Military After Next', *The Washington Quarterly*, Vol 16, No 4, Autumn 1993, p. 167.
47. Lambakis, 'Space Control in Desert Storm and Beyond', *Orbis*, Vol 39, No 3, Summer 1995, p. 425.
48. T Stanage, 'When All Else Fails You Can Trust A Star', *Daily Telegraph Connected*, 23 July 1998, p. 4.

AIR POWER AND THE REVOLUTION IN MILITARY AFFAIRS

But Not Too Far Ahead

Although the US may wish to maintain its technological advantage, particularly in the air, there is a danger that they may become so advanced that they might find themselves isolated from their potential allies. Although the US, in strictly military terms, may wish to keep its technological advantage, this may preclude it operating with its allies who do not possess the necessary technology to enable them to integrate with the US. In political terms this may be unacceptable:

> 'There is a concern that the European allies might fail to keep up with the revolution in military affairs, leading, possibly, to a two-speed Alliance eventually. And we lack the key military assets such as air assets, logistics and lift capability which are required for the type of operations that we are likely to face.'[49]

ASYMMETRY

There are other challenges to the RMA. Whilst an opposing force may face certain defeat if engaged in an all-out war against the an RMA force, if, following on from Freedman's proposal, it has the ability to affect the conditions in which that information-age force has chosen to engage in the conflict, such as low casualty rates, then it could cause it to withdraw from the conflict. For example the withdraw of American forces from UN operations in Somalia and its subsequent hesitancy to commit troops to Haiti as a result of the deaths of 18 soldiers in Somalia is an example of the flimsy basis upon which future information-age armies may be committed to action:

> 'The Somalia debacle, precipitated by the loss of 18 US soldiers, and the Haiti fiasco, caused by the fear that a handful of US troops might be killed while defeating that country's military dictatorship, sufficiently exposed the current unreality of the great power concept. In pride or shame, Americans might dispute any wider conclusion from those events. They would like to reserve for themselves the special sensitivity that forces policy to change completely because 18 professional soldiers are killed (soldiers, one might add, who come from a country in which gun-

---

49. George Robertson. 'Can Europe Keep Up With the Revolution in Military Affairs?', *RUSI Journal*, Vol 44, No 2, (April-May 1999) p. 49.

AIR POWER AND THE REVOLUTION IN MILITARY AFFAIRS

related deaths were last clocked at one every 14 minutes). But in fact the virtue or malady, as the case may be, is far from exclusively American.[50]

This is asymmetric war. Freedman defines asymmetric warfare as:

'When two combatants are so different in their characters, and in their areas of comparative strategic advantage, that a confrontation between them comes to turn on one side's ability to force the other side to fight on their own terms.... The strategies that the weak have consistently adopted against the strong often involve targeting the enemy's domestic political base as much as his forward military capabilities. Essentially such strategies involve inflicting pain over time without suffering unbearable retaliation in return.'[51]

Afghan guerrillas. Asymmetric warfare offers an effective counter to the technological superiority of information-age forces.

---

50. E N Luttwak, 'Where Are The Great Powers?', *Foreign Affairs*, Vol 73, No 4, July/August 1994, p. 23-24.
51. L Freedman, 'Britain and the Revolution in Military Affairs', *Defence Analysis*, Vol 14, No 1, April 1998, p. 58.

Asymmetric warfare offers both the ability to attack not only the moral and philosophical basis upon which an RMA force is committed but also practical 'low-tech' methods of countering the technological advantage which it possesses. For example a billion dollar stealth aircraft can be put out of action by a fifty dollar assault rifle or a ten dollar grenade unless it is secured against determined terrorist attack in secure base areas when not actually flying. Aircrews and technicians essential for the execution of information-age air operations can be attacked by terrorists many hundreds of miles from the operational areas, and the images of their dead bodies beamed into the homes of the information-age force almost instantaneously by satellite news channels. Precision guided weapons are only as good as the targeting information which they receive; this can be confused by concealment, dispersal and deception. The political effects of an incorrectly targeted weapon or malfunctioning weapon can be out of all proportion to the physical results they achieve. Satellite and internet news pictures of dead 'enemy' children may call into question the whole basis upon which the information-age force is committed, as can the deaths of information-age force personnel or their allies through 'friendly fire' incidents. Precision guided munitions may be a double-edged weapon, and this potential weakness can be swiftly exploited by an opponent with rudimentary access to modern communications systems.

SELF INFLICTED LIMITATIONS

Will the RMA make air power even more the cheaper option when military action is considered? Financially, even for the United States, the RMA is not free or cheap, and the development of new technologies must be paid for from within a finite national budget against the competing claims of other sectors of the economy. There is a risk inherent in following new solutions in any situation. It is possible for the United States to identify a wide range of current capabilities, forces and equipment programmes that will be less important when the new 'system of systems' created as a result of the RMA is in place. By reducing these capabilities now it would release the resources necessary to accelerate the acquisition of the new RMA 'system of systems' capabilities. However, is the United States prepared to take the risk of reducing the resources currently committed to systems that ultimately will not be needed in order to acquire more quickly the capabilities that will make them unnecessary?[52] Such a course of action requires tremendous faith in the ability of the new systems to deliver what they promise, with the possibility, however remote, that existing systems may be required in the interim period. There is perhaps prudence in caution.

---

52. W A Owens, 'The Emerging System of Systems', *US Naval Institute Proceedings*, Vol 121, No 5, May 1995, p. 39.

AIR POWER AND THE REVOLUTION IN MILITARY AFFAIRS

In casualty terms the RMA also inflicts limitations. Whilst air power promises a precision strike capability, the application of such a capability is limited and shaped by sensitivity to both friendly casualties and suffering among the enemy civilian population. For example, despite the devastation that resulted from the US bombing in Vietnam, concerns that excessive harm to civilians would undermine support at both at home and abroad severely constrained US target choices.[53] Similarly, the fear of allied casualties from Serbian anti-aircraft defences generally forced NATO aircraft to operate from heights above 15,000 feet in the Kosovo campaign with a consequent limitation on the accurate delivery of air-launched weapons. This limitation in turn prevented many attacks, as accurate delivery could not be guaranteed with consequent fears about inflicting avoidable Serbian casualties.[54] A general trend of western military intervention in the 1990s has been a reluctance to accept casualties, which has in turn led to less than optimum use of military power if it involved the risk of casualties.[55] Perhaps this expectation that an RMA can deliver the military instrument with minimum or indeed no casualties is unfounded. An over-emphasis on technology can unreasonably raise expectations about the tragic but inevitable destructive impact of military force. Like the policy preference for air strikes or cruise missile attacks, exclusive emphasis on technological solutions diverts attention from difficult but necessary choices.[56]

AIR POWER AND THE RMA - A CASE OF WISHFUL THINKING?

Despite the claims that an RMA is occurring and that air power plays a central role within that RMA, the evidence is not compelling. The RMA appears to be built around the capabilities of the United States and applicable in only certain well defined situations against compliant enemies. As with all 'silver bullets' there are conditions and circumstances when they will not work. Within the RMA technology transfer and adaptation, cost, asymmetrical responses and casualty sensitivity in all their guises will impose constraints on the use of air power with a consequent effect upon the RMA. So from this standpoint can we honestly claim that an RMA is occurring, at the heart of which lies air power? My conclusion is that we cannot. A more realistic assessment is that there is currently a period of technical innovation occurring in military affairs that

---

53. Daniel Byman and Matthew Waxman, 'Defeating US Coercion', *Survival*, Vol 41, No 2, Summer 1999, p. 109.
54. Edward M Luttwak, 'Give War a Chance', *Foreign Affairs*, Vol 78, No 4, July/August 1999, p. 40.
55. Adam Roberts, 'NATO's 'Humanitarian War' over Kosovo', *Survival*, Vol 41, No 3, Summer 1999, p. 110.
56. Daniel Byman and Matthew Waxman, 'Defeating US Coercion', *Survival*, Vol 41, No 2, Summer 1999, p. 117.

has the potential to dramatically alter some aspects of the conduct of military operations, but this falls short of a full-scale RMA. The idea of a technology-based RMA at the heart of which lies air power that will produce fast, effective, precise and orderly war is appealing to those who would wish to move away from the squalor and awfulness that human conflict brings. However we are not there yet, and, as events in Kosovo, Bosnia and Chechnya have shown, war remains a brutal, savage and above all irrational act that technology can only make more efficient.

CHAPTER 4

AIR STRATEGY AND THE UNDERDOG
Professor Philip Sabin

DURING THE CLOSING MONTHS of air power's first century of existence, there were several vivid demonstrations of the overwhelming significance which this new form of military power has come to possess. In the Anglo-American attacks on Iraq starting with Operation Desert Fox in December 1998, and in the NATO intervention in Kosovo in the spring of 1999, air power was called on to bear the main burden of the offensive, with surface forces being deliberately held back while the air bombardment did its work. In the Russian attack on Chechyna the following winter, a more integrated strategy was employed, but with precursor air bombardments still playing a much more prominent role than in Russia's previous disastrous intervention in the region.

The other striking common feature of these recent conflicts is the one-sidedness of the air contests themselves. The attacking air forces suffered negligible losses, even in operations sustained for months, while their adversaries did not or could not conduct any aerial counterattacks whatsoever. These trends had been prefigured in several earlier conflicts over the previous two decades - the Lebanon War in 1982, the Gulf War in 1991, Operation Deliberate Force in Bosnia in the summer of 1995, and a whole series of sporadic punitive strikes launched by Israel or the USA against various Muslim adversaries. It seemed as if a new paradigm of asymmetric warfare was developing, based on unilateral aerial coercion by superior air powers of less advanced opponents who incurred their wrath.

A critical question for the future is whether the inter-state wars of the early 21st century will continue to be dominated by such one-sided aerial operations, or whether recent trends will be reversed by yet another twist of the strategic dynamic whereby every successful strategy tends to provoke the development of increasingly potent countermeasures.[1] This leads on to the question of whether Western states, faced as they are with straitened post-Cold War defence budgets, should concentrate their efforts even more heavily on maintaining aerospace dominance as a strategically unanswerable trump card. Would such a strategy in fact prove misplaced or even counterproductive, by impelling potential adversaries to move towards dangerous asymmetric options of their own?

---

1. This pervasive measure-countermeasure dynamic is well illustrated in Edward Luttwak, *Strategy: The Logic of War and Peace* (Cambridge MA: Harvard University Press, 1987).

AIR STRATEGY AND THE UNDERDOG

There has been much discussion of asymmetric warfare in Western defence circles in recent years.[2] As David Caddick explains in Chapter 3, this discussion has been inextricably linked with notions of a 'Revolution in Military Affairs', given the growing imperative for weaker antagonists either to counter or to exploit for themselves the various information-age technologies involved.[3] Several writers have developed chilling hypothetical scenarios to illustrate how a clever opponent could potentially defeat Western air power by capitalising on the many military and political fragilities on which its use depends.[4] However, such 'Red Team' hypothesising is inevitably of rather dubious validity, being based on abstract intellectual speculation rather than on the real passions and constraints surrounding lethal conflicts among diverse masses of people.

To bolster our understanding of the practicalities of asymmetric warfare, we must examine the experience of real antagonists who had to face the challenge of being comprehensively outclassed in the air. There are plenty of useful 20th century precedents which can be used to shed light on the strategic responses available to such inferior air powers, ranging from Germany and Japan in 1944-45 to the Serbs and Chechens in 1999. RAF officers at Staff College have been studying such historical cases for several years, in an assignment called 'Exercise Underdog' which I devised as a corrective to the tendency among Western air thinkers to view the use of air power too much in unilateral terms, rather than as part of a dynamic strategic contest.[5] Analysts like my former student Matt Waxman have taken this perspective to heart, and have produced some insightful recent studies of how Western aerial coercion may be resisted, based on experience in the 1990s.[6]

---

2. For example, Paul Rogers, 'Responding to Western Intervention - Conventional and Unconventional Options', *Defense Analysis* 14/1, 1998, p. 41-54; Nicholas Newman, *Asymmetric Threats to British Military Intervention Operations*, Whitehall Paper 49 (London: RUSI, 2000).
3. One of the best analyses of this wider dimension of the RMA debate is Lawrence Freedman, The Revolution in Strategic Affairs, International Institute for Strategic Affairs *Adelphi Paper* 318, (London: Oxford University Press, 1998).
4. See, for example, Tony Mason, *Air Power: A Centennial Appraisal* (London: Brassey's, 1994) p. 163-6; Francois Heisbourg, *The Future of Warfare*, Predictions 2 (London: Phoenix, 1997); Simon Pearson, *Total War 2006* (London: Hodder & Stoughton, 1999).
5. For a perceptive analysis of how targeting has preoccupied air theorists since early days, see Philip Meilinger, 'Air Targeting Strategies: An Overview', in Richard Hallion, ed, *Air Power Confronts an Unstable World* (London: Brassey's, 1997) p. 51-80.
6. Daniel Byman & Matthew Waxman, *Air Power as a Coercive Instrument* (Washington DC: RAND, 1999), 'Defeating US Coercion', Survival 41/2, Summer 1999, p. 107-20, and 'Kosovo and the Great Air Power Debate', *International Security* 24/4, Spring 2000, p. 5-38; Matthew Waxman, *International Law and the Politics of Urban Air Operations* (Washington DC: RAND, 2000); Barry Posen, 'The War for Kosovo: Serbia's Political-Military Strategy', *International Security* 24/4, Spring 2000, p. 39-84.

AIR STRATEGY AND THE UNDERDOG

In the present chapter, I will adopt a rather broader perspective and assess the relevance for future air contests of the full range of historical experience stretching back to the 1940s, so that we do not become too fixated on what may be evanescent strategic features of the post-Cold War environment. First, I will identify the different components within the strategic responses of past underdogs, and discuss whether technological and political developments have made particular techniques outdated or, on the contrary, have actually increased their potential impact. Then, I will examine the integration of these component elements into overall counter-strategies for aerial underdogs, assessing whether the various elements can be combined synergistically or whether they involve inescapable tensions and trade-offs which will undermine the coherence of possible strategic responses to the kind of one-sided aerial coercion witnessed in recent years. I will conclude by exploring the implications of all this for Western air planners as they strive to maintain and enhance the strategic leverage which superior air power affords.

TECHNIQUES OF RESPONSE

At the most basic and generic level, the political and military approaches employed by antagonists to counter the effects of enemy air superiority may be sub-divided into four broad categories. The first is **limiting the vulnerability** of friendly military forces and supporting infrastructure, including 'strategic' targets, to enemy air attack. The second is **fostering restraint** on the part of the adversary, so that he chooses not to employ his air power to its fullest potential. The third element is **striking back**, either at the enemy air forces themselves or at other targets of direct relevance to the conduct or the strategic object of the war. The final component is **contesting information dominance**, so as to shield friendly and expose enemy vulnerabilities. These four elements are obviously closely interlinked within overall underdog strategies, as I will discuss later in this chapter, but first I will examine each category of response separately to assess the continuing viability of the various individual techniques involved.

Limiting Vulnerability

Reducing the impact of enemy air attack on one's war effort requires a combination of techniques. Besides concealment and active defence measures (which I will discuss in later sections), the most important such techniques are **physical protection** of key targets, **dispersal and redundancy** to reduce the effect of individual attacks, **reconstruction and work-arounds** to aid recovery from earlier airstrikes, and the **maintenance of morale** to avoid progressive demoralisation under the incessant bombardment. I will now discuss how the relative significance of these various techniques is changing as we enter the 21st century.

Physical protection in the form of concrete fortifications, defensive earthworks, bomb shelters and civil defence measures has played an important role in limiting the damage caused by air attacks in the past. In World War II, for example, such defences helped to protect German U-Boat pens and underground factories, and to restrict civilian casualties from Allied bombing to less than 2% of the population, whereas 20% of Germany's housing stock was destroyed or heavily damaged.[7] Earthworks continue to offer valuable protection against area weapons, but the growing availability of PGMs and specialised 'deep penetration' munitions has now made static physical protection of high value targets a much more problematic endeavour. This was illustrated during the Gulf War by the progressive destruction of Iraq's hardened aircraft shelters, and by the precise targeting of command bunkers including, tragically, the Al Firdos bunker.[8]

Precision guided weapons have made concrete fortifications like this Hardened Aircraft Shelter much less effective in protecting the underdog's forces.

---

7. United States Strategic Bombing Survey, *Summary Report (European War)* (reprinted by Air University Press, Maxwell AL, 1987) p. 36.
8. Lawrence Freedman & Efraim Karsh, *The Gulf Conflict, 1990-1991* (London: Faber & Faber, 1993) p. 326-9.

AIR STRATEGY AND THE UNDERDOG

Since air attack works best against key links in an interdependent system, inferior air powers have usually been least vulnerable when their assets have been dispersed and when there has been plenty of 'slack' in the system to absorb damage. In Korea, the Communist forces consisted mainly of light infantry, whose limited supply needs could be met despite the UN interdiction effort reducing rail transport to as little as 5% of its pre-war capacity.[9] The same thing happened 15 years later in Vietnam, despite intensive US efforts to disrupt the 'Ho Chi Minh trail', and it was not until the Communists turned to a more conventional offensive in 1972, with much greater dependence on heavy equipment and supplies, that US bombing in the form of the two Linebacker operations was able to stymie their efforts.[10]

Dispersal alone is not sufficient to protect underdogs from air attack, as long as there remain key 'choke points' on which their war effort depends. Hence, in 1944-45, the dispersed and camouflaged German forces were increasingly hamstrung by the crippling of oil production, while the dispersed armament factories were rendered useless by the destruction of the German railway system.[11] Since societal infrastructure such as the electricity grid and transportation network has become even easier to paralyse with modern PGM-equipped air power, the challenge for future adversaries will be to develop military forces with a more self-reliant, cellular structure, which can use new networked communications technology to work together in an integrated fashion without the dangerous dependence on centralised structures which afflicted Iraq in 1991.

In past campaigns, air operations have often taken the form of a race between the attacker's capacity for inflicting aerial destruction and the defender's ability to reconstruct or work-around the damage. In Korea, for example, bridges were rapidly repaired or by-pass bridges or fords constructed, while rail cuts were repaired in hours or cargo carried from one train to another.[12] Key to the effectiveness of such techniques has been the availability to the underdog of large quantities of manpower to undertake the labour required. The Nazis made extensive use of slave labour from occupied territories to maintain their war effort despite Allied bombardment, and the mass mobilisation of Chinese 'coolies' and Vietnamese civilians played a significant role in hindering interdiction efforts in Korea and Vietnam. Also critical to Vietnamese resistance, of course, were the huge shipments of Soviet and Chinese supplies, which more than made up for the destruction of indigenous production capacity.

---

9. Michael Kirtland, 'Planning Air Operations: Lessons from Operation Strangle in the Korean War', *Airpower Journal*, Summer 1992, p. 37-46.
10. Mark Clodfelter, *The Limits of Air Power: The American Bombing of North Vietnam* (New York: Free Press, 1989).
11. See the masterly analysis in Alfred Mierzejewski, *The Collapse of the German War Economy* (University of North Carolina Press, 1988).
12. Michael Armitage & Tony Mason, *Air Power in the Nuclear Age, 1945-84* (London: Macmillan, 2nd edn., 1985) p. 35-9.

AIR STRATEGY AND THE UNDERDOG

Today, it is much harder for underdogs to rely on such techniques during an ongoing campaign. Equipment and infrastructure is harder to produce or repair, often relying on imported components which may be unavailable to a blockaded state now that the great power support which characterised the proxy conflicts of the Cold War can no longer be counted upon. Moreover, the shift from serial to parallel attack made possible by dominant PGM-equipped air power gives the attacker a huge advantage in any race between destruction and reconstruction efforts.[13] Hence, although finding ways to recover from the impact of aerial destruction will remain an important priority for future underdogs, other techniques for the protection of existing assets or the concealment of effective work-arounds are likely to assume greater salience.

The final way in which underdogs may limit their vulnerability to enemy air power is through the maintenance of morale. Attackers have often fondly hoped that the privations and suffering inflicted by air bombardment would lead the population to turn against their regime, especially a regime which had started the campaign partly to distract attention from its existing unpopularity. However, experience has usually demonstrated the reverse. Goebbels was able to use the horrors of Allied bombing to make the German people more committed to total war, and more recently both Saddam Hussein and Slobodan Milosevic have exploited similar nationalist reactions and have remained in power, despite suffering abject military defeats. Although bombing seems to foster apathy and fatalism as much as active hostility among civilian populations, experience suggests that a judicious combination of inspirational rhetoric, 'creative' reporting and internal repression will usually allow underdog regimes to overcome the challenges involved.

A greater problem is the demoralisation which air attack often causes among military forces themselves.[14] It was the psychological as much as the physical impact of Coalition air power which destroyed the Iraqi army's ability to resist in 1991, and more recently, Saddam Hussein might even have been toppled in a military coup had his pre-emptive countermeasures been less ruthlessly efficient. Only where armed forces are more ideologically committed to the struggle and have a greater sense of successful achievement on the ground, as in Vietnam and Afghanistan, are they likely to be able to resist such demoralisation in the face of incessant air attack. It is a measure of the German Army's discipline and sense of honour that it was able to hold together so well on the Western front in 1944-45, despite suffering successive defeats at the hands of a much less demonised foe than the Red Army in the East. A key challenge for underdogs facing US-led coalitions in the future will be to retain the conviction among their troops that standing up to the adversary is justified and worthwhile, despite the losses and sacrifice involved.

---

13. John Warden, 'The Enemy as a System', *Airpower Journal*, Spring 1995, p. 54.
14. This aspect is well explored in Andrew Lambert, *The Psychology of Air Power*, Whitehall Paper 30 (London: RUSI, 1995).

AIR STRATEGY AND THE UNDERDOG

Fostering Restraint

The second broad group of responses to superior air power involves reducing or constraining the enemy's willingness to employ it. This is a complex area embracing multiple response options, but for present purposes we can consider underdog responses in terms of the exploitation of three generic factors - **fear, humanity** and **politics**.

The exploitation of fear involves deterring the adversary from using his air power to its fullest extent, by credible threats of unacceptable counter-action. Key elements of such counter-action obviously include inflicting losses on the attacking air forces themselves, as well as launching strikes against enemy surface forces and strategic targets. I will discuss these responses in the next section, along with questions of the practicality of underdog retaliation. For now, I will limit my consideration of deterrence to two more specific aspects - the threat of resort to weapons of mass destruction (WMD), and the use of hostages to encourage enemy self-restraint.

Possession by an underdog of a WMD capability does seem to have had a significant restraining influence on superior air powers in past crises. In the confrontations over Cuba in 1962 and North Korea more recently, a powerful argument against the air strike option was that some nuclear weapons might survive and might even be launched in retaliation.[15] Van Creveld argues that the gradual proliferation of nuclear capability will make conventional inter-state war increasingly unthinkable, thereby giving future underdogs a shield against the kind of aerial coercion suffered by Iraq and Serbia in the 1990s.[16] However, deterrence works both ways, and it is noteworthy that (like Germany and Japan in World War Two) both Iraq and Serbia were engaged and defeated without provoking a resort to their chemical arsenals.[17] Nuclear and biological weapons certainly raise the stakes much higher, but as I will discuss in due course, their attempted acquisition by past underdogs has been a distinctly mixed blessing with regard to encouraging enemy self-restraint.

---

15. Robert Kennedy, *Thirteen Days: A Memoir of the Cuban Missile Crisis* (New York: Norton, 1969); Michael Mazarr, 'Going Just a Little Nuclear: Nonproliferation Lessons from North Korea', *International Security* 20/2, Fall 1995, p. 113-4.
16. Martin van Creveld, *Nuclear Proliferation and the Future of Conflict* (New York: Free Press, 1993).
17. On the disincentives involved, see my chapter on 'Restraints on Chemical, Biological, and Nuclear Use: Some Lessons from History', in Efraim Karsh, Martin Navias & Philip Sabin, eds, *Non-Conventional Weapons Proliferation in the Middle East* (Oxford: Clarendon Press, 1993) p. 9-30.

The use of hostages to influence enemy (and allied) decisions has a much longer ancestry. Thucydides records how a threat to kill captured Spartan troops succeeded in preserving Attica from invasion for several years during the Peloponnesian War.[18] It is interesting that similar methods were not at first employed to deter air attacks. Despite their ruthless slaughter of civilian hostages in response to resistance attacks, the Axis powers in World II Two did not exploit their prisoners of war to try to head off Allied air bombardment - indeed, US fears that Allied prisoners might be moved to any pre-announced demonstration target for the first atom bomb were one reason why it was dropped by surprise on Hiroshima instead.[19] Hostages played a marginal role during the long-running Arab-Israeli conflict, but it was not until the 1990s that hostage-taking became clearly linked to air operations, with Iraq's detention of Western civilians prior to the Gulf War, the Bosnian Serb capture of UN peacekeepers in 1995, and the snatching of three US soldiers by the Serbs during the Kosovo campaign.

Given the attention these hostages commanded in the Western media, the tactic seemed to be having some effect, especially when the prisoners were chained to likely strategic targets. However, in each case, the hostages were eventually released, thus freeing the Allies from some very difficult choices during their subsequent escalation of air operations.[20] Why hostages were not used in earlier campaigns, and why the respective underdogs in the 1990s apparently threw away their trump cards in this way, is a complicated issue, and one to which I will return when I discuss the practicality of integrated underdog strategies.

The next factor which underdogs may exploit to encourage enemy self-restraint is the humanity of their adversaries. The key variable here is obviously the sensitivity of their opponents to moral qualms. In the total war of 1939-45, the air forces of the liberal democracies incinerated enemy civilians as a matter of routine, and even killed large numbers of citizens in occupied countries such as France as a regrettable by-product of the liberation struggle. More recently in Afghanistan and Chechnya, Soviet and Russian leaders have shown similar indifference to the suffering of the civilian population. However, a combination of factors - the immediacy of television coverage, the availability of precision weapons which *can* minimise 'collateral damage', and the comfortable security of Western nations now that the Cold War is over - has made Western publics extremely sensitive to the direct infliction of human suffering in the 'wars of choice' in which they now engage, especially when the motive for such interventions is to relieve humanitarian crises as much as to secure traditional national interests.[21]

---

18. Thucydides, *History of the Peloponnesian War* (Harmondsworth: Penguin, 1972) 4.41.
19. Len Giovanetti & Fred Freed, *The Decision to Drop the Bomb* (London: Methuen, 1967) p. 104.
20. Lawrence Freedman & Efraim Karsh, *The Gulf Conflict, 1990-1991* (London: Faber & Faber, 1993) p. 131-9, 154-7 & 238-40; 'Unshakable Vacillation', *Time*, June 12th, 1995; 'Serbs agree to release three American soldiers', *The Sunday Times*, May 2nd, 1999.
21. Adam Roberts, 'NATO's "Humanitarian War" over Kosovo', *Survival* 41/3, Autumn 1999, p. 102-23.

AIR STRATEGY AND THE UNDERDOG

Media images such as this have greatly reduced the willingness of liberal democracies to risk inflicting civilian casualties.

Underdogs such as North Vietnam, Iraq and Serbia have sought to exploit this new humanity in several ways. Media coverage has been welcomed, and used to broadcast atrocity stories by focusing on the human consequences of errant or ill-targeted weapons.[22] Military forces have been deliberately mingled with civilian populations or stationed near sensitive sites such as mosques or monuments, thereby either gaining immunity from attack or provoking episodes like the Al Firdos bunker bombing which cause greater self-restraint by the adversary in the future.[23] Sometimes the civilian population has been sufficiently motivated to form its own 'human shield', as on the Danube bridge in Belgrade. In other circumstances, as in Kosovo itself, the very people whom the attackers are trying to save have been pressed into unwilling service for this purpose.[24] As traditional forms of protection such as concrete fortifications become increasingly redundant in the face of precision weaponry, so this new 'human armour'

---

22. Mike Bratby, 'Air Power and the Role of the Media', in Andrew Lambert & Arthur Williamson, eds, *The Dynamics of Air Power* (Bracknell: RAF Staff College, 1996) p. 86-102; 'Serb lies duped media, claims No 10', *The Times*, July 10th, 1999.
23. Wayne Thompson, 'After Al Firdos: The Last Two Weeks of Strategic Bombing in Desert Storm', *Air Power History* 43/2, Summer 1996, p. 49-65.
24. 'Bombs fail to halt defiance in Belgrade', *The Times*, April 5th, 1999; 'Harriers hit Serb tank convoy as 'human shield' tactics limit targets', *The Times*, April 8th, 1999.

seems likely to grow in importance for underdogs facing air attacks by the sensitive forces of the Western democracies.[25]

Finally, underdogs may seek to exploit the politics of the situation in order to constrain air operations by their adversaries. The key variable here is the amount of international disagreement and division regarding the use of force and the political issues at stake. In 1944-45 there was very little scope for the Axis powers to use this approach, given the concerted and uncompromising opposition which they faced. However, as hostility grew between East and West during the subsequent Cold War, it became much more feasible for smaller states to exploit the situation, not only to garner military and economic aid from one or other bloc, but also to foster restraint on the part of their adversary, lest the proxy conflict escalate into World War III. Fear of such escalation was a key reason for the various 'sanctuaries' which the US observed in Korea and Vietnam, and it also helped to constrain Israeli air operations during the War of Attrition with Egypt, once Soviet personnel became directly involved.[26]

Now that the Cold War is over, underdogs have had to operate in a more multi-polar context, by playing on the doubts of less committed states in order to constrain the air bombardment. One important technique has been to try to convince neighbouring states in the region not to support the air attacks, thereby depriving the adversary of nearby bases and airspace. Saddam Hussein has used a mixture of threats and appeals to Muslim solidarity in this connection, and his Scud attacks on Israel during the Gulf War seem to have been expressly designed to provoke a response which would fracture the Arab coalition against him.[27] The Serbs have made similar efforts to play on the doubts of neighbours such as Greece and Italy, and to highlight the regional economic damage caused by attacks like those on the Danube bridges.[28] Equally important has been careful diplomacy and negotiation at the international level, making just enough compromises to avoid complete isolation within the UN framework. Iraq performed poorly in this regard in 1991, but has done better since, to the point where Operation Desert Fox and the subsequent attacks have become a rather lonely Anglo-American crusade.[29]

---

25. Matthew Waxman, *International Law and the Politics of Urban Air Operations* (Washington DC: RAND, 2000).
26. Mark Clodfelter, *The Limits of Air Power: The American Bombing of North Vietnam* (New York: Free Press, 1989) ch.4; Chaim Herzog, *The Arab-Israeli* Wars (London: Arms & Armour Press, 1982) p. 216.
27. Lawrence Freedman & Efraim Karsh, *The Gulf Conflict, 1990-1991* (London: Faber & Faber, 1993) chs. 24-5.
28. Barry Posen, 'The War for Kosovo: Serbia's Political-Military Strategy', *International Security* 24/4, Spring 2000, p. 66-9.
29. Marc Weller, 'The US, Iraq and the Use of Force in a Unipolar World', *Survival* 41/4, Winter 1999-2000, p. 81-100; 'Iraq: Poisoned Cigars, Perhaps?', *Jane's Defence Weekly*, April 12th, 2000.

AIR STRATEGY AND THE UNDERDOG

However, one should not exaggerate the constraints imposed by a lack of international consensus in the post-Cold War environment. NATO in Kosovo and the Russians in Chechyna waged protracted and escalating air operations despite vocal reservations from many major and minor powers. There is a world of difference between recent diplomatic frictions and the active hostility during the Cold War, when both blocs could be relied on to back up their support for regional clients with military and economic aid in order to spite and frustrate their opponents. Future underdogs cannot count on anything like the outside assistance received by the North Vietnamese and the Afghan *Mujahadeen*, and their resistance will have to depend much more on their own resources.

Striking Back

The third broad group of responses which we must consider involves attempts by the underdog to strike back rather than waiting passively for the bombardment to end. Potential targets for such retaliation fall into three main categories - the **attacking air forces** themselves, **enemy surface forces**, and various kinds of **strategic targets** including those directly related to the object of the war. I will now discuss each of these in turn.

The most common way for underdogs to strike back against the attacking air forces has been through the employment of air defences in the form of fighters, flak and surface-to-air missiles. In World War II, Korea, Vietnam, and the Yom Kippur War, such defences imposed very significant attrition upon the attackers.[30] However, as I discussed in an earlier volume produced by this study group, the growing dependence on electronic warfare has produced much more asymmetric loss-rates in recent counter-air contests, by exposing the underdog's defences to jamming and radar-homing techniques, and by allowing attackers to shield themselves through stealth technology and stand-off attacks.[31] Hence, in Lebanon and the Gulf War, sophisticated air defence systems were quickly smashed with very little loss to the attackers, while over Iraq and the former Yugoslavia more recently, it has become routine for attacking aircraft to operate with virtually no risk of being shot down, despite the presence of dense air defence networks.

---

30 On the contribution made by surface-based defences, see Kenneth Werrell, *Archie, Flak, AAA and SAM* (Maxwell AL: Air University Press, 1988).
31 See my chapter on 'The Counter-Air Contest', in Andrew Lambert & Arthur Williamson, eds, *The Dynamics of Air Power* (Bracknell: RAF Staff College, 1996) p. 18-39.

Does this mean that air defences have ceased to be a worthwhile response for future underdogs? The answer is clearly no, for two main reasons. First, as Tony Mason argues in Chapter 9, some forms of surface-based defences remain extremely potent. Stinger missiles caused very significant losses in Afghanistan, and similar Serbian systems prompted NATO aircraft in 1999 to stick to high altitude, with consequent penalties in effectiveness.[32] As passive tracking systems improve and ways are found to counter stealth technology, air defence performance may well recover from the nadir it reached during the 1990s.[33] The second key consideration is that the *sensitivity* of Western states to air losses has increased enormously, due to a variety of factors including the lower political commitment to recent interventions, the ability of the media to amplify the slightest setback, and the 'revolution of rising expectations' which the low level of recent air losses has produced. The reactions caused by the shooting down of a single F16 in 1995 and of a single F117 in 1999 illustrate that it remains worthwhile for underdogs to pursue even such minimal air defence successes.[34]

Past underdogs have made some attempts to use captured aircrew for political purposes, by coercing them into broadcast recantations as in Vietnam and the Gulf War, or by using them as bargaining chips in prisoner exchanges as in the Arab-Israeli conflict.[35] However, as with hostages from other sources, underdogs have found it difficult in practice to undertake effective blackmail over the conduct of the air operations themselves, and the few aircrew captured during Operations Desert Storm and Deliberate Force were subsequently released without much fuss. This illustrates that underdog responses based on the political exploitation of militarily marginal levels of success need to be subtly judged if they are not to backfire.

---

32. William McManaway, 'Stinger in Afghanistan', *Air Defense Artillery* Jan-Feb 1990, p. 3-8; 'General admits NATO exaggerated bombing success', *The Times*, May 11th, 2000.
33. 'Chinese radar may trap stealth planes', *The Sunday Times*, November 28th, 1999.
34. 'Downing a Top Gun', *Newsweek*, June 12th, 1995; 'Stealth fighter "shot down" as Serbs slaughter hundreds', *The Sunday Times*, March 28th, 1999.
35 On the travails of US presidential candidate John McCain as a Vietnamese POW, see 'Home from Hell', *The Sunday Times*, January 9th, 2000.

AIR STRATEGY AND THE UNDERDOG

A key reason for the growing Western sensitivity about aircrew losses has been the wish to avoid further media images like these from the Gulf War.

AIR STRATEGY AND THE UNDERDOG

Some Western commentators have argued that future underdogs could enjoy much greater *military* success in the counter-air contest by employing more proactive techniques. Favourite 'nightmare scenarios' have included concerted fighter attacks on high value assets like tankers and AWACS aircraft, guerrilla strikes against vulnerable airfield flight lines or off-duty aircrew, or sabotage by agents infiltrated into the maintenance system.[36] There is certainly scope for some success against a careless or vulnerable adversary, as illustrated by the various guerrilla attacks on airfields in Vietnam and Afghanistan, and by the terrorist bombing of USAF personnel in Saudi Arabia in 1996.[37] However, infiltrating agents into enemy countries to launch such attacks is a difficult business even for a former superpower like the USSR with its vaunted *spetsnaz* forces, and historical experience suggests that this is not an option readily available to lesser powers, especially if they wish to foster enemy self-restraint.

The use of the underdog's own air forces in a more proactive and symmetrical role is very much of a gamble. The Luftwaffe's surprise airfield raid on New Year's Day 1945 cost the Germans as many planes as it did the Allies, together with far more of their precious aircrew.[38] Although such an exchange would be a massive improvement on the asymmetric loss rates of more recent conflicts, it is far from clear that future underdogs attempting such a mass sortie in the face of today's much improved surveillance and missile technology would not simply be playing into the hands of the waiting enemy fighters. Having seen the one-sided annihilation of Syrian fighters over Lebanon in 1982, it is hardly surprising that the Iraqi and Serbian air forces subsequently adopted a much more passive stance in the face of superior air power.

If causing serious attrition to the opposing air forces themselves remains highly problematic, what of the second option, namely attacks on enemy surface forces? Conducting such attacks has traditionally been very difficult for underdogs in the face of overwhelming enemy air superiority, as illustrated by the bloody repulse of the Germans at Mortain in August 1944 and of the Iraqis at Al Khafji in 1991.[39] However, light infantry forces in suitable terrain have been better able to undertake offensives despite enemy air power, as in Korea, Vietnam, and Afghanistan. Suitably committed forces have on occasion been able to cause serious casualties quite against the conventional odds through their self-sacrificial behaviour, as with the Japanese *Kamikazes* in 1944-45

---

36. For example, Simon Pearson, *Total War 2006* (London: Hodder & Stoughton, 1999) ch. 12.
37. Alan Vick, *Snakes in the Eagle's Nest* (1995); 'Bombing makes hard role harder for USA', *Jane's Defence Weekly,* July 10th, 1996.
38. Danny Parker, *To Win the Winter Sky: Airwar over the Ardennes, 1944-1945* (London: Greenhill, 1994) ch. 20.
39. Ian Gooderson, *Air Power at the Battlefront: Allied Close Air Support in Europe, 1943-1945* (London: Frank Cass, 1998) p. 110-17; Lawrence Freedman & Efraim Karsh, *The Gulf Conflict, 1990-1991* (London: Faber & Faber, 1993) p. 364-6.

and the suicide bombers in Lebanon more recently. It has been surface force losses, rather than the far lower casualties inflicted on their aircrew, which have been instrumental in prompting US withdrawals from Vietnam, Lebanon and Somalia, Israeli withdrawal from Lebanon, Soviet withdrawal from Afghanistan, and Russia's initial withdrawal from Chechyna.[40]

The down side of this clearly effective underdog response is that it has often prompted adversaries to hold their surface forces back out of harm's way, and to focus even more on exploiting their air power advantage. One reason for America's lack of restraint in the fire bombing and atomic bombing of Japan was its fear of the potential US casualties should an invasion of the home islands be required as at Okinawa. Saddam Hussein's belief that the prospect of 10,000 casualties would deter a US liberation of Kuwait proved misplaced when the Coalition's lengthy precursor air operation broke Iraqi resistance and restricted overall losses to a few hundred.[41] NATO had its fingers burnt in Bosnia through the vulnerability of UN peacekeepers on the ground, and in Kosovo it eschewed the problematic option of a ground invasion and placed its faith in air power alone. The prospect that precursor air attacks could similarly limit their casualties in Chechyna encouraged the Russians to re-invade the region, with strong popular support, in 1999.[42] Attacking enemy surface forces is clearly a fruitful tactic for underdogs where such forces are accessible, and is of major importance in dissuading the opponent from seeking the synergistic benefits of a simultaneous air-surface campaign, but it does not offer a reliable way of countering enemy employment of air power itself.

The final proactive option available to underdogs is to attack some form of 'strategic' target instead of focusing exclusively on the enemy military forces. Sometimes such targets exist within the actual territory in dispute, and so are accessible to the underdog's troops despite enemy air superiority. Examples include the cities and official buildings attacked by Viet Cong guerrillas during the 1968 Tet offensive, the Kuwaiti oil stocks released into the Gulf or set ablaze by the Iraqis in 1991, the Kurds and Marsh Arabs repressed by Saddam's troops after the Gulf War, and the Muslim populations subjected to ethnic cleansing by Serb forces in Bosnia and Kosovo. Where such attacks change the realities on the ground in an irreversible fashion so as to achieve the underdog's strategic objectives in the ongoing conflict, they obviously offer an attractive means of prevailing despite aerial inferiority. However, the example of Kosovo shows that even the most ruthless such actions can sometimes be fruitless or counterproductive if enemy air power

---

40. US sensitivity to casualties is not in fact as straightforward as some might suggest - see Eric Larson, Casualties and Consensus: The Historical Role of Casualties in Domestic Support for US military operations (Santa Monica: Rand, 1996).
41. Lawrence Freedman & Efraim Karsh, *The Gulf Conflict, 1990-1991* (London: Faber & Faber, 1993) ch. 20.
42. 'Chechen war makes hero out of a political nobody', *The Times*, November 23rd, 1999.

cannot be withstood. Despite Pape's argument that aerial coercion is doomed to fail unless it can directly frustrate an underdog's achievement of its strategic objectives, the Serbs eventually withdrew voluntarily from Kosovo, whose Albanian population has now seized *de facto* independence thanks in part to the bitterness caused by earlier Serb repression.[43]

Underdogs have also in the past attacked targets located in enemy territory, in retaliation for the damage they themselves were suffering from enemy air power. Since their own air forces have had great difficulty in reaching such targets safely, underdogs have tended to rely on other weapons. Rocket launchers and artillery have been used against enemy population centres when these have been sufficiently close, as in the Iran-Iraq War and the long-running confrontation on Israel's northern border. In both of these cases, the superior air power was prompted to accept mutual constraints on the bombardment of civilian targets, but these limited truces proved fragile, and were not extended into wider leverage over the course of the conflict.[44]

Other underdogs wishing to bombard enemy civilian populations have had to resort to longer range missile systems. Hitler's V-weapon attacks and Saddam's 'Scud war' in 1991 share some significant characteristics, in that they inflicted little military damage, but did serve to bolster morale at home and to impel the enemy to divert considerable air effort to countering them. Although the Iraqi attacks caused far fewer casualties than the V-weapons, this was offset by media amplification of their impact, since they received equal billing with the thousands of much more effective sorties being launched by the Coalition. However, neither Hitler nor Saddam succeeded in translating the terror caused by their missiles into real constraints on the employment of enemy air power.[45]

Another similarly indiscriminate but more belated form of long distance retaliation which may be available to underdogs is terrorism, either through the attempted assassination of political leaders or through the detonation of bombs in airliners or crowded public places. Terrorism is used routinely by sub-state groups such as *Hizbollah* and the followers of Osama bin Laden, and there are plenty of instances of such attacks being threatened or carried out in response to aerial bombardment.[46]

---

43. Robert Pape, *Bombing to Win: Air Power and Coercion in War* (Ithaca: Cornell University Press, 1996); 'West abandons dream of a unified Kosovo', *The Sunday Times*, February 13th, 2000.
44. See my article on 'Escalation in the Iran-Iraq War', in Efraim Karsh, eds, *The Iran-Iraq War: Impact and Implications* (London: Macmillan, 1989) p. 280-95; 'Hezbollah threatens revenge for airstrikes', *The Times*, February 9th, 2000.
45. Peter Cooksley, *Flying Bomb* (London: Robert Hale, 1979); Martin Navias: 'Non-Conventional Weaponry and Ballistic Missiles during the 1991 Gulf War', in Efraim Karsh, Martin Navias & Philip Sabin, eds, *Non-Conventional Weapons Proliferation in the Middle East* (Oxford: Clarendon Press, 1993) p. 49-66.
46. For example, 'Chechens threaten terrorism', *The Times*, February 7th, 2000; 'CIA exposed Serb plot to assassinate Lord Robertson', *The Daily Telegraph*, March 28th, 2000.

AIR STRATEGY AND THE UNDERDOG

However, as the Lockerbie inquiry illustrates, direct *state* sponsorship of terrorism is a murky and uncertain affair, and unlike with sub-state groups, there are no clear instances of states using this means as an explicit and acknowledged strategic response to an enemy air operation.[47] Where terrorist attacks have been conducted, as in Israel and Russia over the past decade, their impact on the employment of air power by the target state has been equivocal to say the least.

The *potential* for future underdogs to strike back against the home territory of their adversaries seems likely to grow, as long range missile systems and WMD capabilities gradually proliferate, and as hackers exploit the growing reliance of all sectors of society on complex computer networks. The current Western preoccupation with missile defence systems and computer security illustrates the degree of concern about the capabilities involved.[48] However, whether future underdogs will actually *choose* to retaliate by such means is less certain. As with other potential responses like the use of hostages, underdogs will have to weigh the benefits of such action against the risks, as they construct an overall strategy to counter the superior air power with which they are faced.

Contesting Information Dominance

The fourth and final group of underdog responses concerns the intelligence contest. A major benefit of air superiority has always been the information advantage it has brought to the side enjoying secure overflight of enemy territory. The consequences of this information asymmetry were clearly demonstrated during the Gulf War, when Coalition forces with unprecedentedly precise information from air and satellite systems on their own and the enemy locations faced Iraqi forces almost blind to what was happening beyond their own immediate horizons. To contest such information dominance, underdogs have two forms of response - **concealment and deception** to limit the impact of enemy air reconnaissance, and **intelligence gathering** of their own, to build up a picture of enemy activities and vulnerabilities despite the blanketing fog of air inferiority. I will discuss each of these two aspects in turn.

As air power has become more capable of knocking out any target it can locate (and less prone to inflict area devastation in the process), so the importance to the underdog of concealment and deception has risen apace. Terrain is a key variable in this regard, and hiding forces has proven much easier in the mountains of Afghanistan or the jungles

---

47. 'New evidence hits Lockerbie case', *The Times*, May 15th, 2000.
48. Ivo Daalder, James Goldgeier & James Lindsay, 'Deploying NMD: Not Whether, but How', *Survival* 42/1, Spring 2000, p. 6-28; Andrew Rathmell, 'Cyber-Terrorism: The Shape of Future Conflict?', *RUSI Journal*, Oct.1997, p. 40-5.

AIR STRATEGY AND THE UNDERDOG

of Vietnam than in the deserts of the Middle East. The ingenuity of the underdog's forces in camouflaging their activities is also very important, and historical experience suggests that such measures can be far more elaborate than adversaries used to enjoying the security of air superiority tend to expect. The following description by Pierre Clostermann of an overflight of a German airfield in June 1944 is instructive in this regard.

> *'Saint-Andre seemed to have had a terrible pasting - sticks of bombs criss-crossed over the runway, the hangars were in ruins. On the other hand, all around were trim villages and barns in clumps of trees, connected by little roads.*
>
> *Mm! Those roads seemed very straight. We came down to 10,000 feet. Just so! Those roads were taxi-ing strips and the barns were hangars, perfectly camouflaged...*
>
> *The details began to show up more clearly. Between the destroyed hangars there were others, of a different type, half buried and covered with turf... The large main runway was carefully repaired and the craters which pitted it (as we thought, from 13,000 feet) were dummy ones, artistically painted to give the impression of an unserviceable runway...*
>
> *I levelled out two or three miles from the airfield and kept right down on the deck, to keep the flak off... In the shade of a clump of trees about 20 brand-new emerald green Focke Wulfs were warming up... This airfield, which at 13,000 feet had seemed deserted, was simply swarming with aircraft and personnel.'*[49]

As this passage makes clear, concealment works best when accompanied by the construction of dummy artefacts to distract enemy attention. The Iraqis during the Gulf War made extensive use of dummy Scud launchers, and the Serbs during the Kosovo campaign placed mock armed convoys on dummy roads - in both cases, confirmed kills of the real target vehicles were very disappointing.[50] Although the growing multi-spectral capabilities of sensors aboard aircraft, UAVs and satellites will make such concealment and deception more difficult than in the past, there will remain real practical limits to what aerospace assets alone can discern. Only two of the more than twenty sites associated with Iraq's nuclear weapons programme were known of before the UN ground

---

49. Pierre Clostermann, *The Big Show* (London: Corgi, 1979) p. 153-5. The airfield was in fact Dreux.
50. Martin Navias, 'Non-Conventional Weaponry and Ballistic Missiles during the 1991 Gulf War', in Efraim Karsh, Martin Navias & Philip Sabin, eds, *Non-Conventional Weapons Proliferation in the Middle East* (Oxford: Clarendon Press, 1993) p.54-60; 'NATO dropped thousands of bombs on dummy roads, bridges and soldiers and hit only 13 real Serb tanks', *The Times*, June 24th, 1999.

inspections after the ceasefire in the Gulf, and biological weapons programmes of the kind now causing so much anxiety in the USA are even easier to hide.[51] Hence, deception and concealment are likely to remain crucial techniques for aerial underdogs in the future, with traditional espionage activities being at least as important in uncovering these secrets as high-tech aerospace surveillance.

As regards intelligence gathering by the underdog itself, one important technique is to employ aerospace assets despite enemy air superiority. The difficulty of intercepting fast lone reconnaissance aircraft made these vehicles useful even for the Axis powers at the end of World War II, although the inevitable limitations imposed by enemy air superiority helped to make concerted Allied deception operations, like the phantom preparations for an invasion of the Pas de Calais, successful regardless.[52] As interception technology improved during the Cold War, aircraft reconnaissance became more problematic, but this was offset in some cases by the provision of satellite intelligence by a supporting superpower. Future underdogs will be less dependent on great power goodwill in this regard, thanks to the growing commercial availability of high resolution satellite imagery of any part of the planet. Real time aerial intelligence on the developing battle situation will remain the prerogative of superior air powers, though even here, the proliferation of inconspicuous reconnaissance drones may level the playing field to some degree.

Past underdogs have also made the most of other intelligence sources not affected by the air balance. This has been easiest in guerrilla conflicts like Vietnam and Afghanistan, where the intertwined and asymmetric nature of the forces, and the availability of informers in the enemy camp, allowed the insurgents to have better overall intelligence than their adversaries, despite their aerial inferiority. The communications revolution has offered underdogs like the Serbs increasingly timely and pervasive insight into the activities of the open societies of the West, through instant media reporting, the proliferation of mobile phones, and growing reliance on the Internet. It is especially difficult for coalitions of many nations to maintain military secrecy in such an environment, as illustrated by the recent NATO controversy over Serb intelligence gathering during the Kosovo campaign.[53]

---

51. *Gulf War Air Power Survey Summary Report* (Washington DC: US Government Printing Office, 1993) ch.3; 'Clinton predicts "miniature" terrorism', *The Times*, December 29th, 1999.
52. Michael Howard, *Strategic Deception in the Second World War* (London: Pimlico, 1990) ch. 6.
53. 'NATO spy blamed for Stealth loss', *The Times*, August 28th, 1999; 'Officials admit NATO headquarters was open house for Serb eavesdropping', *The Times*, March 10th, 2000.

AIR STRATEGY AND THE UNDERDOG

Underdogs thus have available a very wide range of techniques with which to counter the advantages of superior air powers. Although technological and political changes have made some of these techniques (such as physical hardening of potential targets or a reliance on support from a superpower patron) much less useful in modern times, those same changes have made other techniques (such as the use of the media to gather intelligence or to magnify enemy tactical failures into strategic events) much more powerful than they were hitherto. The key question is whether this shifting menu of available techniques can be used to develop coherent overall strategies to overcome enemy air superiority and prevail against the odds. I will now examine what past experience tells us about the prospects of future underdogs constructing such integrated and flexible strategies to defeat the kind of unilateral aerial coercion witnessed in recent years.

STRATEGIC DILEMMAS

One of the biggest challenges facing warring states in general is to translate their tactical and operational advantages into integrated overall strategies which allow them to secure victory, rather than simply prompting their opponents to return to the fray having devised effective responses. There are plenty of historical examples of states achieving tactical and operational triumphs against the conventional odds, but then failing to convert this initial success into lasting victory - Carthage under Hannibal, France under Napoleon, and Germany under Hitler, are three famous instances which spring to mind. The strategic dynamic of action and reaction is a key reason why superior air powers should not rely on simply repeating their recent triumphs in years to come, but the same logic applies to underdogs themselves. Unless such states can combine the various responses discussed earlier into coherent overall strategies, they are unlikely to overturn the many advantages which superior air power bestows.

This does not mean that underdogs can prevail only by devising an explicit and infallible strategic 'master plan'. In the few historical cases where underdogs have triumphed against the odds - notably Vietnam and Afghanistan - their victory has come more from a combination of favourable circumstances, deep commitment and 'muddling through' than from their chosen strategies, which were often flawed and (like the Tet offensive) succeeded only in unexpected ways.[54] What *does* matter is that the techniques employed by the underdog combine (whether by accident or design) in a synergistic rather than a mutually destructive fashion. Since no single element of the many

---

54. On Communist expectations of the Tet offensive, see Phillip Davidson, *Vietnam at War* (London: Sidgwick & Jackson, 1988) p. 475-7.

techniques which I have outlined is remotely sufficient in itself to offset the huge advantages bestowed by modern air superiority, it is vital that multiple elements can be pursued simultaneously so that their combined effect may achieve the result desired.

Historical experience reveals many significant instances of synergy among the various responses employed by underdogs. Perhaps the most pervasive is the way in which active air defence efforts interact with other techniques. Hence, although Serb air defences in the Kosovo campaign achieved practically no success in shooting down NATO planes, the fact that NATO aircraft operated at such high altitudes to avoid the defences was decisive in keeping the attrition of Serb forces in Kosovo so low and in fostering tragic and politically damaging mistakes like the bombing of refugee convoys. There are plenty of instances from Korea, Vietnam and elsewhere of dummy targets being set up as 'flak traps' to entice enemy aircraft into range of the guns, and in 1973, the Arab ground attacks under a dense air defence umbrella provoked the Israelis into costly and not very effective airstrikes on the advancing tanks.[55]

However, such examples of synergy among underdog responses are outweighed by significant tensions and trade-offs, which help to explain why past underdogs have found it so difficult to achieve overall victory. Three main types of strategic tensions may be identified - between **asymmetry and flexibility** in the structuring of the underdog's forces, between **deterrence and provocation** in the underdog's coercive strategy, and between **activity and endurance** in the underdog's conduct of military operations. I will now examine each of these tensions in turn.

Asymmetry versus Flexibility

A clear lesson of the past sixty years is that some force structures are far more vulnerable to superior air power than others. Heavy equipment which depends on an extensive support and logistic infrastructure can be effectively targeted, as in 1944-45 and 1991, whereas light forces like those in Korea, Vietnam and Afghanistan present much more elusive targets and have much lower logistic needs. This might suggest that even those states capable of fielding a conventional military panoply of armoured vehicles, warships and combat aircraft should, if faced with the likelihood of enemy air superiority, eschew these options in favour of a deliberately asymmetric arsenal combining light infantry with carefully chosen modern technology in the form of mobile surface-to-air defences and offensive missile systems. However, there are two major problems with such a complete reorientation, which suggest that most future underdogs are likely to retain more balanced force structures.

---

55. Kenneth Werrell, *Archie, Flak, AAA and SAM* (Maxwell AL: Air University Press, 1988).

AIR STRATEGY AND THE UNDERDOG

For one thing, there is likely to be very strong resistance from military forces to the adoption of an asymmetric stance, if it involves giving up the high-tech 'toys' which in all states are so bound up with the prestige and self-image of the military profession. Civil-military relations in many potential underdog states are such that it would be a brave civilian government which tried to force through such a reorientation, in the face of the tendency of the military to intervene in politics. Past experience suggests that governments instead often allow the acquisition of high status hardware of very dubious practical utility, in order to keep the military quiet. It would, in any case, be very difficult for most states to inculcate into their personnel the kind of individual commitment needed for the conduct of truly asymmetric war, as displayed by the Viet Cong and the *Mujahideen*. In many cases, the necessary degree of initiative and decentralisation would be highly corrosive of established authority structures within the state.[56]

The second problem with deliberately asymmetric force structures is that they are inherently limited in coping with contingencies other than resistance to a superior air power. Heavy weapons which prove a liability under overwhelming air attack may be invaluable force multipliers against less capable regional adversaries. One need only think of the use which Iraq made of tanks and helicopter gunships against Iran in the 1980s and against the Kurdish and Shia rebels after the Gulf War, or of how the tanks and artillery inherited from the Yugoslav Army have helped the Serbs to counter their numerous but less well-equipped ethnic adversaries. Light infantry may be well suited to defence and guerrilla raids in appropriate terrain, but they are not very capable in more organised offensive operations - the Communist forces in Korea and the Iranian Revolutionary Guards in the 1980s suffered appalling losses for very mixed overall results, and the North Vietnamese finally succeeded in seizing the south only when the withdrawal of US air power allowed a more conventional attack.

Underdogs thus face an inescapable tension between the theoretical potency of an asymmetric force structure in resisting superior air powers and the real advantages, in political stability and the flexibility to tackle other security challenges, associated with a more balanced force posture. When asymmetric military structures have been used by underdogs in the past, this has almost always been through force of circumstance rather than deliberate choice. Antagonists like the North Koreans, *Mujahideen*, Somalis and Chechens simply did not have access to significant stocks of heavy weaponry, and so had to make the most of what they possessed. When Egypt shifted to an asymmetric strategy based on surface-to-air defences in 1973, this was less a deliberate reaction to the one-

---

56. S Biddle & R Zirkle, 'Technology, Civil-Military Relations and Warfare in the Developing World', *Journal of Strategic Studies*, June 1996; Christopher Parker, 'New Weapons for Old Problems: Conventional Proliferation and Military Effectiveness in Developing States', *International Security* 23/4, Spring 1999, p. 119-47.

AIR STRATEGY AND THE UNDERDOG

sided destruction of Arab air forces in 1967 than it was a virtue of necessity, given problems in pilot training and given Soviet reluctance to supply modern combat aircraft lest they encourage the Arabs to break the peace.[57] Although future underdogs may be less resistant to making such radical choices, having seen what happened to Iraq in 1991 and Serbia in 1999, the signs at present are that new technology is being integrated into established force structures rather than displacing traditional weapons systems altogether.

Deterrence versus Provocation

The second major tension within underdog strategies concerns the fostering of enemy self-restraint. I argued earlier that this could be attempted through the exploitation of **fear, humanity** and **politics**. The trouble is that the policies needed to exploit these various factors are often in conflict, so that a stance which is successful in one dimension may be counterproductive in another. To attract sympathy and reduce international support for air attacks, states usually need to appear weak and to portray themselves as innocent and helpless victims of the unwarranted aggression. Conversely, if they take the opposite stance and seek ways to strike back at the adversary to create a situation of deterrence, this can erode sympathy, forfeit political support, and perhaps even provoke the very attack which they are trying to avoid.

There are plenty of instances in which missile or terrorist attacks launched by the victims of air bombardment have themselves provoked an aggressive response, thereby fuelling a cycle of mutual reprisals. Israel and *Hizbollah* have been locked in such a spiral of revenge and attempted counter-coercion for many years, and a similar situation has developed over Iraq, with attempts to shoot down Allied aircraft prompting attacks on Iraqi installations, thereby giving further reason for air defence activity.[58] The US air raids on Libya in 1986 and on Sudan and Afghanistan in 1998 were launched in response to terrorist outrages, and the apartment bombings in Moscow in 1999 were a key factor in consolidating Russian support for a renewal of hostilities against Chechnya.[59] Experience thus suggests that 'reprisals' by underdogs are just as likely to provoke as to deter enemy air attacks.

---

57. See the unpublished PhD thesis by my former student Marouf Nader, on *The Evolution of Egyptian Air Defence Strategy, 1967-1973* (King's College London, 1990).
58. Kenneth Schow, *Falcons against the Jihad: Israeli Airpower and Coercive Diplomacy in Southern Lebanon*, SAAS thesis (Maxwell AL: Air University Press, 1995); 'Cost of forgotten war mounts', *The Times*, Aug 23rd, 1999.
59. 'Moscow in panic as bomb kills 70', *The Times*, September 14th, 1999; 'Voters stand firmly behind warmongers in Duma campaign', *The Times*, December 16th, 1999

It might be thought that the best strategy for underdogs in the face of these problems would be to seek retaliatory capabilities so fearsome that they can establish mutual deterrence without risking the cycle of reprisals associated with the actual *use* of force. However, past experience suggests that attempts by underdogs to acquire WMD capabilities may in themselves provoke attack if the countries concerned are considered 'rogue states' unfit to be trusted with such awesome military potential. Iraq's WMD activities have served to attract air strikes by fearful adversaries on no less than three occasions - in 1981, 1991 and 1998 - and the United States also seriously considered pre-emptive air attacks during the controversies in the 1990s over Libya's chemical weapons plant and North Korea's nuclear programme. Even if an underdog can get through this dangerous transitional period and develop a WMD capability secure against pre-emptive attack (by no means an easy matter for such an outclassed state), the fact that this capability cannot actually be *used* without provoking overwhelming retaliation significantly limits its effectiveness as a deterrent threat.

Nothing better illustrates the difficulty underdogs have in striking a balance between deterrence and provocation than their attempted use of hostages. Although threatening hostages with harm if air strikes are launched might seem to create the perfect relationship of deterrent conditionality, the very act of holding hostages tends to revolt international opinion, and is extremely difficult to sustain for an extended period while also conducting a 'charm offensive' to ward off air attack - hence the eventual release of hostages by Saddam Hussein before Operation Desert Storm and by the Bosnian Serbs before Operation Deliberate Force. Once air strikes are under way, actually harming defenceless hostages in retaliation would have catastrophic consequences in the image war. Slobodan Milosevic did not dare even to hold for long the three US servicemen captured on the Macedonian border, and his attempted ethnic cleansing of the Kosovan population, although seemingly intended to demonstrate that NATO's bombing was counterproductive, served instead to confirm his demonisation and to harden his enemies' resolve, since at least the tragedies which their own bombs inflicted were accidental rather than deliberate.[60]

---

60. Barry Posen, 'The War for Kosovo: Serbia's Political-Military Strategy', *International Security* 24/4, Spring 2000, p. 52-4 and 68-9..

AIR STRATEGY AND THE UNDERDOG

Nothing better encapsulates the dilemmas of a hostage strategy for underdogs than this media image of Saddam Hussein with Stuart Lockwood before the Gulf War.

Given the irreconcilable tensions which underdogs face in trying to foster enemy self-restraint, it might be thought that they would be better off abandoning the balancing act and going all out for one extreme or the other. However, such simplicities are illusory. Underdogs are by definition militarily inferior, and so cannot afford the luxury of basing their strategy entirely around the confident Latin epithet *Oderint dum metuant* (Let them hate, so long as they fear).[61] Indeed, deterrence may be positively undermined if an impression is given of unrestrained frightfulness, leading adversaries to see their least bad option as being to overwhelm the underdog as soon as possible, as happened to Nazi Germany in 1944-45 and to Chechnya in 1999-2000.[62] On the other hand, seeking sympathy by adopting an entirely passive approach is unlikely to do more than to prompt sensitive adversaries to win gracefully and with as little collateral damage as possible, since there will be so little risk of casualties in pursuing what they presumably consider

---

61. Lucius Accius, *Atreus*, 140 BC.
62. The Chechens also forfeited much potential international sympathy through their barbarous behaviour. See 'Chechens filmed murder of Britons', *The Sunday Times*, November 21st, 1999; 'Impact of world outrage will be limited', *The Times*, December 8th, 1999.

to be a justified grievance. Hence, future underdogs will have to balance carefully their exploitation of fear, humanity and politics when encouraging enemy self-restraint, and even then, experience suggests that they are very unlikely to obtain the best of both worlds.

Activity versus Endurance

The third fundamental strategic dilemma facing past underdogs has been that of how to achieve strategic success and conflict termination in a situation where seizing the initiative militarily usually results in much greater exposure to enemy air power. Traditional military doctrine stresses the need for an offensive spirit, so as to impose one's own will on the course of the war, but the ill-advised application of such ideas by inferior air powers has often led to catastrophe. On the other hand, underdogs which have taken the opposite approach of playing a waiting game have often seen the adversary able to dictate the course of the confrontation and to play to his own strengths so as to win at leisure, without suffering prohibitive setbacks along the way.

As regards the surface battle, one way in which underdogs have traditionally tried to square this circle is by launching ground offensives at times when enemy air operations are hindered by poor weather, as with the Battle of the Bulge and the Chinese intervention in Korea. However, adverse weather also complicates surface movement itself, and it rarely lasts long enough to provide a complete shield.[63] An alternative approach is to launch a surprise attack before enemy air power can be fully mobilised. This was a key reason for the near success of the initial North Korean invasion in June 1950, and it has been argued that Saddam Hussein should have made a similar all-or-nothing gamble forty years later by ordering his forces to drive straight on to the Saudi airfields rather than allowing the Coalition to build up at their leisure for the liberation of Kuwait. However, the rapid and complete collapse of the over-extended North Korean forces in September 1950 in the face of the Inchon counter-offensive illustrates the perils of an all-or-nothing approach.[64] Had Iraqi forces continued their offensive beyond Kuwait, they would have forfeited any hope of fostering US self-restraint, and they would have found themselves even more strung out in the open desert as helpless targets for the rapidly gathering air armada.

---

63. Danny Parker, *To Win the Winter Sky: Airwar over the Ardennes, 1944-1945* (London: Greenhill, 1994); Conrad Crane, 'Raiding the Beggar's Pantry: The Search for Airpower Strategy in the Korean War', *Journal of Military History* 63/4, Oct 1999, p. 894-904.
64. Max Hastings, *The Korean War* (London: Michael Joseph, 1987) chs. 4-6.

AIR STRATEGY AND THE UNDERDOG

The Vietnam and Yom Kippur Wars, despite their very different character, illustrate well the conflicting pressures on inferior air powers as regards land offensives. The Arabs in 1973 achieved striking initial successes through their surprise assault, but then hunkered down behind their missile defences to defend their limited territorial gains. This protected them against the initial enemy air and armoured counterattacks, but the enraged Israelis now held the initiative and were able to mobilise to defeat the Arabs in detail, and to smash the Egyptian armoured reserves when they ventured out to resume the offensive in support of their beleaguered Syrian allies. In Vietnam, guerrilla tactics and the exploitation of US self-restraint and their own intense commitment allowed the Communists to maintain their war effort for years as US patience eroded, but the Communists still felt impelled to launch major offensives in 1968 and 1972 in an attempt to break the deadlock and secure victory. Both these offensives, like the Arab attack in 1973, ended in abject military defeats in the face of enemy air superiority, but in each case the *political* effect was to shock the adversary into loosening his commitment to the territory in dispute. Hence, only through a careful and complex blend of activity, endurance and diplomacy were the underdogs able to secure such gains as they eventually achieved.[65]

Seizing the initiative, as with this mortar attack on a US airbase in Vietnam, can bring significant results, but also exposes the underdog's own forces to easier destruction.

---

65   Chaim Herzog, *The Arab-Israeli Wars* (London: Arms & Armour, 1982) book 5; Phillip Davidson, *Vietnam at War* (London: Sidgwick & Jackson, 1988)

AIR STRATEGY AND THE UNDERDOG

The same tension between activity and endurance affects the strategies which past underdogs have adopted as regards the air battle itself. In Lebanon in 1982, the Syrians offered an active air defence, but this merely resulted in the rapid and one-sided annihilation of their air and surface-to-air forces.[66] Iraq in the Gulf War and Serbia during the Kosovo campaign adopted a much more cautious and passive air defence posture, and this resulted in a much lower rate of attrition to their forces, but because their adversaries were suffering only minimal losses, they were able to prolong the air operations for the weeks and months needed to achieve a slower but equally inexorable triumph. Only in Operation Desert Fox has the underdog's ideal of being able to 'ride out' a brief aerial storm been achieved, and even here, the continued pressure of UN sanctions has provoked Iraq into air defence countermeasures which have produced a continuing and still heavily one-sided air war.[67] As with surface operations, future underdogs will need a careful balance of active air defence, passive endurance and diplomacy if they are to find the 'least bad' strategy by which to minimise the impact of enemy air superiority.

CONCLUSION

There is a wide variety of techniques which underdogs may employ to counter enemy air power. One clear lesson of the past 60 years is that superior air powers often fall into the 'fallacy of the passive opponent', through too great a preoccupation with their own targeting dilemmas, or through too narrow or conventional an approach to characterising 'sensible' enemy options. Hence, underdogs can often spring some very nasty surprises, as with Hitler's Ardennes offensive and V-weapons bombardment, the Japanese *Kamikazes*, Chinese intervention in Korea, the Tet offensive, the Yom Kippur assault, Saddam Hussein's Scud launches and Al Khafji attack, and Milosevic's expulsion of the Kosovar Albanians. Although these actions often appear irrational in purely military terms, they may bring important political benefits for the underdog, as with the Tet and Yom Kippur offensives. Hence, superior air powers like those in the Western world need to think more strategically about possible enemy responses, and to place themselves more in the cultural and political framework of their adversaries rather than engaging in mirror imaging and artificial 'Red Team' hypothesising, if they are not to be caught out in the future as they have been in the past.

---

66. Michael Armitage & Tony Mason, *Air Power in the Nuclear Age, 1945-84: Theory and Practice*, 2nd ed., (London: Macmillan, 1985) p. 139-40
67. Ronald Lewis, 'Saddam out Foxed', *Air Forces Monthly*, Mar.1999, p. 22-8; 'Saddam Wins on Points', *The Middle East*, Jan 1999.

AIR STRATEGY AND THE UNDERDOG

However, past experience also suggests that it is very difficult for underdogs to translate individual techniques of response into overall victory, because of the inescapable tensions which inhibit the development of coherent, synergistic strategies to defeat enemy air power. The most important such tensions are between asymmetry and flexibility in the structuring of the underdog's forces, between deterrence and provocation in the underdog's coercive strategy, and between activity and endurance in the underdog's conduct of military operations. Although in some cases these tensions can be reconciled sufficiently to permit overall victory, this is usually due more to favourable individual circumstances than to clever underdog strategies which could be applied on a more universal basis. Hence, although superior air powers often finds it much harder to prevail than the promises of the enthusiasts might suggest (the recent experience in Kosovo being a prime example), only rarely are they thwarted in the end. As air power enters a new century, an appropriate aphorism would seem to be Damon Runyan's reworking of *Ecclesiastes 9/11*:

> *'The race is not always to the swift nor the battle to the strong - but that's the way to bet!'*

AIR STRATEGY AND THE UNDERDOG

CHAPTER 5

EUROPEAN AIR POWER
Sir Timothy Garden

LESSONS OF THE 90s

THE END OF THE COLD WAR left NATO with a vast and expensive set of military forces, which had been training to fight a single campaign for over 40 years. The planning assumptions for an all-out war in Europe were relatively simple. The enemy was well defined and consisted of the aggregate forces of the Warsaw Pact. The exact locations, strengths of forces, tactics to be used and phases of the war were studied by generations of soldiers. The fall of the Berlin Wall, the unification of Germany, the demise of the Warsaw Pact and the Soviet Union, all changed the strategic landscape in Europe in little more than a 3-year period. NATO's purpose was suddenly in question as nations scrambled to cash in on the peace dividend. Yet in the event, the decade of the 90s had more diverse military action by the Western nations, under various banners, than at any time previously. Kuwait, Iraq, Somalia, Rwanda, Bosnia, Haiti, Albania, Kosovo and East Timor have seen western military force deployed to less than benign environments. A new doctrine for peace support operations has replaced the manuals on flexible response and the air-land battle in the military staff colleges of the Alliance.

This series of military experiences is sufficient now to have established a strong consensus on the new rationale for NATO, which was articulated in the Strategic Concept launched at the NATO summit in Washington in April 1999. The accumulation of data from real operations, rather than deterrence postures, has highlighted major shortcomings in the security capabilities available to the Alliance for these new tasks. The Gulf War, while not a NATO operation, was conducted by an ad hoc coalition drawn for the most part from NATO members. It was conducted using NATO procedures with forces drawn from NATO formations. It was a relatively clear-cut case for the international community to react to aggression, and thus an almost ideal trial for the concept of enforcing international law. Iraq had broken international law by invading Kuwait, and the UN could authorise military action to expel the invaders. Iraq had few friends among its neighbours; had an oppressive regime with potentially dissident groups; and was remote to US and European publics.

The US-led coalition was able to take its time in building up military presence in the surrounding area. The then novel doctrine of a prolonged precursor air campaign was tested successfully. Lack of casualties to the allies made the 6 weeks of offensive air action acceptable to politicians and public. The much greater availability of precision guidance for bombs had also set a precedent in terms of what was to become acceptable collateral damage in this type of operation. Nevertheless in 1991, even after the air campaign phase, there was a general expectation that the ground phase would involve traditional levels of casualties to the attacking forces. In the event, the ground campaign was short and almost casualty-free for the allies. The 4 days of ground war reinforced a new vision of war: ground forces sent in only when it was safe to secure the victory that had been won relatively bloodlessly from the air.

The Gulf War showed that the US was both quantitatively and qualitatively in a different capability league from all the other nations involved. As the French discovered, if you could not operate to US/NATO procedures, then you were kept out of the action. In the air, it was a war primarily of offensive air operations, and these had to be conducted from medium to high altitudes, where advanced defence suppression methods were more effective. Air defence fighters had relatively little work to do. The European nations had invested heavily in fighters to protect themselves from the long-range Russian bombers of the Cold War. For their offensive operations, they had depended on low flying tactics to improve their survivability against Warsaw Pact air defence systems, while accepting that there would be a significant attrition rate. In a war that was expected to last only 5 days before going nuclear, training and equipment were posited on achieving rapid results. The European military equipment was not well structured to the new doctrine.

The UN operation in Somalia reinforced the perception, both in America and internationally, that the US was only prepared to remain engaged if their troops were kept safe. The predominance of air power solutions to international crises was underlined by the continuing air operations over both Northern and Southern Iraq. Operation Provide Comfort had successfully, through air operations, given relief to the displaced Kurds who had fled from their homes in Northern Iraq. It was less clear that the results for the Marsh Arabs in the South were as positive. While there was a need for some fighter capability to police the air exclusion zones, this could be carried out as the secondary role of either bomber or reconnaissance aircraft.

The sequence of events in Bosnia reinforced the US view that offensive air power could provide the necessary coercion to bring recalcitrant leaders to the negotiating table. That the history of the region up to the Dayton accord is considerably more complex is unimportant. There is a widespread perception among American decision makers that the threat and application of air strikes was critical to obtaining Milosevic's agreement to the Dayton proposals. Again, in this short air campaign, publics and politicians expected precision attacks with no collateral damage and no losses to our own side. When an airman was lost over hostile territory, combat search and rescue effort became the overriding priority.

The 1999 Kosovo air campaign brought together all the political and military lessons that had been learned in the post-Cold War operations. The US had expended a good deal of research on improving its precision weapons. Nevertheless, the use of laser designation remained a significant constraint if the target was obscured by weather. The two other precision systems (GPS navigation and TERCOM ground mapping) were available both in bombs and cruise missiles, but were significantly more expensive and limited to fixed targets. They required access to US national data. Nevertheless, this mix of weaponry allowed the campaign to be planned on a requirement for no casualties to NATO forces, and minimal collateral damage from attacks.[1] These constraints undoubtedly prolonged the air campaign, but given that the required outcome was ultimately achieved, we can expect future operations to have similar assumptions about the requirement for very low numbers of casualties.

The contributions from the 14 NATO nations which took part were varied as shown in the pie chart below,[2] but all were overshadowed by the US, which provided 61% of the sorties flown.[3] For example, the UK carried out 1618 of the total of 38,004 NATO sorties flown, or just over 4%.[4] 102 of these sorties were the Sea Harriers doing little more than defending the small anti-submarine warfare carrier that they were deployed on. 324 were air-to-air refuelling aircraft mainly supporting the Tornados that operated from their bases in Germany. The UK E3-D airborne early warning aircraft clocked up 184 sorties. The sorties which directly influenced the outcome were those carrying out offensive attacks, and here the total UK effort was in the range 4% to 10% depending on the method of calculation (the lower figure reflects munition numbers and the higher missions flown), and we know that in many of these cases it was not possible to release weapons.[5] From 1008 RAF bombing sorties just 1011 weapons were released. Of these three quarters were non-precision weapons.[6] The story is similar for the other non-US NATO air forces. The US provided 70% of the total aircraft and 80% of the total weapons delivered.[7] Europe was shown to be good at providing political support for the operation, but poorly equipped to contribute to an offensive air campaign in an effective way.

---

1. The Kosovo/Allied Force After Action Report to Congress, of 31 January 2000. Page xxi of the Executive Summary warns however that casualties were expected, and should be planned for in future operations.
2. Ibid, Chapter VII Figure 16.
3. Ibid, p. 78.
4. 'Kosovo: An Account of the Crisis' by Lord Robertson of Port Ellen, United Kingdom, Ministry of Defence, October 1999, p. 30.
5. Ibid. *Lessons of Kosovo*: 1011 UK munitions out of NATO total of 23,614; UK 1008 strike sorties out of NATO total strike sorties of 10,484.
6. Ibid. Weapons used were 230 x 1000 lb bombs, 226 x Paveway II, 18 x Paveway III, 532 x RBL 755, 6 x ALARM.
7. 'The Military Balance', IISS, 1999-2000, p. 30.

EUROPEAN AIR POWER

An F16 of the Royal Netherlands Air Force. But in Operation Allied Force, the US provided 70% of the total aircraft and 80% of the total weapons delivered.

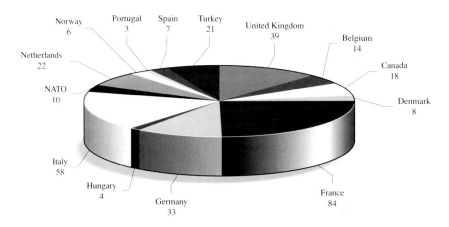

Non-US Aircraft Participating in Operation Allied Force

WHAT AIR ASSETS ARE AVAILABLE OR PLANNED

The United States Defence budget for 1998 was $267 bn from a GDP of $8.1 tr. Out of almost exactly the same total GDP, the EU nations together spent some $173bn on defence or 64% of the US total.[8] The US fields some 1.4 million professional forces and almost as many ready reserves. The EU runs 1.8 million troops of which 700,000 are conscripts and retains 3.6 million reservists at various stages of readiness. These raw budget and personnel statistics show clearly why Europe is so far behind the US in its military hardware development. Europe fields more full-time troops, and very many more reservists, than the United States, yet spends only half as much on defence. It is often claimed that the major factor in differences in US and EU capabilities stems from an all-regular force in America being compared with a largely conscript force in Europe. As can be seen from the figures, this is not the main issue. If all conscription were eliminated, and two thirds of the reservists were released, the EU could field over one million professional soldiers, sailors and airmen. Adding in the 6 non-EU European NATO members (Czech Republic, Hungary, Iceland, Norway, Poland and Turkey) would raise the regular forces to almost exactly the 1.4 million of the United States and lift the total current European aggregate defence spending to 70% of that in the US

If Europe, however defined, wishes to be a more equal partner with the United States in its ability to intervene internationally, it needs to spend its defence money differently. It is currently trying to support far too large a number of regular forces, conscripts and reserves on too few funds. This means that little is available for funding research, development and the procurement of equipment and weapon stocks. While the United States is scarcely a perfect example of tight control of defence spending, it is nevertheless achieving a different order of military capability for its expenditure. This suggests that Europe needs either to raise its defence spending, or reduce and restructure its forces to match the current spending more effectively. It is unlikely that there will be much political enthusiasm among nations for raising defence expenditure, and it is therefore more sensible to look at how European nations might work together at restructuring their military forces to provide more appropriate capabilities to the likely demands of the future.

---

8. Figures derived from IISS Military Balance, 1999-2000.

EUROPEAN AIR POWER

FINDING A DEFENCE ROLE FOR EUROPE

Before making any assessment of the appropriate size and shape of future European armed forces, we need to examine the nature of the current and future security need. NATO members remain firmly committed to the organisation's collective defence task. Individual national governments have a responsibility for the territorial defence of their lands, which they exercise through NATO membership. Yet the current threat to their territorial integrity is very remote, and the planning assumption is that there would be a long warning time of any newly emerging threat. It is important that European governments analyse the degree of risk that they are prepared to take in this area if there is to be a sensible allocation of defence resources.

Much of the force structure in Europe is still drawn from the Cold War days, when the priority was to deter the threat of a short warning time invasion by Warsaw Pact forces across the Inner German Border. The nature of such a threat determined the requirement for forward defensive positions on the ground supported by heavy armour with limited need for range. In the air, the need was for very good early warning detection to direct large numbers of air defence fighters and ground-based surface-to-air missiles. Those countries, such as the United Kingdom, which were further distant from the Warsaw Pact forces, could develop air defences on the basis of long range engagement of incoming bombers. At sea, anti-submarine warfare was a high priority. Overlaying the force planning process for this set piece campaign was the assumption that if the conventional battle were lost, then nuclear weapons would be used. For some European nations, this meant that there was little investment in conventional (non-nuclear) long-range interdiction capability. Air-to-ground capability was designed more to assist the ground battle and halt the advance of Warsaw Pact armour. In sum, the long period of the Cold War produced a force structure in Europe that was designed for a short, high intensity conflict, where air power assets, with the exception of nuclear forces, were primarily defensive or in a support role. Air strategists might articulate the arguments for interdiction and offensive counter-air campaigns, but in practice their most effective bombers needed to be reserved against the potential need for early nuclear options.

While the fall of the Berlin Wall in 1989 could change the security context in less than five years, it is not easy to restructure the armed forces of Europe as quickly. Some changes in balance were possible through the cuts that took place throughout NATO nations in the early 90s. However, some of the reductions were made soon after the end of the Warsaw Pact, when it was still thought possible that Russia might be able to pose a threat in a relatively short time. Thinking, as the 1991 NATO Strategic Concept showed, still looked primarily at maintaining a defensive posture, although with significantly lower readiness for most forces. By the end of the decade, three members of the Warsaw Pact (Hungary, Poland and the Czech Republic) had become full members of NATO, while the rest, including Russia, had become formal partners with the Alliance. Russia was so weak that it was finding great difficulty in winning a conventional war in Chechnya. Only her decaying nuclear weapon arsenal remained as a potential residual threat to the security of the rest of Europe.

The UK Strategic Defence Review (SDR), which was started in 1997 and was published in mid 1998, is a thoughtful analysis of the security concerns of one European nation.[9] It identified the positive results from the collapse of Communism and the emergence of democratic states throughout Europe. It stated that there was no direct threat to Western Europe, and that none was foreseen, provided that efforts were made to continue to promote and develop the constructive relationships between all nations of Europe. On the negative side, the SDR identified a number of new security risks. In particular, it pointed to instability inside Europe, citing Bosnia and Kosovo, as a threat to the UK's security. The SDR went on to say:

'Instability elsewhere - for example in Africa - may not always appear to threaten us directly. But it can do indirectly, and we cannot stand aside when it leads to massive human suffering.'[10]

This was the first statement of humanitarian intervention as a national security driver. The Review also identified the growing threat from proliferation of nuclear, biological and chemical technologies, particularly from a number of hostile regimes. Finally, it reminded the reader of the new risks to security from drugs, organised crime, environmental degradation, terrorism and new information technology vulnerabilities.

The security threats as perceived by the UK were in line with the general thrust of, and indeed helped to shape, European and NATO thinking. The successive crises in the Gulf, Bosnia, Kosovo and East Timor have also had an effect on political perceptions of the utility of military force. NATO decided to formulate a new Strategic Concept, which would be launched at its 50th anniversary summit meeting in April 1999 in Washington. As officials from member states began drafting they drew on the recent experience in Bosnia, and were already contemplating what might happen in Kosovo. The United States was seeking to extend the NATO mandate beyond its collective defence remit and possibly beyond Europe. The concerns felt by some European nations changed as the Kosovo crisis showed how necessary this change had become in practice.

---

9. *'The Strategic Defence Review'* (London: The Stationery Office, July 1998).
10. Ibid, p. 5.

When the Washington Summit took place, NATO found itself fighting a major air campaign against Serbia and showing that it was prepared to intervene beyond its national boundaries. The official summit communique was summed up as: 'NATO says it will expand its numbers and its functions'.[11] It announced that the 19 member countries had:

- approved an updated Strategic Concept;
- reaffirmed their commitment to the enlargement process of the Alliance and approved a Membership Action Plan for countries wishing to join;
- completed the work on key elements of the Berlin Decisions on building the European Security and Defence Identity within the Alliance and decided to further enhance its effectiveness;
- launched the Defence Capabilities Initiative;
- intensified relations with Partners through an enhanced and more operational Partnership for Peace and strengthened consultations and co-operation within the Euro-Atlantic Partnership Council;
- enhanced the Mediterranean Dialogue; and
- decided to increase Alliance efforts against weapons of mass destruction and their means of delivery.

These seven elements are all important not just for the future of NATO, but for the part that the European members have to play. The Strategic Concept recognised the changes in the strategic environment since the 1991 NATO Strategic Concept was produced.[12] The main elements were:

- **Collective Defence:** The Strategic Concept underscores the enduring core mission of NATO as the collective defence of its members under Article 5 of the North Atlantic Treaty.
- **Military Capabilities:** The Concept reaffirms Allies' determination to strengthen Alliance defence capabilities by ensuring forces that are more mobile, sustainable, survivable and able to engage effectively on the full spectrum of NATO missions.
- **New Missions:** The Concept calls for improvements in NATO's capability to undertake new missions to respond to a broad spectrum of possible threats to Alliance common interests, including: regional conflicts, such as in Kosovo and Bosnia; the proliferation of weapons of mass destruction and their means of delivery; and transnational threats like terrorism.

---

11. NATO Summit Communique, Washington, April 1999.
12. *NATO Strategic Concept*, Washington, April 1999.

- **New Members:** The Concept underscores NATO's continued openness to new members and Allies' commitment to enlargement as part of a broader effort to enhance peace and stability throughout the Euro-Atlantic community.
- **Strengthened Partnerships:** The Concept reinforces Alliance efforts to build wide-ranging partnerships with the aim of increasing transparency and mutual confidence in security matters and enhancing the capacity of allies and partners to act together.
- **European Capabilities:** The Concept highlights development of a European Security and Defence Identity within NATO as an essential element of NATO's ongoing adaptation, enabling European allies to make a more effective contribution to Euro-Atlantic security.

This last point of the Strategic Concept recognised the work that had been going on in parallel to develop a more coherent EU approach to foreign and security policy.

TOWARDS AN EU DEFENCE CAPABILITY

The development of a coherent defence policy for the EU had been an area of great difficulty for most of the 90s. The UK had been particularly unhelpful, fearing that any enhancement of the EU's role would be at the expense of NATO cohesion. The logjam was broken by the Anglo-French summit at St Malo in December 1998. Despite having predicated the just completed UK defence review on a continuing NATO-centred Atlanticist foreign policy, within six months of its publication, Prime Minister Tony Blair was advocating a much more significant role for Europe. The St Malo Declaration[13] made it clear that 'the Union must have the capacity for autonomous action, backed up by credible military forces, the means to decide to use them, and a readiness to do so, in order to respond to international crises'.[14] The declaration went on to say:

> *'In order for the European Union to take decisions and approve military action where the Alliance as a whole is not engaged, the Union must be given appropriate structures and a capacity for analysis of situations, sources of intelligence, and a capability for relevant strategic planning, without unnecessary duplication, taking account of the existing assets of the WEU and the evolution of its relations with the EU. In this regard,*

---

13. St Malo Declaration official text, December 1998.
14. Ibid, paragraph 2.

the European Union will also need to have recourse to suitable military means (European capabilities predesignated within NATO's European pillar or national or multinational European means outside the NATO framework).'[15]

This was a radical change of position for the British and opened the way to the further developments in 1999 in European defence.

The Western European Union (WEU) had in the past been seen as the main focus for European defence efforts. It had been circumscribed in terms of access to capability, a lack of an adequate planning staff, and a degree of uncertainty over the types of operation that it could take on. A consensus was emerging that it would be necessary to hand over the task of providing European defence capability from the WEU to the EU. The WEU ministerial meeting in Bremen at the end of May 1999 took forward the thinking that had started at St Malo and had been confirmed in Washington. The apparently insurmountable difficulties of the differences in membership between NATO, WEU and EU appeared to be no longer a sticking point. They agreed that there was a 'need for WEU to be operationally effective with the involvement and participation of all WEU nations in accordance with their status and to continue its cooperation with the EU and NATO, in preparation for any new arrangements which may be agreed in the light of ongoing developments'.[16]

The Cologne European Council Declaration, the following month, put this into a wider context, but picked up the same points, when they committed themselves in paragraph 2

'to further develop more effective European military capabilities from the basis of existing national, bi-national and multinational capabilities and to strengthen our own capabilities for that purpose. This requires the maintenance of a sustained defence effort, the implementation of the necessary adaptations and notably the reinforcement of our capabilities in the field of intelligence, strategic transport, command and control.'

It is significant that this was a declaration by all 15 members including four neutral EU countries.

Work continued in the UK to keep up the pace of European defence developments. The Anglo-Italian declaration of 20 July 1999 produced some concrete proposals on what needed to be done. It widened the requirement from a need for an EU capacity for

---

15. St Marlo Declaration, paragraph 3.
16. Bremen declaration, 10-11 May 1999, Official Text, paragraph 4.

EUROPEAN AIR POWER

doing its own humanitarian, crisis management and peace support operations (the Petersberg tasks). The need for a more effective European role in NATO was promoted as a clear lesson from Kosovo. The declaration sought to develop a timetable to achieve European-wide goals for enhanced military capabilities, and a set of national capability objectives to achieve this European requirement. The declaration proposed a peer review process with meetings of EU Foreign and Defence Ministers twice a year to check progress towards the agreed goals. This would take place in parallel with NATO's Defence Capabilities Initiative (DCI) work. The DCI made the point that NATO members would have to be able 'to make a fair contribution to the full spectrum of Alliance missions regardless of differences in national structures.' The DCI, like the Anglo-Italian declaration, highlighted the need to develop a common assessment of future requirements. However, it recognised the importance of the resource dimension as well as the need for better co-ordination between defence planning disciplines.

In November 1999, the first joint meeting of EU Foreign and Defence Ministers took place with Javier Solana, the new EU high representative for Common Foreign and Security Policy, in the chair. They looked at how Europe might be more effective in the defence field and in particular provide capabilities for Kosovo-like crises. A further Anglo-French summit occurred in the same month, when the two main defence players in Europe launched their vision for a new rapid deployment force of up to 60,000 men.[17] This would require the EU to develop a Corps sized capability, which could be deployed within 60 days and sustained for at least a year. The force would be militarily self-sufficient with the necessary command, control and intelligence capabilities, logistics, combat support and appropriate naval and air combat elements.

All this work was brought together at the EU Summit in Helsinki on 10/11 December 1999. In the European Council declaration, it was stated that[18] 'building on the guidelines established at the Cologne European Council and on the basis of the Presidency's reports, the European Council has agreed in particular the following:

- cooperating voluntarily in EU-led operations, Member States must be able, by 2003, to deploy within 60 days and sustain for at least 1 year military forces of up to 50,000-60,000 persons capable of the full range of Petersberg tasks;
- new political and military bodies and structures will be established within the Council to enable the Union to ensure the necessary political guidance and strategic direction to such operations, while respecting the single institutional framework;

---

17. Joint Declaration by the British and French Governments on European Defence, London, 25 November 1999.
18. Presidency Conclusions, Helsinki European Council, 10-11 December 1999, paragraph 28.

- modalities will be developed for full consultation, cooperation and transparency between the EU and NATO, taking into account the needs of all EU Member States;
- appropriate arrangements will be defined that would allow, while respecting the Union's decision-making autonomy, non-EU European NATO members and other interested States to contribute to EU military crisis management;
- a non-military crisis management mechanism will be established to coordinate and make more effective the various civilian means and resources, in parallel with the military ones, at the disposal of the Union and the Member States.

The more detailed Annex spells out the scale, types and readiness of the forces which are proposed.[19]

To develop European capabilities, Member States have set themselves the headline goal: by the year 2003, cooperating together voluntarily, they will be able to deploy rapidly and then sustain forces capable of the full range of Petersberg tasks as set out in the Amsterdam Treaty, including the most demanding, in operations up to corps level (up to 15 brigades or 50,000-60,000 persons).

These forces should be militarily self-sustaining with the necessary command, control and intelligence capabilities, logistics, other combat support services and additionally, as appropriate, air and naval elements. Member States should be able to deploy in full at this level within 60 days, and within this to provide smaller rapid response elements available and deployable at very high readiness. They must be able to sustain such a deployment for at least one year. This will require an additional pool of deployable units (and supporting elements) at lower readiness to provide replacements for the initial forces.

Member States have also decided to develop rapidly collective capability goals in the fields of command and control, intelligence and strategic transport, areas also identified by the WEU audit. They welcome in this respect decisions already announced by certain Member States which go in that direction:

- to develop and coordinate monitoring and early warning military means;
- to open existing joint national headquarters to officers coming from other Member States;
- to reinforce the rapid reaction capabilities of existing European multinational forces;

---

19. Presidency Conclusions, Helsinki European Council, 10-11 December 1999, Ibid, Annex IV

- to prepare the establishment of a European air transport command;
- to increase the number of readily deployable troops;
- to enhance strategic sea lift capacity.

The UK Government published its annual (although this was the first since 1996) White Paper on Defence immediately after the Helsinki Summit.[20] In examining the European dimension, the White Paper argues that European nations must be able to pull their weight, and have an international influence commensurate with their size and economic presence.[21] To do this they must find ways to provide genuine capability improvements, and that the Helsinki European Council declaration provides the way forward. The Prime Minister emphasised his commitment to improving the European defence capability when he reported to the House on the Helsinki summit:

> *'However, it would be a tragic mistake—repeating mistakes of British European policy over the past few decades—if Britain opted out of the debate on European defence and left the field to others. This is a debate that we must shape and influence from the start, because our vital strategic interests are affected by it.'*[22]

We have now, in theory, an outline plan for progress in improving European defence capabilities in a way which works with the grain of NATO. That is a remarkable step forward given the reluctance of the US and the UK in past years to address these issues. But there are many difficulties ahead. NATO would claim to have a planning process, and to have expended much effort over the years on coercing nations into setting more challenging force goals for themselves. In practice, the achievement of the process has been limited, particularly in the past decade. The institutional arrangements will almost certainly delay the development of the agreed capability. Nevertheless, there are a number of measures that might be taken in the field of air power capabilities, which would make practical sense in any case.

---

20. Defence White Paper, London, December 1999, Cm 4446.
21. Ibid, paragraph 17-22.
22. Hansard, 13 December 1999, col 22.

EUROPEAN AIR POWER

HOW MUCH AIR POWER DOES EUROPE NEED?

In order to look at the air power capabilities that the European Union nations should field, we need to make some assumptions about the scale of effort that it would be appropriate for the EU to seek to provide. The EU and the US are just about equal in terms of absolute wealth. The EU is more populous and has more potential conflicts in its backyard than the US. However, the US has formal security obligations in Japan and Korea as well as in Europe. Taking all these factors into account, it might seem a reasonable initial benchmark for European nations to seek to contribute a usable military capability of the same order of magnitude as the United States plans for NATO. The United States is seeking to generate ten air expeditionary wings, each with about 15,000 personnel and 200 aircraft. Certainly Europe would not need to aim for any greater capability than this. This would not be a recipe for duplication, but a significant challenge for Europe. It would make the Europeans equal partners when operating within NATO, and would ensure a capability for operations on a European basis when necessary. While in theory such a force should be affordable, in practice it would require massive restructuring of the way military forces are provided within Europe.

The UK Government has taken this need for restructuring as a strong lesson of the Kosovo operation:

'...... in co-operation with our Allies, we need to examine ways in which member states can increase their qualitative and quantitative military contribution to NATO's overall capabilities. The priority lies in such areas as precision attack weapons, secure communications and strategic movement assets. Interoperability of systems will, of course, be a key component of this.

..... there is a particular need to boost European capabilities. In order to strengthen our ability to use force effectively, we Europeans need to improve the readiness, deployability and sustainability of our armed forces and their ability to engage in both high intensity operations and those of an expeditionary nature. This would strengthen our contribution to NATO, which remains the sole instrument for collective defence. NATO will still be the natural choice for the conduct of non-Article 5 crisis management operations which North American and European Allies might choose to undertake in the future. A strengthened European capability would allow us to undertake European-led crisis management operations, in circumstances in which the whole Alliance is not engaged. We strongly support the focus of the European defence debate on these key capabilities and the more effective targeting of defence resources. We

EUROPEAN AIR POWER

will pursue these aims through NATO's Defence Capabilities Initiative, and the Western European Union's audit of European capability. The work on performance criteria which we launched with the Italians in July will help to achieve this.[23]

The key elements for early work in improving European capability are contained in this analysis. Readiness, deployability and sustainability are identified as prime drivers for force structures. Precision attack weapons, secure communications and strategic movement assets are highlighted as areas for priority work. There are significant implications for air power in all of these six issues. Europe needs to completely restructure its expensive, but unusable, military capability to meet these challenges. While the focus of this volume is on air power issues, it is impossible to look at air power in isolation. The funds provided for defence purposes throughout Europe are unlikely to increase without a significant change in threat perception. This means that restructuring of capabilities will need to be achieved within broadly the same resource assumptions as today. Thus, a balance will need to be struck between the different elements of the joint force structure. Nevertheless, it is possible to start by making an initial unconstrained assessment of what air power assets Europe should be able to deploy, and then assess how they might fit into the resource priorities.

A THEORETICAL EUROPEAN AIR POWER CAPABILITY

Using the Kosovo campaign as a benchmark for a modern military operation which should be within the capability of European nations, we can break out the scale of effort that might be needed in future. The campaign needed to be able to call upon the traditional mix of air defence fighters, bombers, close air support, reconnaissance, airborne early warning, air-to-air refuelling, strategic airlift, tactical fixed-wing and rotary transport capabilities. Although the maritime aspects of the operation were limited, it must be assumed that some future campaigns might need the appropriate mix of maritime reconnaissance, air defence, attack and anti-submarine warfare air assets.

The EU nations together have elements of all of these air power capabilities. They field some 3235 combat aircraft with a total air force manpower of 380,000. If the NATO non-EU members are added (Czech Republic, Hungary, Iceland, Norway, Poland and Turkey) the numbers rise to 4281 combat aircraft and 530,000 men.[24] These large air power assets, as discussed earlier, are however balanced to provide the defensive posture

---

23. *'Kosovo: An Account of the Crisis'* by Lord Robertson of Port Ellen, United Kingdom, Ministry of Defence, October 1999,
24. Figures drawn from data in IISS, The Military Balance, 1999-2000.

that was appropriate to the static defence requirements of the Cold War. All forces have a strong air defence element reflecting the requirement to defend their own territory. While many of the fighters can be used in a bombing role, they are not all-weather capable and aircrew will not have undertaken primary training in this role. For offensive air operations, the only EU nations with a significant capability are France, Germany, Italy and the UK, who can field around 500 aircraft in an all-weather bombing mode. Looking at the scale of offensive air capability needed for the Gulf and Kosovo, Europe needs to work at providing perhaps 50% more all-weather bombers than it can at present. This is an achievable aim if the priority given to the air defence role is reduced.

However, the platform is only part of the question in modern air campaigns. It has become very clear that in future operations, precision weapons will be the norm. Figures for weapons stocks are not readily available, but inferences can be drawn from the data of weapon usage in the Kosovo air campaign. Only 250 of the 1011 UK aircraft weapons used were precision, and for France the total was 582 laser-guided bombs.[25] The French Defence Ministry is quoted as saying that they had an inadequate stockpile of such weapons.[26]

APPROACHES TO IMPROVING EUROPEAN DEFENCE CAPABILITIES

In any discussion about improving European defence capabilities, the argument usually begins with a plea for more spending on defence. It is also argued that greater integration of defence industries would be beneficial. Neither approach has much prospect of early success, and there can be no confidence that either would generate real enhancements in capability without a radical restructuring. Putting aside the political difficulties, Europe could undoubtedly organise its defence spending more efficiently if it was done on an integrated basis in the same way that the United States organises its armed forces at the Federal level. Such an approach for Europe will not be possible for many years (if ever), as it will be necessary for EU member nations to give up national sovereignty to what is currently an unacceptable extent. There are similar, although slightly less acute, difficulties with moves towards allocation of military tasks to particular nations. This 'Role Specialisation' was much studied during the later stages of the Cold War. Even with a common view of the mission, nations were reluctant to become reliant on other Allies for particular capabilities. Nevertheless a *de facto* specialisation has occurred as European nations have been unable to match the technology of the US. It may be that

---

25. *'Kosovo: An Account of the Crisis'* by Lord Robertson of Port Ellen, United Kingdom, Ministry of Defence, October 1999, p. 30.
26. *International Herald Tribune*, 11 November 1999, p. 4.

there will be a greater willingness for each European nation to undertake fewer roles, but make those that they field more effective. This approach will require close co-ordination if it is not to open up yet more gaps in capability.

The proposals agreed at the 1999 Helsinki Summit could provide an appropriate mechanism for co-ordinating efforts between EU nations, and also keeping less enthusiastic contributors up to the mark. It would allow nations to move towards as much specialisation as they felt comfortable with, and to be credited with real military contribution to the EU force component. However this will take some years to develop. In the meantime there is a danger that European capability will degrade further. What is needed is some early action to improve capability without assuming large budget increases. This can only be achieved by looking for ways to reduce nugatory expenditure by cutting duplication, unnecessary support overheads, and inappropriate capability. This is a painful process even when carried out on a national basis. It will be yet more difficult if it is to be carried out on an EU basis. Nevertheless, it is the only immediate option available, and can be done relatively rapidly given the political will.

If we look at the European forces as a whole, we see duplication of headquarters, planning, training, logistics support, procurement, research, bases and other facilities. This would be bad enough if the scale of the frontline in each nation justified the scale of the support infrastructure, but it does not in nearly all cases. For the final section of this chapter, we will look at how this opportunity for rationalisation could be exploited to provide Europe with a more effective and appropriate air power capability.

Opportunities for more effective operation of European military forces are apparent in land, sea and air capabilities. However, the air capabilities offer more easily achieved improvements for a number of reasons. Air procedures are already better harmonised between nations than is the case for land and sea power. This is partly because of air safety issues and partly because speed of operation means that communications, standard operating procedures, rules of engagement, planning methods and terminology must all be agreed, standardised and practised between air forces which are likely to operate together. English has become the universal language of the air, and this considerably eases the problem of mounting international combined air operations. Given the high unit cost of air force platforms, it is not surprising that many nations operate common equipment. This also eases the problems of rationalisation. Finally, the high costs of infrastructure to support air operations means that modest rationalisation can pay high dividends in achieving greater military capability at lower cost.

EUROPEAN AIR POWER

NEAR TERM EU AIR POWER RATIONALISATION

In looking for opportunities to provide more effective European military power, the leap is too often made towards a full-scale integrated European army. Indeed the Helsinki proposals are in danger of trying to achieve this step, which remains impossible unless the EU becomes a much more politically integrated entity. In the near term (the next 5 years), it would be much more productive to look for opportunities to rationalise forces in being which can be operated more efficiently on a multilateral or EU-wide basis. The model for such a supranational activity is the NATO AWACS force, which has successfully provided an airborne early warning capability to NATO members at much lower day-to-day operating cost than would have been the case if operated on an individual national basis.

The NATO AWACS force has successfully provided an airborne early warning capability to NATO members at a much lower operating cost than would have been the case on an individual national basis.

What capability does Europe need which it could operate on a similar basis to NATO AWACS? Airlift is an obvious example. If forces are to be deployed rapidly, they need to be able to call on a significant airlift capability. In looking for an opportunity for early rationalisation, we need to identify a capability which is common to many EU members. The air tactical transport role is a capability which most nations need, and many provide for it at least partly using the C130 aircraft. Pooling of some of these widely used C130 Hercules could provide an immediate European tactical fixed-wing transport capability. Provided that nations structured their contributions sensibly, they could make operating cost savings at the national level through closure of bases, training units, and headquarters. The level of saving would depend on the degree to which each nation felt able to rely on the supporting infrastructure being provided by a European facility.

Some ten EU nations operate C130 aircraft.[27] It would be possible to imagine a pooled fleet of 70 aircraft, which would look after all the national C130 needs of Belgium (who operate 11), Denmark (4), Italy (10), Netherlands (2), Spain (12), Sweden (8) and Portugal (6). France with 14 C130s and the UK with 55 have larger transport aircraft fleets; and they could provide a partial contribution of perhaps 6 and 10 aircraft respectively to the pooled arrangement. Greece (15) might choose not to depend on pooled aircraft. For those nations that were prepared to put all of their C130 fleets into a common pool, there would be significant savings in operating costs. They would also have a much better assurance of availability on a day-to-day basis, given the ability to plan routine servicing across a larger fleet. For Europe there would be a usable airlift capability for humanitarian operations as well as for use within NATO. Also nations would not lose the option to withdraw their airframes and aircrews if they felt the need for some national purpose. The force would not be rendered useless if one or more nations declined to take part in a particular operation for national reasons.

However, for lower costs to be achieved this would have to be a quite different arrangement from current on-call multinational arrangements. The force would operate from a single main base located centrally in Europe, but would have dispersed flights to service national needs. There would be a single headquarters, manned by personnel from the contributing EU nations. Aircrew would be multinational and not tied to the airframes provided by their nations. There would be a single planning, servicing and logistics organisation to support the force. Most importantly, the manpower, headquarters, infrastructure and other savings would have to be realised in the military structures of the contributing nations. Those resources could then be redeployed to updating and enhancing other capabilities.

Over time, the management and operation of this common fleet would lead to a common perception among participating nations of the characteristics of the next generation transport aircraft. This would have great benefits in terms of reducing duplication of defence research and procurement costs in this particular area. The extra costs of operating on a national basis rather than a pooled basis would also become clear, and it is likely that nations would begin to see the advantages of contributing to such a force element. This would also increase the pressure for common equipment procurement programmes for successor aircraft.

---

27. All statistics on C130 aircraft are drawn from IISS, The Military Balance, 1999-2000.

In a slightly longer time-scale, the requirement for a large strategic airlift capability could be tackled. The operation of such a fleet could easily be managed by the same organisation that would look after the tactical C130 pooled capability. It would be possible to procure a new capability of C17s or Antonov strategic transport aircraft that could either be operated by the military or on a leased basis from a commercial company. In either case the costs would be lower than each nation trying to operate a very small fleet of large and expensive aircraft.

Air-to-air refuelling capability is also needed by all European air forces, and would be a natural candidate for a European fleet operation. There is consideration being given to procuring the UK air-to-air refuelling capability through a public private partnership arrangement. This would be particularly easy to enlarge to encompass those nations in Europe which sought such a facility. The economics of the operation would improve for the larger fleet and there would be no sovereignty issues to worry about given the service is being provided by the private sector.

It is possible to draw up similar proposals for transport helicopters, although care must be taken to ensure that sufficient assets are based within easy flying range of their normal tasking. This will tend to require dispersed deployments and the efficiencies from pooling short-range assets will therefore be less.

Reconnaissance and Combat Search and Rescue (CSAR) are two roles, which are expensive in equipment and training, but which could offer opportunities for building up EU capabilities to operate with the US forces available to NATO. There will be considerable development in the use of UAVs for the tactical reconnaissance role, and there is a need for a European satellite-based strategic reconnaissance capability. Both of these capabilities will be expensive, but are essential if Europe is serious in its intention to provide real military capability. The information exploitation organisation will again be much more cost-effective if operated at the supranational level. This capability needs to be considered in the context of an EU intelligence capability, which given the political, military and financial complexities is dealt with below as part of medium term integration.

None of the air transport, air tanker, reconnaissance or CSAR pooling proposals would undermine national capability. Indeed for the smaller nations it would both increase available capability and reduce costs. It is thus possible to see opportunities for enhancing the support element of air power in Europe in a relatively short time-scale through aggressive rationalisation of forces in being, and exploiting the moves towards public-private partnerships. Significant defence funds would be released provided that nations took the consequent manpower and infrastructure savings which would flow. There would remain a problem of the 'free-rider' nation, although the audit and capability criteria proposals of the Helsinki Summit may help to stimulate contributions from EU member nations. At an early stage, it will be necessary to establish a European Defence Budget to which members contribute either capability or money.

MEDIUM TERM EUROPEAN AIR POWER INTEGRATION

While the support area offers opportunities for pooling and rationalisation of air power forces without too many issues of national sovereignty, real increases in capability will need a similar approach to combat air power. It is unlikely that major EU defence players will be attracted to giving up their combat capabilities to a supranational authority until some confidence has been gained through the less contentious pooling of air transport and air-to-air refuelling capability.

Offensive and defensive air power capability is politically the most difficult element to pool and operate at the European level. Nations are prepared to make arrangements for multinational forces, but insist on retaining the ability to operate their forces nationally. The effect of this approach was seen in the divergence of the national Tornado enhancements over the past 20 years. The Tri-national Training Unit was closed down in 1999 because the aircraft it operated were no longer representative of each nation's own Tornados.

As soon as it became politically acceptable, some of the existing common combat air equipment capabilities could be pooled in a similar manner to that described for the C130 force. An obvious example would be an EU F16 force. Belgium, Denmark, Greece, Netherlands and Portugal operate 424 F16s between them.[28] This could provide some support for the new deployable Helsinki agreed force. Despite the divergence in Tornado IDS updates, Germany, Italy and the UK could look at how pooled arrangements might allow them to contribute some of their 570 aircraft to an early offensive capability to the Helsinki force.

The introduction into service of Eurofighter from 2002 to five European nations (UK, Germany, Italy, Spain and Greece) offers a good opportunity to enhance capabilities and reduce costs through pooling of assets. Sharing training, engineering, logistic, and operational planning facilities would throw up significant operating cost savings. These would be greatly increased if the number of bases required could be reduced as a result. Most importantly common fleet management would play a vital role in retaining system configuration control so that all Eurofighters remain fully interoperable. From a political viewpoint, if as a result Europe were able to offer a force of 500 of the most modern combat aircraft for future NATO operations, it would be a capability contributor more equal to the United States in any Gulf or Kosovo type operation. A pooled fleet would also ensure that a common approach to weapons procurement was adopted. Indeed, it would become an attractive club to join: other EU nations would calculate the additional cost savings to be achieved by procuring Eurofighter as their successor combat aircraft.

---

28. All aircraft statistics are drawn from IISS, The Military Balance, 1999-2000.

The introduction into service of the Eurofighter from 2002 to five European nations offers a good opportunity to enhance capabilities and reduce costs through pooling of assets.

The development of an EU precision attack capability would be a key part of this medium term plan. The provision of adequate stocks of appropriate munitions would allow nations to contribute in other ways than just aircraft and aircrew. Starting the process early would allow a common view to emerge about the platform/weapons combination which should be developed. Leaving France, Germany, Italy and the UK to research their own future offensive capability will inevitably result in a sub-optimal solution. A united EU view on both the importance and the nature of the next generation offensive air power requirement would be a very powerful driver towards procuring an effective capability. There is time for this process to begin, provided that nations start to operate in this role together. Under the current arrangements, Europe is likely to perpetuate the mix of systems of limited effectiveness in the offensive role.

One of the more expensive air power capabilities is provided by the aircraft carrier, which is examined in Dr Goulter's chapter on expeditionary warfare. Few European nations can afford to field such a force; for those which stay in the role, the opportunity costs are very high. The UK plans to provide 2 carriers in 2012, and it is likely that France, Spain and Italy will wish to retain the role as well. Operated on a national level, one or two carriers do not constitute a viable and reliable force, and the opportunity costs are severe for other defence capabilities. The time-scale is sufficiently long for interested EU nations to look at how they might jointly contribute to a force of 5 or 6 aircraft carriers with their supporting ships and aircraft.

Intelligence requirements permeate every aspect of military operations, and an independent intelligence capability will be needed if EU forces are to be able to operate truly autonomously. Pooling of current intelligence related air power capabilities will be difficult for a number of reasons. The equipment used by nations is diverse, and much of it outdated; the national exploitation is jealously guarded; and there are bilateral difficulties with wider information sharing. For these reasons, it would probably be more effective to build up a new EU intelligence capability from scratch. This would be expensive, but would allow a fully integrated modern system to be established relatively quickly. If the EU wanted to focus on one area for priority action, then intelligence would provide it. The platforms, communication, fusion, exploitation and dissemination systems could be built up to be fully interoperable with NATO, but also independently usable. Kosovo showed that the inability to share digital intelligence data was a problem throughout the operation.[29]

LONG TERM: THE EUROPEAN AIR FORCE

In the much longer term, it is possible to contemplate the gradual development of a European Air Force as experience of pooling forces is gained. Confidence would grow as to the greater availability of air power assets to individual nations, to the EU and to NATO. Such a force would be a part of a wider integration of European defence capabilities, which would require the development of a European defence budget. The mechanisms for operating such a budget are beyond the scope of this chapter, but are an essential part of moves towards more efficient use of European defence resources.[30] Nations would still be able to retain independent national air capabilities if they so wished, but such national air power would not count as a contribution in European defence budget terms.

There is a close parallel in these proposals with the original evolution of independent national air forces. Armies and navies wanted to own their own air power, and were concerned about becoming too dependent on an independent air force, which would be centrally controlled at the higher level. The costs, confusion and inefficiencies of maintaining army and naval air forces eventually led nations to form a third service which could procure and use air power effectively. The next stage for such sensible

---

29. *The Kosovo/Allied Force After Action Report to Congress*, of 31 January 2000, p. 49.
30. The argument for a European defence budget is outlined in *'Pooling Forces'*, by T Garden and J Roper, in the December 1999 issue of Centre for European Reform Newsletter.

rationalisation must be an integration of air power across national boundaries. Those national boundaries may have had physical meaning on the ground and at sea, but are irrelevant in the air. If the political will were there, Europe could produce effective modern air power, and could even do it more cost effectively than does the United States.

CHAPTER 6

THE AIRMEN'S DILEMMA: TO COMMAND OR TO CONTROL?
Air Commodore Stuart Peach

INTRODUCTION

MANY PEOPLE IN AND OUT of the military lump the terms command and control together in one phrase of military jargon. In fact, they mean different things to a politician, soldier, sailor or airman. In an era of participation in conflicts of 'choice' rather than wars of national survival, if command and control procedures are convoluted or confused, and they often are, the initiative can be handed to the enemy. This is particularly true in complex emergencies involving the intervention of western military forces either drawn from an Alliance such as NATO, or an *ad hoc* coalition. Thus, the study of command and control is important in the context of contemporary air power.

Command defies easy or neat definition. The exercise of command over men and women in an operational situation is a human function. Thus, commanders adopt widely differing styles and 'ways' of command. Furthermore, since the birth of aviation, airmen do not apply command in the same way as soldiers and sailors; commanding formations of machines in the air requires different skills and considerations in the exercise of command. Their efforts have been complicated by the baggage surrounding the birth of their version of operational art. Throughout the short history of air power, the struggle for independent air forces and arguments and debate over subordination and support have dominated the issue of command and control of air power.

Airmen have always believed that freedom from the friction of ground warfare and the inherent perspective and speed of response of air power means that air power needs to be controlled in a centralised manner if it is to be concentrated where and when it is needed. In consequence, a philosophy of centralisation for air generals placed in command bunkers with airfields remote from the command centre has developed. Cinematic images of the Battle of Britain and the Bomber Offensive reinforce the historical perception. The bunker mentality solidified during the Cold War with centralised command centres proliferating around Europe. Since the birth of the information age, airmen procured vast quantities of computer systems designed to improve air command centres. In fact, the millions of defence dollars spent in this way have barely kept up with the rise in the quantity of information that is passed to and from

THE AIRMEN'S DILEMMA: TO COMMAND OR TO CONTROL?

military headquarters.[1] Sifting the data into what is important and time-critical becomes a genuine challenge, since concentrating on the wrong thing could lead to mission failure. The drive to streamline procedures and handle ever more data has had an important side-effect; airmen have become driven by process not strategy.

Recent air operations have highlighted the centralising 'pull' of computers and information systems into air command centres, which have 'pushed' air commanders away from decentralised execution. For example, in August 1995, during air operations over Bosnia, code-named Operation Deliberate Force, the air commander placed himself at the tactical level in the Combined Air Operations Centre at Vicenza in Italy and took direct control of the Air Tasking process with a small, specially selected team of air advisers.[2] During the air war over Kosovo in 1999, the air commander, Lieutenant General Mike Short, again chose to locate himself close to the 'action' at the tactical level so that he could directly influence events.[3]

If NATO or the US had followed its agreed doctrine, in both of these recent events, the Air Commander could have located himself at the operational level alongside the Joint Force Commander to influence targeting and overall campaign planning. Of course, commanders can argue that their hand was forced by the lack of secure, reliable, interoperable communications, but that reinforces the point. Despite the money lavished upon the systems and sensors, air operations planners have proved remarkably reluctant to divorce strategy from process. With Air Tasking Orders running into hundreds of pages requiring large numbers of airmen to create and sustain the process, the inherent reluctance to change the plan is understandable. Von Moltke's aphorism that 'no plan survives contact with the enemy' remains relevant today.

This chapter will examine the contemporary labels for command and control, offer a brief overview of air power history from the perspective of command and highlight thoughts for the future.

---

1. Peter Emmett, *Perspectives on Air Power*, edited by Stuart Peach (London: TSO, 1998) ch. 6.
2. T Ripley, *Operation Deliberate Force* (Lancaster University: CDISS, 1999).
3. Lt Gen Mike Short, USAF, speaking on 'Balkans Air War', BBC TV, January 2000.

THE AIRMEN'S DILEMMA: TO COMMAND OR TO CONTROL?

CONTEMPORARY AIR COMMAND AND CONTROL

With the Allied experience of World War Two as a guide, in the 1950s NATO defined and refined command and control terms to cater for the needs of the Cold War. Common, agreed strategy and common goals were assumed. The Royal Air Force defines command as "the military authority and responsibility to issue orders to subordinates" and control as "the authority exercised by a commander over subordinates to implement orders".[4] NATO embraces terms such as full command, operational command, operational control, tactical command, tactical control, functional command, and administrative control, which have been carefully crafted in NATO 'smoke-filled rooms.' The problem is that these elegant terms no longer work.

NATO Command States

Full Command - The military authority and responsibility of a superior officer to issue orders to subordinates. It covers every aspect of military operations and administration and exists only within national services.

Operational Command (OPCOM) - The authority granted to a commander to assign missions or tasks to subordinate commanders, to deploy units, to reassign forces, and to retain or delegate operational and/or tactical control as may be deemed necessary.

Operational Control (OPCON) - The authority delegated to a commander to direct forces assigned so that the commander may accomplish specific missions or tasks which are usually limited by function, time, or location; to deploy units concerned, and to retain or assign tactical control of those units.

Tactical Command (TACOM) - The authority delegated to a commander to assign tasks to forces under his command for the accomplishment of the mission assigned by higher authority.

Tactical Control (TACON) - The detailed and, usually, local direction and control of movements or manoeuvres necessary to accomplish missions or tasks assigned.

Functional Command - A command organisation based on military functions rather than geographic areas.

---

4. RAF Air Operations Manual, (First Edition) III, 1.

THE AIRMEN'S DILEMMA: TO COMMAND OR TO CONTROL?

Administrative Control - Direction or exercise of authority over subordinate or other organisations in respect to administrative matters such as personnel management, supply, services, and other matters not included in the operational missions of the subordinate or other organisations.

The taxonomy is bewildering and formal definitions mask a simple truth. Unity of effort is a sensible goal, but remains elusive. Ever since the days of the 'Great Game', national interest will prevail in setting the conditions for engagement in any form of military activity. In warfare, one nation is never entirely happy to place its military forces under the command or control of the forces of another nation. Thus, a single commander is unlikely to have complete freedom of action over the forces of another sovereign nation. Indeed, this is enshrined by Presidential decree in the United States.[5] If the ingredient of voluntary participation in a conflict of choice rather than a war of national survival is added, the reality is that the designated national commander will always retain a national 'red card'.

To address the 'so what' issue, does this matter for air forces? Yes, because national interest issues apply equally to the use of air power, especially bomber aircraft. Western aircraft (except US stealth fighters and bombers) generally operate together in formations combined into force packages. In modern parlance, these are known as composite air operations. A single package commander is nominated who controls the formation in the air. He reports to a mission commander. The mission commander may be located in an airborne control aircraft such as the airborne warning and control aircraft (AWACs) or on the ground in a combined air operations centre (CAOC). His (or her) boss will be the designated air component commander or joint force air component commander (JFACC), who will report to the joint force commander (JFC). He, in turn, will issue clear unequivocal guidance and intent for the conduct of air operations. Typically, the JFC will be located in or near to the political centre of gravity for the designated Theatre of Operations so that he can 'sniff the prevailing political wind' and control his forces free from the interference of politicians, non governmental organisations (NGOs) and supranational bodies such as the UN, OSCE or EU. That is the job of the strategic commander.

Meanwhile in UN New York, HQ NATO in Brussels or in national capitals, the strategic or joint commander (Jt Cdr) will issue deliberately vague directives couched in military language. The aim is to offer the theatre commander freedom of action to plan, mount and sustain military operations aimed towards achieving an agreed End State.

---

5. Presidential Defence Directive No 25 (PDD 25 states that US forces will not serve under command of another nation). This limitation affects all form of coalition operations involving the US and can lead to increased friction with allies as the US insist on maintaining a separate command chain, regardless of local agreements.

THE AIRMEN'S DILEMMA: TO COMMAND OR TO CONTROL?

Military commanders invariably complain that the guidance they receive is too vague or hopelessly unrealistic. Politicians and academics respond that the 'realpolitik' of international organisations or international relations makes this necessary. Nonetheless, military staff officers turn this vague direction into a campaign plan. They use techniques or tools developed over many years of military experience.[6] This campaign plan is then translated for each component into specific tasks and missions. The air component commander issues his direction to his staff who, in turn, develop a master air attack plan (MAAP) which is transmitted to participating units via an Air Tasking Order (ATO). This order tells the mission commander when to take off, where to find his tanker, what frequency to call the airborne mission commander, what his target is and - critically - how to attack it. In a phrase: centralised command and centralised execution.

NEW REALITIES - CENTRALISED CONTROL, CENTRALISED EXECUTION

Intervention forces operating in multinational operations will reflect their way in warfare, economic circumstances and motive for participation in that particular operation.[7] They may not have the equipment, political will, or rules of engagement to be able to carry out the mission as stated. Ten years of post Cold War peacekeeping have created, by inspection, a range of informal command states:

Realities of Peacekeeping Command and Control

OPWILL - We understand our mission and will comply, but may need assistance.

OPWONT - We understand our mission but will not comply for national reasons not specified.

OPCAN - We understand our mission and can comply without support.

OPCANT - We understand our mission, but cannot comply because of a lack of equipment etc.

---

6. In military doctrine this process is known as campaign planning and is conducted through campaign planning tools, which largely stem from Clausewitzian notions such as centres of gravity, lines of operation, decisive points and so on. Military students in staff and war colleges learn how to apply this 'process'.

7 For example, the motives for participation in the Gulf War coalition ranged from perceived national survival to economic interest.

THE AIRMEN'S DILEMMA: TO COMMAND OR TO CONTROL?

OPMAYBE- We understand our mission and may be able to comply but we will need to check with an unspecified number of national agencies.

The frustration caused by attempting to build and maintain unity of effort with so many agendas being pursued at the same time can only be hinted at. Understandably, commanders with direct experience of the phenomenon (including this one) are reluctant to speak out. The plain fact is that the challenge of high command in the multinational environment is profound. Lt Gen Short has made clear that frustrations surfaced regularly within the air coalition during Allied Force. Indeed, as the historical survey below indicates, they always have. The conclusion is that NATO formal command states were established at a unique time for a unique purpose when unity of effort could (probably) be guaranteed in the face of Soviet aggression. Now, the operational situation has changed. The realities of coalition warfare are that some form of 'contract' needs to be negotiated and sustained with each participating nation.

Thus in reality, theory, doctrine and practice collide with process. Airmen claim one thing (centralised command and decentralised execution) and in fact practice another (centralised command and centralised execution). Freedom of action for the airman in the cockpit lies within very narrow parameters. This conclusion challenges military doctrine. Behind the flickering screens and growling generals, a deep understanding of politics, strategy and history is needed to develop a coherent campaign plan. Just as airmen created a distorted perception of the accuracy of precision guided munitions during the Gulf War, so air generals have created a distorted perception of the 'ease' of command and control amongst their land and maritime colleagues. Smart computers and tailored software allow 'air' operational art to be smothered by process. There is simply insufficient time to analyse the data flooding into the air command and control centre which, anyway, lies at the tactical or execution end of air operations. Mastering and sustaining the process consumes the time available.

Although technology appears to be taking command and control procedures forward enabling more rapid decision-making, the opposite is happening. In consequence, synchronisation across several time zones with the 'man on the ground' of the naval, special forces or logistics component is not only difficult, it is wasting valuable 'thinking' or analysis time; surely the crux to operational art. And it is getting worse. Many middle ranking air commanders wish to hone the process even further. Staff officers in safe, rear headquarters - possibly thousands of miles away from the crisis itself - will carry out campaign planning by committee surrounded by experts to take advantage of modern communications systems. The product will then be delivered by electronic means to the units who will carry out the air operations. This process, known as 'reachback', is now a reality. Driven by US concerns over force protection and the vulnerability of deployed forces to missile or terrorist attack, the process is accelerating. Just as the Gulf War of 1991 was the last conflict that employed Cold War doctrine and procedures, air operations over Kosovo in 1999 may have been the last time where commanders at local level operated in physical contact with each other. In future, coalition partners who participate in US-led air power coalitions may find themselves located in continental USA, not in the theatre of operations.

This will enable the US policy makers to enjoy a position of geographical advantage and, in theory, interfere directly in operations. Thus, the parallel phenomenon of 'reachdown' where decisions are reached in capitals not in Theatre or campaign headquarters will accelerate even faster. In military colloquialism, this is known as 'the long screwdriver'. Throughout history, politicians have interfered, or have wanted to interfere in military operations. Often their future employment depended upon it. Fortunately for many commanders over many centuries, the means were not available. Now they are.

Any study of recent conflicts over the last 10 or 100 years would suggest that simply applying technology to the process of command and control provides no 'silver bullet' to victory in warfare. Whether leather chair-bound air generals like it or not, command remains a stressful human function which cannot be delegated to a computer. Operational art remains an ephemeral subject. Education, study, experience, psychology, personality, social interaction, language skills and political acumen all play a part to build what Clausewitz called 'genius' in warfare. Genius, it could be argued, remains the quintessential element of generalship. If airmen have come so far away from the Clausewitzian view of generalship, perhaps a brief look at air power history with an eye to command and not to results might offer a glimpse as to 'how' this has happened.

GLIMPSES IN THE MIRROR FROM HISTORY - THE FIRST WORLD WAR - AIR FORCES ARE BORN

Even the most visionary of early airmen would not understand the highly centralised command and highly centralised execution of modern air power. Why, because they were practical men who saw aircraft as extended eyes for armies and navies. Aircraft were for observation, reconnaissance and artillery spotting - the means of directing the indirect fire of the day - artillery. The other roles were in support of that function. The visionaries came later with their talk of air power as a war-winning weapon on its own. By the time of the spring offensives of 1918 on the western front, the pioneering airmen understood how to apply air power to the principles of war and concentrated force to allow air power to shape the battle. Lessons were learned, doctrine and tactics developed on all sides which were to have a profound impact on the future development of air power.

Thus, although many air power historians gloss over or dismiss the influence of World War I on contemporary command and control for air power, this stance could be mistaken. After all, the flight and squadron commanders of WWI became the air

THE AIRMEN'S DILEMMA: TO COMMAND OR TO CONTROL?

marshals and air generals of World War II. Furthermore, if we accept the overall thesis that we are shaped by our national 'ways' in war[8], the foundling experience of nations in bearing arms from the air is important to understanding the subsequent development of air power.

The German Air Force represents a good example. Outnumbering the French and British air arms at the outbreak of war, the Germans saw the offensive potential for air power early. Although the Berlin establishment balked at the notion of a separate service, as early as 1916, the German Air Service (Luftstreitkraefte) had its own Commander-in-Chief, General Headquarters, separate arm of the General Staff and centralised control of all air assets of the German Army. This principle of centralised control was much more pervasive than we would understand in the modern context, extending to production of aircraft, engines, weapons, the training of airmen and pilots, logistics and administration. If that was not enough, in a move with long term strategic impact, all civil defence and anti-aircraft artillery defences - active and passive, came under control of the Air Service.[9]

The approach of the Allies was somewhat different. As Air Marshal Tony Mason has lamented in his writing, by 1917 the British and French aircraft industries were producing a bewildering variety of aircraft and engines, instead of standardising on successful designs.[10] Indeed, in the Dardanelles, III Squadron had to cope with 8 different types of aircraft and 10 different types of engine in a single squadron. Although some progress was made in logistic support through the creation of aircraft parks and centralised servicing, these were innovations born of 1918 not of 1916.[11] British air command and control remained reactive and fragmented throughout the First World War.

After the War, the victors settled to dealing with the problems that faced them. Although they made half-hearted attempts to make tactical progress, they generally failed to learn the lessons at the operational and strategic level. Divisions between rather than harmony within the Allies marked the post-war era. Nonetheless, air power was established as a major factor in warfare. The very fact that the Treaty of Versailles demanded (in Articles 198-202) the complete emasculation of all forms of German military aviation is testament to allied respect for the Luftstreitkraefte. Meanwhile, even if German air power was destroyed, this did not prevent Germany thinking about air power. General Hans von Seeckt, Chief of the German General Staff from 1920 to 1926 concluded (as did Tutachevsky and others in Russia), that manoeuvre and mobility were the key to future warfare.

---

8. D French, *The British Way in War* (London: Unwin Hyman, 1998).
9. James Corum, *The Luftwaffe - Creating the Operational Air War, 1918 - 1940* (Kansas: University Press, 1997) ch. 1.
10. R A Mason, *A Centennial Appraisal* (London: Brasseys, 1996).
11. Peter Dye, 'Logistics and Air Power - a failure in doctrine', *RAF Air Power Review*, Vol. 2 No.1, Spring 1999, for an excellent summary of WWI RFC logistics.

THE AIRMEN'S DILEMMA: TO COMMAND OR TO CONTROL?

Air power was the key enabler for von Seeckt's vision. He envisaged the creation of a separate air force. What made von Seeckt different, however, was that he did not claim air power could be a war-winning weapon; instead, he took a more Clausewitzian line claiming that attacks against military fielded forces would remain the most important target since they embodied the enemy's will to resist.[12] Thus, although Guderian, rightly, lays claim to be the father of the Blitzkrieg doctrine, von Seeckt is the father of the air/land manoeuvre strategy, which influenced both Soviet and German thinkers in the 1920s and 1930s. Moreover, Luftwaffe command structures were integrated into Army headquarters and were not separated in a functional model.

For the Royal Air Force, survival as a separate Service was Trenchard's main effort rather than lessons learned from WWI. The politics of defence in London in the early years after WWI, the penury of the economy and the obsession with Empire shaped the debate over command and control. The doctrine, organisation and structure which emerged was a functional air command and control system which focused upon the role - 'fighter', 'bomber', 'coastal' - rather than synergy with armies and navies. The fledgling Service grew its own versions of Cadet, Technician and Staff College charged with developing a separate but sustainable culture. Of note, it is interesting that from 1922 to 1996, the Royal Air Force trained its senior officers in a 'Staff' not a 'Command' or 'War' college. The reason is because Trenchard believed staffwork would be the key to survival as an independent Service.[13] Thus, the obedience to the Trenchard 'way' has to be viewed in the context of 'survive or die' as an independent Service.

---

12. R Suchenwirth, 'The Development of the German Air Force, 1919-39', *USAF Historical Study 60* (Maxwell: AU Press).
13. See Jackson & Bramall, *The Chiefs* (London: Brasseys, 1992) ch. 5, for a description of the acrimony in the British War Office of the 1920s.

THE AIRMEN'S DILEMMA: TO COMMAND OR TO CONTROL?

Lord Trenchard. The survival of the Royal Air Force as a separate Service was Trenchard's main effort, rather than lessons learned from the First World War.

If history offers a glimpse in the mirror, the inter-war period was dominated by different approaches within nations to the development of air power.

INTER-WAR YEARS - THE GROWING PAINS

The battles between the prophets and the doubters of the potential of air power were not limited to Britain. In the US, the frustration and acrimony surrounding Brigadier General Billy Mitchell's court martial and dismissal from the US Army Air Corps in 1925 had a profound and lasting impact on the Corps. Meanwhile in Continental Europe, different lessons were being drawn from the First World War.

In France, the Army was completely opposed to the development of a separate air service and put all manner of real and spurious obstacles in the path of the development of air power. This resistance from an Army slowly recovering from the strategic shock of the First World War did not stop junior officers thinking about air power. Indeed, the French were the most zealous in the appreciation of the ideas of Giulio Douhet and actually developed his generic idea of creating a multi-role battle aircraft into a lumbering reality. The French Air Force became independent in 1936, but was tied to a regional command structure subordinate to the Army Regional Commander. The French adopted the worst of both systems: neither integrated into a manoeuvre force as in Russia or Germany or organised on functional lines as in the UK or US. Again this suited the

THE AIRMEN'S DILEMMA: TO COMMAND OR TO CONTROL?

French 'way' in war at the time with strong links to regional structures. Just as with the Royal Air Force system of functional control, this system broke down when exposed to the reality of air/land combined tactics as espoused by Blitzkrieg.

In Italy, the inter-war development of the Italian Air Force is not as many might suppose the preserve of Douhet. Instead it was the ideas of Mecozzi and the practical skills of Marshal Italo Balbo[14] which led to the development of a balanced force of aircraft supported by sound doctrine. The Italian Air Force performed well during the Spanish Civil War with air commanders collocated with allied ground commanders in support of the campaign main effort. What let them down was not operational level command and control, but misplaced strategic thinking, endemic technical obsolescence and poor logistic support. Mussolini was proud of his air force. This made his air generals proud. Unfortunately this pride reflected a hollow capability. Regional air commanders flew aircraft from base to base ahead of Mussolini's visits to give the impression of a much larger force. The realities of combat exposed the myth and the commanders. Moreover, when pressed, the Italian military/industrial complex simply could not keep up with technology.

In Russia, despite the enormous strategic disadvantages of the legacy of revolution and civil war and a devastated technological base, Frunze and later Tukhachevski became the true prophets of the offensive use of air power as a key enabler of manoeuvre warfare. Army commanders were encouraged to 'think' air in a way that was anathema to many western armies. In particular, the Soviet forces developed the airborne force concept and tried it for real in Manchuria in 1929. Furthermore, Soviet tactical experience in Spain confirmed Tukhachevski's ideas and related command and control concepts. Soviet air arms were completely integrated at Corps level. The results were dramatic. At Guadalajara in March 1937, Soviet air power secured a little-known yet impressive victory. Just 125 Soviet aircraft flying battlefield interdiction sorties under the direct command and control of the local divisional commander destroyed an Italian motorised column of some 50,000 troops.[15] Western commentators and media concentrated on terror bombing and Guernica because that suited 'the bomber will always get through' doctrine in London and Washington. The Guadalajara battle was not even noticed by western military observers preparing for the coming war.

---

14. Marshal Balbo invented the notion of large numbers of tactical aircraft swamping enemy defences, thereby developing what is now known as the composite air operation or COMAO in NATO parlance; hence the enduring description in airman's language of the 'Balbo' to describe a melee of tactical aircraft.
15. Corum, *The Luftwaffe - Creating the Operational Air War, 1918 - 1940* (Kansas: University Press, 1997) ch. 6.

THE AIRMEN'S DILEMMA: TO COMMAND OR TO CONTROL?

Operations for the RAF throughout the inter-war period focused on the 'doctrine' of air control to police the troublesome lands and mandates of the British Empire. This doctrine appeared to work in the 1920s when those it was directed against fled at the sight of an aeroplane. It failed when the opponents stood their ground or fought back. And, most importantly of all, this 'doctrine' allowed the RAF to relegate command and control issues to squabbles with the British Army over who should be the local potentate.[16] This squabbling became enshrined in the geographical global British model with Air Officers Commanding Near, Middle and Far East matching Army commands. This structure may have made administrative sense, but it would not prove conducive to warfighting. In the UK, the RAF blithely ignored the lessons emerging from Spain of collocation and synergy of air within a joint campaign plan. They were focused upon a separate 'strategic bombing' strategy and chose examples from Spain to match their views. The priority afforded to the build-up of Bomber Command at the expense of other forces bears testimony to this conclusion. Thus, despite extensive operational experience, British command and control procedures remained wedded to the functional command model.

The inter-war period shaped the war to come. Each nation learned and applied different lessons from the First World War. By 1939, although all nations understood that air power would play a significant part in the war to come, their approach to the command and control of it was very different. It is only surprising that air forces could work together at all, when the war began.

THE WORLD WAR TWO LEGACY - AIR POWER COMES OF AGE?

In the Second World War, many cherished RAF tactical doctrines were rapidly abandoned. The RAF fighter doctrine, which had led to the 'tight' formation tactics of 1939, proved ineffective in the face of the Luftwaffe and the operational doctrine with strategic impact called Blitzkrieg. Moreover, RAF day bomber tactics in 1939 proved disastrous, with huge losses for little tangible gain. The functional command structure did not respond well to requests for changes in tasking and procedures as a result of lessons learned from operations. As John Terraine makes clear in 'The Right of the Line', the response was to change the commanders rather than question the structure; the British way to this day.[17]

---

16. David Omisi, *Air Power and Colonial Control 1919-39* (MUP, UK, 1990) ch. IV.
17. John Terraine, *The Right of the Line* (London: Hodder and Stoughton, 1985).

THE AIRMEN'S DILEMMA: TO COMMAND OR TO CONTROL?

The Luftwaffe, on the other hand, had produced and implemented a lessons-learned report from the Polish campaign by October 1940. It included several command and control recommendations such as the collocation of 'Luftflotte' (air fleet) commanders with Corps Commanders to control air apportionment according to campaign main effort or Schwerpunkt. Thus, when Blitzkrieg struck France and the Low Countries in May 1940, the Luftwaffe was integrated into the overall campaign plan in a way that was anathema to the RAF and US Army Air Force. This organisational technique granted enormous impact for German air power during the campaign in the offensive support role. For example, during the height of the Battle for Sedan in May 1940, the JU87 Stukas and ME109s of Luftflotte 2, commanded by Major General Wolfram von Richtofen,[18] were flying 7 sorties per day with the air commanders collocated with the forward ground commanders. The Stukas, 109s, Storch and Henschel spotter aircraft and tanks, artillery, AAA and troop carriers were all on the same secure radio net carrying out dynamic retasking and targeting. Once the Germans achieved air superiority, every single aircraft was focused upon offensive support - with ME109s even flying missions without bombs or ammunition for psychological effect. It was this sheer concentration of command and control effort at the Schwerpunkt which enabled a truly combined air and ground force to break the French line and set the conditions for Guderian's 'expanding torrent' to the French coast.

---

18. Wolfram von Richtofen, a colourful figure and cousin of the 'Red Baron', had been the German air commander during the Spanish Civil War and ruthlessly and passionately believed in combined air/land operations.

THE AIRMEN'S DILEMMA: TO COMMAND OR TO CONTROL?

JU87 Stukas in action. In the German Blitzkrieg of May 1940, the concentration of command and control at the campaign's main effort enabled a truly combined air and ground force to break the Allied line.

THE AIRMEN'S DILEMMA: TO COMMAND OR TO CONTROL?

Meanwhile on the allied side, the beleaguered Blenheims, Battles and Hurricanes supporting the British Expeditionary Force were tasked with 'armed reconnaissance of the Sedan area' - hardly targeting for effect. The French were little better. At the height of the battle for France, several French squadrons in the forward area went several days without receiving any tasking; a profound failure in command and control. Anglo/French 'combined' air support was a shambles. The cries for help from Air Marshal Sir Arthur 'Ugly' Barratt, the British air commander, grew ever more strident but met with a distinct lack of response from the Air Ministry. As the Battles and Blenheims rode the 1940 equivalent of the 'Valley of Death' on 15 May 1940, Air Marshal Sir Charles Portal, Commander-in-Chief Bomber Command, launched the strategic bomber offensive against Germany. The German Army's bridgehead at Sedan had created a massive military traffic jam stretching back through Belgium to Germany - in modern parlance 'a target-rich environment'. On that night, the entire strength of Bomber Command bombed Bremen and inflicted moderate damage upon a single warehouse in Bremen containing confiscated Jewish furniture. This was hardly joint campaign planning.

The Battle for France was lost. Thousands of aircraft and valuable pilots were killed or missing, but as the focus switched to the Battle of Britain, the lessons from France were either forgotten or ignored. Too late, the RAF formed Army Co-operation Command but it was always 'cardboard cut-out' in its make-up because the main effort lay with Bomber Command taking the war to the enemy. It fell to another Theatre, the Middle East, to develop command and control procedures for the tasking of air power in joint operations which actually worked. Air Marshal Arthur 'Mary' Coningham set up his headquarters alongside Montgomery's 8th Army HQ to allow air power to be focused where and when it was needed. Although the two generals later fell out with strategic consequences in Normandy, this was a good harbinger for future campaigns. But again lessons were noted rather than learned and often the 'not invented here' notion in the Air Ministry ensured that the very notion of collocation with the Army somehow implied subordination. In consequence, in Sicily, Italy and the Far East, separation of air and land commanders remained the British way.

By 1944, however, the strategic balance had shifted. The UK became and would remain a junior partner to the US. But, at the time, egos had to be massaged and the scale of the British high command 'air' contribution was impressive. Senior British airmen had a reservoir of experience which the US could not match. Nonetheless, it was inevitable that a preponderance of British airmen in the top jobs would rankle with the USAAF desperate in its struggle for independence from the US Army. Following Eisenhower's appointment as Supreme Commander, Churchill argued and won to appoint Tedder as his deputy. Tedder was 'good' with the Americans and 'sound' on strategy. Tedder's pedigree and experience as an airman was irrelevant; he was there to help to frame strategic guidance.

THE AIRMEN'S DILEMMA: TO COMMAND OR TO CONTROL?

The operational level air commander was Air Chief Marshal Sir Trafford Leigh-Mallory, as Commander-in-Chief Allied Expeditionary Air Forces. History has not been kind to Leigh-Mallory who did not survive the war, implying he was stuffy and out of touch with reality: an air 'chateau' general. In fact, he offered full and complete support to the campaign main effort to gain and secure the bridgehead and plan for the breakout. His position was undermined by his colleagues, particularly USAAF officers annoyed that they had not been given the top 'air' job.[19] Air Marshal Sir Arthur Coningham was appointed as Commander Advanced Allied Expeditionary Air Force, in modern parlance, the JFACC forward. Air command for deployed air elements after the landings was exercised through 2nd Tactical Air Force, Coningham's second hat, with Air Vice-Marshal Harry Broadhurst for the RAF and Major General Pete Quesada for the USAAF as tactical level group commanders.

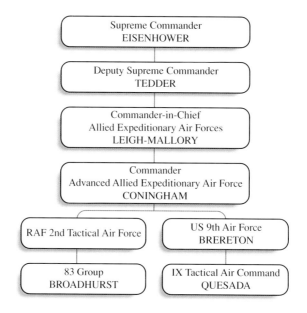

Allied Air Command - Normandy Campaign 1944

---

19. S Cowlan, 'Leigh-Mallory', *RAF Air Power Review*, Vol 2, No 3, Autumn 1999, p. 76-92.

THE AIRMEN'S DILEMMA: TO COMMAND OR TO CONTROL?

Inevitably friction between commanders rose as the Allies became bogged down around Caen with libraries full of accounts of spats - real and imagined - between all the commanders. The role of heavy bombers in direct support of ground forces was the most controversial and exposed the fundamental weakness of the functional command model during joint and combined operations.

The most publicised example of the difficulties of operating heavy and medium bombers in support of ground forces came during the preparatory bombardment for Operation Cobra, the breakthrough attack at Saint-Lô on 25 July 1944, that led to the breakout across France. The bombing in support of Operation Cobra killed approximately one hundred American soldiers and wounded approximately five hundred others. A large number of fragmentation bombs were dropped short of the German positions and fell on friendly lines. There is no question that the bombing missions were badly executed, and that serious command errors established conditions whereby the short-bombings occurred.[20]

The failure to address the lessons learned from the fall of France four years earlier meant that even when airmen understood the difficulties of offensive air support, particularly close air support, they were powerless to coordinate and control tactical aircraft in a coherent way. Procedures remained rudimentary, communications near to non-existent, with nowhere near enough forward air controllers. For example, each British Mechanised or Armoured Division had a single vehicle which was ground-to-air radio equipped. Doctrine placed that vehicle at the front of the line of departure. Unsurprisingly, few of these lightly armoured vehicles survived the first contact with the enemy. Result: no communications for land/air operations.[21] Thus, in reality most missions were armed reconnaissance or battlefield interdiction, not close air support. The USAAF did better as Major General Pete Quesada unilaterally (and without authority) removed radios from his serviceable aircraft to place them in armoured vehicles. As Ian Gooderson has made clear in his recent book, 'Air Power at the Battlefront', it was the vast amount of air power, total air superiority and a lack of effective opposition from the Luftwaffe, rather than an effective system of command and control, which led to victory.[22]

---

20. Richard Hallion, *Strike from the Sky: The History of Battlefield Air Attack 1911 - 1945* (Washington: Smithsonian Institution Press, 1989) p. 208.
21. Ian Gooderson, *Air Power at the Battlefront* (London: Frank Cass, 1998) covers this subject extremely well.
22. Ibid.

THE AIRMEN'S DILEMMA: TO COMMAND OR TO CONTROL?

History is invariably kind to the victors and many of the surviving air marshals dashed off their memoirs to ensure their place in history. But the evidence is clear. Air main effort lay in proving air power as a war-winning weapon and ensuring continued independence for air forces. High air commanders, perhaps with the exception of Tedder, did not 'grip' joint warfare. Indeed, those operational level air commanders that did, such as 'Mary' Coningham, Pete Quesada and Harry Broadhurst, did not find favour in the post-war period.[23] The bravery and courage of those flying and commanding the missions at the tactical level rescued air power's influence and place in history rather than the performance of high command. Moreover, the dawning of the Cold War and the nuclear age played into the hands of the bomber barons rather than the joint commanders.

THE COLD WAR NUCLEAR LEGACY - COMMAND OR CONTROL AGAIN?

As the Cold War became a reality, post-WWII air forces were in rapid, almost precipitous, drawdown. In the United States, the long struggle for independence was won by the newly formed United States Air Force in 1947. Both the RAF and the USAF continued with the functional command model with deployed forces carrying out air policing roles as small conflicts simmered on. Unexpectedly in 1950, a larger conflict erupted in Korea, which demonstrated again the need to think about command and control.

There were very few strategic targets available in North Korea, but a strategic bomber offensive was waged anyway to prove that the USAF could do it on their own. In the air-to-air war, fighter pilots and commanders were shocked by their first encounters with the MiG 15. The USAF was so confident that they would always hold the qualitative edge that losses in combat assumed a disproportionate impact. Command arrangements for the ten air forces participating meant subjugation within a US system. Co-ordination and co-operation between US air arms was particularly poor with several avoidable fratricide incidents, incompatible communications equipment and deep mutual suspicion and hostility. Complexity was required to satisfy institutional paranoia. As in WWII, at the tactical level, units worked well together; the problem lay further 'up' the command chain. Of course there were exceptional individual commanders such as Lt Gen Earl Partridge, but the whole campaign was not well executed. Even the official

---

23. Trenchard's influence on the RAF cannot be overstated. Throughout the Second World War, Trenchard called on CAS (Lord Portal) weekly. After the war Portal's and Tedder's influence shaped the next generation and procured the V Bombers. The 'joint' air commanders who succeeded in Normandy were eclipsed in the UK and the US by the bomber barons well into the Cold War.

THE AIRMEN'S DILEMMA: TO COMMAND OR TO CONTROL?

USAF history reads more like a summary of treaty negotiations between uneasy allies rather than a joint campaign record of sister services facing a common enemy.[24]

The air command and control specialists of the 1950s did not absorb the abundant lessons from Korea. They had other priorities. Political and social scientists developed the theories of existential nuclear deterrence, which underpinned the air doctrine for the Cold War. The 'nuclear' influence ran deep in both NATO and Soviet air forces. In the 1950s and 1960s, NATO air doctrine focused on the nuclear role and tactical operations in support of that role; a deep lacuna developed in planning for conventional air operations at the operational level. Although formulated by the Harmel Report of 1967, it was only in the 1970s and 1980s that NATO's strategy of 'flexible response' became remotely achievable as specialist weapons for airfield attack and precision guided munitions for interdiction slowly entered service. Belatedly and largely pushed by armies, NATO planning focus switched back to planning for large-scale conventional air operations.[25]

If few lessons were learned from the Korean War, it should be no surprise that the mistakes made in Korea were repeated in Vietnam. The USAF, in particular, found it difficult to apply Cold War command and control procedures to a 'small' war. As the campaign progressed, doctrines and procedures such as the 'single manager' concept helped, but again they were invented and implemented at the higher tactical level. At the operational level, the horns of vested interest remained locked. The USAF remained wedded to its Cold War functional command model. That said, the strategic failure of Vietnam did lead to a 'widening' of USAF thinking to embrace not just the spectrum of air power roles and missions, but the whole spectrum of conflict with a shift away from nuclear to conventional operations.[26] Cold War careers for airmen were built in air command bunkers, not in the field with the Army or at sea with the Navy. Given this organisational bias, refining the process of airspace control orders, air tasking orders and air task messages became the performance criteria, rather than creative and bold operational ideas or campaign plans.

---

24. Winnefeld & Johnson, *Joint Air Operations* (Santa Monica: RAND, 1993) ch. 5.
25. NATO Tactical Air Doctrine (RAND, 1985).
26. This shift in thinking is exemplified by the publication of Colonel John Warden's *The Air Campaign* (London: Brasseys, 1989).

THE AIRMEN'S DILEMMA: TO COMMAND OR TO CONTROL?

AIR COMMAND IN THE GULF WAR - COLD WAR PROCEDURES IN NEW BOTTLES

The Gulf War was the apogee of the application of air command and control procedures developed during the Cold War. US forces set out to exorcise the ghosts of Vietnam with the slogan: 'overwhelming force overwhelmingly applied'. They succeeded at the tactical level by throwing huge numbers of resources into the campaign. At the operational level, the campaign again highlighted the differences between navies, armies and air forces rather than the similarities; strategic main effort lay in keeping the disparate coalition of 38 nations together. Coalition cohesion held, but it required a great deal of work. At the strategic level, US commanders went out of their way to accommodate the wishes of allies. At the operational level, however, sharing information with coalition partners proved more difficult. Detailed campaign planning and development of target sets was carried out by a USAF special planning group with very limited access to certain specified allies who were read into the plan. This caused resentment amongst those excluded; resentment which rankled throughout the campaign.

A propaganda leaflet heralding the arrival of B52s. In the Gulf War, the US set out to exorcise the ghosts of Vietnam by adhering to the principle of 'overwhelming force overwhelmingly applied'.

THE AIRMEN'S DILEMMA: TO COMMAND OR TO CONTROL?

Moreover, there were frictions within the USAF. The 'Checkmate' team, influenced (and led initially) by Colonel John Warden, a well known air power theorist, developed a plan which included specific attacks against the Iraqi leadership.[27] These ideas were briefed 'off the record' to journalists by General Mike Dugan, Chief of Staff USAF, remarks for which he was dismissed.[28] Furthermore, not all of Warden's ideas were welcomed by the JFACC, Lt Gen Chuck Horner, who envisaged a more 'traditional' air campaign modelled on Cold War theory and doctrine.[29] Once the campaign began, many tactical level accommodations were made in the interest of coalition unity. On one occasion, Horner grounded French and Qatari Mirage F1 aircraft for fear they might be mistaken for same-type Iraqi aircraft - a sensible command decision which caused friction.[30]

Friction abounded over targeting. The debate between the 'strategic' targeting exponents who predicted disproportionate impact from attacks against strategic targets, and the remainder, who followed the logic train of NATO doctrine towards traditional roles such as offensive counter- air and battlefield air interdiction, was vigorous. The rigid distinction that was drawn between the 'strategic' and 'non-strategic' target sets was perilously close to dogma. Consultation over 'downtown Baghdad' targeting was non-existent with French and British air commanders regularly rejecting targets for their forces because of different interpretations over what, in legal terms, constitutes a legitimate target. More difficulties were avoided because many allies accepted US dominance willingly and merely did as they were told or were not tasked into Iraq. Consultation took place within the Coalition Command Co-ordination Centre (C3IC), but was often cosmetic - whatever the memoirs or the lecture circuit presentations state.

Thus, NATO Cold War doctrine and procedures worked at the tactical level and, at the strategic level, there was little disagreement with the aims of the campaign - to evict Iraqi forces from Kuwait. Unity of purpose was maintained. The problem, which has been skipped or dismissed by most writers, was at the operational level. Air operations continued to strike targets on the US CENTRAL COMMAND approved list; allocation of tactical air assets to shape the battlespace for the ground invasion was viewed by many airmen as a distraction. In fact, these sorties were vital to the rapid success of the ground

---

27. Warden's The Air Campaign, Op Cit, has become a benchmark of air campaign planning. Warden has exerted a great deal of influence on USAF thinking. In the event, Gulf War targeting was more 'traditionally' based upon NATO/Cold War air campaign planning with 'flashes' of Warden's ideas. He has criticised this piecemeal approach. See J Warden, 'The Enemy as a System', *Air Clues Air Power Supplement,* 1997.
28. See Richard Hallion, *Storm over Iraq* (Washington: Smithsonian Institution Press, 1992) for the circumstances surrounding General Dugan's dismissal and Colonel Warden's recall to Washington.
29. Ibid.
30. Stuart Peach, *Air Power in Peace Operations* (Cambridge, 1997).

offensive phase and, thereby, the campaign as a whole. Joint campaign planning did not really take place. Although B52s flew in the battlefield area and tactical aircraft flew deep into Iraq, it proved difficult to integrate US Navy and US Marine Corps aircraft into 'combined' air operations. They had been allowed to develop methods of air tasking and control which were incompatible with those of the USAF. Few studies have exposed this schism because the campaign met its objectives and air power was perceived to have had a good war.[31]

AIR COMMAND AND PEACEKEEPING - A CONTRADICTION IN TERMS?

The Bosnia Experience

If the Gulf War was the high point of the application of air power command and control procedures developed during the Cold War, NATO's experience in Bosnia was the opposite. In 1992 and 1993 air power was given a bad press. The perception was created that air power could not be used for 'complex peacekeeping'. This perception was misleading. The fact that air power was applied nine times over two years and was largely ineffective is not the fault of individual commanders, nor those who flew the missions. The problem lay with the Byzantine complexity of the command and control arrangements between the UN and NATO. Operating without mission statements, guidance or any form of unity of purpose, it is not surprising that air power was applied haphazardly. Senior air commanders did their best but, in addition to the usual problems of dual-key command arrangements, airmen faced hostility to the use of air power on all sides. Army doctrine did not cater for joint operations in support of peacekeeping.[32]

By 1995, however, after the embarrassment of the hostage-taking following the Pale raids, the determination and resolve of the international community hardened and allowed the planning and execution of joint operations with a warfighting flavour under a peace enforcement banner. Operation Deliberate Force took place in August and September 1995. NATO flew over 3,500 missions in three weeks. Air power increased the operational tempo with results - as broadcast by the global media - that appeared extremely impressive. Through the precise and coercive application of military force, air

---

31. One of the few exceptions is Winnefeld & Johnson, *Joint Air Operations* (Santa Monica: RAND, 1993) ch. 9, which exposes the myths of US 'joint' air command and control.
32. See Christopher Bellamy, *Knights in White Armour - The New Art of War and Peace* (London: Hutchinson, 1996) and T Ripley, *Operation Deliberate Force* (Lancaster University: CDISS, 1999), for details.

THE AIRMEN'S DILEMMA: TO COMMAND OR TO CONTROL?

power helped to apply pressure on the Serb leadership to bend to the will of the international community. Again this is only part of the story. In campaign terms, targeting was 'difficult'. As Richard Holbrooke, the US Chief Negotiator, makes clear in his account 'To End a War', once the bombing began, there was little co-ordination between military activity and diplomacy. Perhaps most significantly, political interest in the targeting process was intense, sustained and intrusive. After this short operation, military leaders lamented this intrusion as a distraction or difficulty. In fact, it is axiomatic for any form of operation that in democracies military operations need to be adapted to the needs of the politicians; there is no point pretending that military operations can be conducted in isolation.[33] Again, after the event, commentators focused on the tactical successes. At the operational level, although there was close harmony between the air and land commander, after 3 weeks NATO was running out of targets; an indicator and a warning for the next Balkans campaign.[34]

The Defining Moment? - Perhaps Not - Kosovo 1999

Even a brief study of Balkans history would have suggested that the limitations which NATO placed upon itself would limit the effectiveness of NATO air power during the Kosovo campaign in 1999. Unsurprisingly, the Serbs employed a combination of Soviet concealment and camouflage techniques and 'hide' tactics similar to those employed by Tito against the Germans during the Second World War. They ruthlessly exploited their decision/action cycle advantage in information operations and used their air defence systems extremely well. As post-war interviews with Serbian commanders showed, they understood the US-led NATO way in air war and managed to ride out the first few days, leaving NATO with no option but escalation. Throughout the 78 days of air operations, all NATO air commanders agree that Serbian air defences remained a potent threat and required a great deal of effort, which inevitably reduced the number of aircraft available for tactical or strategic effect targets.[35]

NATO's success at the strategic level was to maintain cohesion. After 78 days Milosevic agreed to sign the Military Technical Agreement which allowed the entry of NATO's Kosovo Force (KFOR) into Kosovo to stabilise the situation. NATO had flown over 38,000 missions for the loss of two combat aircraft and no aircrew killed or taken prisoner. Air power had achieved a victory, despite the shackles and constraints applied. Nonetheless, the lessons for command and control for future operations are important

---

33. General Mike Ryan, speaking at RAF Air Power Conference, London, 1996.
34. See T Ripley, *Operation Deliberate Force* (Lancaster University: CDISS, 1999).
35. Confirmed by Lt Gen Mike Short, USAF, speaking on 'Balkans Air War', BBC TV, January 2000.

THE AIRMEN'S DILEMMA: TO COMMAND OR TO CONTROL?

and must be learned not noted. In essence, many of the trends identified earlier, reachback, reachdown, domination of operational art by time consuming protocols and process, different motives for participation, lopsided military capabilities, experience and personalities of commanders all played a part in limiting creativity and operational art during Operation Allied Force. Indeed, it is a testimony to the dogged determination and leadership of Lt Gen Short that NATO air power achieved so much given the deluge of constraints.

The limitations of NATO formal command states and the importance of the 'red card' within the coalition also emerged on a number of occasions. In theory, NATO doctrine was followed with strategic direction offered by the North Atlantic Council, translated into strategic guidance by the Supreme Allied Commander Europe (SACEUR, a US Army 4 Star General) and passed to the Theatre Commander (a US Navy 4 Star Admiral) based in Naples. In turn, the air component commander, (Lt Gen Short, a 3 Star USAF Officer), based forward at the NATO Combined Air Operations Centre within 5ATAF in Vicenza, Italy, planned and executed air operations. In practice, parallel national command and control procedures were established and, although they could be justified for national reasons and - possibly - for operational security, they intensified multinational friction at the operational level and prevented effective campaign synchronisation. Thus, although all the high commanders were from one nation, the friction of multinationality reduced the overall effectiveness of the campaign.

Returning to the 'process' problem, the strength of the CAOC went from 300 to 1400 in a few weeks. By May 1999, this staff was planning and controlling up to 900 sorties per day by NATO aircraft. In terms of organisation, the operation was a triumph as procedures were refined and honed to minimise risk. The sheer complexity of conducting air operations on such a scale in such a small area could be compared to conducting a symphony orchestra. Tactical air operations were carried out with exemplary skill, precision and discipline. Despite deep concerns over interoperability, 13 air forces flew together in harmony and, at the point of execution, the CAOC was a model of integrated international command and control; at the tactical level multinationality worked.

As in the Gulf and Bosnia, however, the balance sheet for the operational level is mixed. The level of interference from above and differences in interpretation over targeting constrained the air commander's freedom of action. Again the sheer volume of data reaching the CAOC swamped the ability of analysts to carry out coherent combat assessment to feed targeting for strategic effect.[36] Despite the capabilities of advanced manned and unmanned reconnaissance systems, the ability to receive the data and fuse

---

36. The proliferation of different communication systems between national detachments in Italy - despite the NATO banner - prevented the timely analysis of mission reports to improve targeting for effect.

THE AIRMEN'S DILEMMA: TO COMMAND OR TO CONTROL?

it to offer the commander rapid battle damage assessment proved again to be beyond current command and control systems. Moreover, the demands of the media for video copy to feed daily press conferences and investigations into alleged mistakes in bombing and targeting slowed the decision/action cycle even further. Endless speculation by retired officers and armchair strategists - common since the Gulf War - created a further distraction and irritant to those involved in live operations as air operations continued over weeks and not days.

In the event, as air operations continued, commanders, airmen and politicians 'got smarter', and NATO nations slogged on with grim determination, gradually escalating the pressure upon Serbia. As in the Gulf and Bosnia, it was not a shortage of aircraft, weapons and aircrew that constrained operations, it was the lack of an agreed coherent strategy for targeting and the number of politically agreed and cleared targets. Since the end of the Cold War the process of tasking and employing air power has reached new heights of sophistication. The application of creativity - especially in developing coherent, agreed, legally acceptable, targeting strategies has plumbed new depths. If this lesson is not learned and the 'way' air power is targeted is not matched from strategy to task, next time air power could fail. NATO doctrine teaches targeting through the creation of a 'joint targeting co-ordination board'. This process does not chime with legal clearance procedures in capitals at the strategic level, the ability to switch - at Theatre level - to take advantage of changes in campaign emphasis or, at the tactical level, the ability to exploit fleeting opportunities. Targeting for effect requires a thorough overhaul of targeting procedures and doctrine; probably the major lesson of recent operations.

THE DANGERS OF TECHNOLOGY REPLACING COMMAND

Technology continues to grab the headlines in the defence press rather than the human frailties exposed by modern operations. The zealots of the putative Revolution in Military Affairs (RMA) tell us that technology will allow greater emphasis on long-range, precision strikes carried out by Unmanned Aerial Vehicles (UAV), reducing the risk of casualties in conflicts of choice. Corresponding improvements in information and communication systems will provide commanders with fast and accurate information, improving the quality of their decision-making. New technologies will allow increased stealth, mobility, dispersion and a higher tempo of operations.

THE AIRMEN'S DILEMMA: TO COMMAND OR TO CONTROL?

Phoenix UAV. Despite the advances of the information age and technology such as UAVs, the act of command remains fundamentally a human function.

None of this, however tells us where the commander is expected to find his 'genius' amongst his myriad team of co-commanders reflecting their national ways in command, or his (or her) moral courage in the face of reporting a single loss of a manned aircraft in these days of casualty-free warfare. The blame culture associated with losses is not new. Commanders throughout history have been sacked, relieved or retired. What is new is the threshold of acceptability. It may be set as low as the loss of a single pilot or aircrew. In this technological world, force protection concerns will come to dominate operational art. Even if the strategy is agreed and the campaign plan coherent, the mission could stand or fall on the willingness - in an era of conflicts of choice - to accept any losses at all. If we are to challenge this trend, first we need to frame our thinking and our doctrine for command.[37]

---

37. Military college students are encouraged to think 'outside the box'; few do. Most change in military thought or structures stems from defeat in war or the imposition of a new political system. Few military officers who advocate radical change achieve high rank viz Liddel Hart and Fuller in the UK and Mitchell and Warden in the US.

THE AIRMEN'S DILEMMA: TO COMMAND OR TO CONTROL?

THE CENTRALISERS - THE NEW LUDDITES?

Strategy should be all about balancing ends, ways and means. Command involves achieving some harmony between these elements and imposing a certain order on the inevitable chaos of war. Technology may assist process, but it does not determine the ends or ways. They have to take account of a wider canvas, which incorporates political, diplomatic and military factors in the campaign plan. Despite the advances of the information age and technology such as video conference links, the collocation of commanders is always important and, on occasion, critical.

Demand for information will always expand to meet, and then exceed, the capacity to supply information. Expectations from commanders are rarely satisfied on operations because of the friction involved - too many people are always chasing too much data on too few links with too little bandwidth. Furthermore, two-dimensional bean-counting style intelligence tells us little about the attitudes, perceptions or intent of the enemy. This is why human-based intelligence (HUMINT) should never be ignored if it is available - intangible human factors which help us to determine whether he will stand and fight or not. For air power, these intangible factors are needed to target for strategic effect rather than simply flicking down the target list - intuition and moral courage are just as important as they have always been.

Taking the experience of recent operations and current trends together, a new approach to command and control of air power would appear appropriate. If multinational operations to deal with complex emergencies are here to stay, a more flexible approach to command and control is the only solution. Rather than replicate Cold War structures by a new name with component commanders, an alternative model would be to place a small, integrated air staff forward with the commander who is designated as main effort or the 'supported' commander. The strategic command function would be carried out in a remote multinational headquarters such as SHAPE with the staff and expertise to handle broad issues and offer guidance to the Theatre Commander. The 'air forward' commander would become the *de facto* air component commander with power to deal for day-to-day tasking and targeting. The operational level air commander would operate in the supporting role, providing air power for the effect required by the designated forward-based joint commander and relayed to him by his air forward commander. Thus, the Air Tasking Order would become generic and not specific, drawing down the numbers of staff and simplifying the process.

The Theatre Commander would be drawn from the 'environment' designated as main effort; it should not be seen as the domain of soldiers. Furthermore, recent operations have confirmed the limitations of the formal command states and the need to retain national control. This should be recognised by a national role for a designated joint headquarters for each participating nation. They would handle the 'red card' function which would remove the 'national business in a multinational environment' strain from the forward-based commander. The national headquarters (the Permanent Joint Headquarters in the case of the UK, the Major Regional Command in the case of the US and so on) would carry out horizontal liaison and many of the 'reachback' functions such as legal advice and political clearances. This approach would formalise a great deal of what already happens, but could radically reduce the amount of overlap in the command chain. Such an approach is more radical than it appears because it challenges directly the vested interest within the multi-layered geographical or functional command chain. The rationale for many intervening levels of headquarters would disappear. Within the headquarters that remain, staffs would be fully integrated rather than replicated.

For air power, this latter approach would build upon existing doctrinal changes at the tactical level such as developing further the airborne mission command function in AWACs and flexible targeting to support (if necessary) a large number of small forward-based teams. The role of fixed CAOCs would be reduced to a supporting and sustaining function. If complex emergencies are throwing up a number of problems to the *status quo*, it is time for change. This suggested amendment owes more to the successful application of air power in Normandy in 1944 than the process and procedures of the component command model. If air power has 'come of age', perhaps it is time to take a post- 'coming of age' approach to command and control and cease to operate either on the Prussian General Staff model of 1820 or the Trenchard functional model of 1920.

CONCLUSION

Throughout the first century of war waged in and from the air, the style of command exercised by airmen has developed in a different way from that of other environments. Inevitably, the nature of the medium has drawn airmen towards a centralised 'way' of command. Technology has aided and accelerated this process, but advanced information-based technology has not always 'delivered' on time and to cost. The casualty-free, high-technology 'western way of warfare' may neglect to develop effective counters to strategies which employ different ways and means to attack us. Thus the dangers of asymmetric warfare should not be underestimated. If war remains based on a complex interaction of political, economic, social and cultural factors, there is surely much more than technology at work. Strategy remains the bedrock upon which the campaign plan is built. If we are facing a more general 'Revolution in Strategic Affairs' as proposed by Lawrence Freedman,[38] we need to look beyond technology in

---

38. Lawrence Freedman, *The Revolution in Strategic Affairs* (Oxford: Oxford University Press for the International Institute for Strategic Studies, April 1998).

THE AIRMEN'S DILEMMA: TO COMMAND OR TO CONTROL?

order to understand how warfare may develop. For airmen in particular the application of ever more process to the existing hierarchy of air tasking and control orders has reached a point where the volume of information threatens to swamp the commander and his staff alike.

The act of command remains primarily a human activity. Of course technology assists commanders in their exercise of command, but does not offer a substitute for it. As we face military operations around the spectrum of conflict, so we need a spectrum of response. The levels of conflict, and types and dimensions of war remain relevant, but only insofar as they are used as a guide and adapted to each operational environment or circumstance. Rather than develop mobile bunkers to replace the Cold War fixed bunker leviathans, we need to examine light mobile command tools which allow integrated and synchronous activity with fellow military commanders. Changing the model will not be easy. There is no substitute for study and analysis in an attempt to understand the 'whys' and 'whats' of command, but to understand the 'hows' still requires an acceptance that command remains more of an art than a science. Doctrine for command should reflect the need for study, education and creativity rather than process.

If air power is to develop the politically stated goal of 'high aims but limited resources' and develop air operational art, a common understanding of the nature, conduct and command of future war is vitally important. Yet there is much more to study than just the process itself. The product in terms of achieving the strategic ends, often with limited means, will require imaginative ways. This puts a premium on creative and flexible command, on enhancing confidence, mutual trust and understanding amongst our friends and allies. The human brain spurred on by the emotion and stress of war can rise to the challenge. By acknowledging the complexity of modern operations, airmen should aim to apply technology selectively to employ air power for decisive effect within an overall campaign. Command and control should be achieved through an integrated, not separate, staff. The component command model may already be past its 'sell-by date'. An integrated flexible approach offering a widely different course of action for each scenario should ensure our prospective opponents develop a healthy respect and understanding for our strategic competence and political will, as much as for our military hardware and associated technical and tactical skills.

Sharing ideals will be as important as sharing doctrines and technologies. Air power has always been associated with technology. If we are not careful, applying the technology we crave to what is quintessentially a human emotional function could become our Achilles' heel. If air power has matured into a military first option of choice, airmen owe it to those that they command and those that they support to demonstrate that they understand command. The jury is still out.

THE AIRMEN'S DILEMMA: TO COMMAND OR TO CONTROL?

CHAPTER 7

THE LAND/AIR INTERFACE: AN HISTORICAL PERSPECTIVE
Brigadier Mungo Melvin

INTRODUCTION

IN A BOOK ABOUT AIR POWER it is surely not surprising, and hardly very original, to include a contribution on the land/air interface. After all, the interdependence of air and land operations is nothing new as many campaign records show, and the accounts of the senior practitioners involved confirm its fundamental importance to operational success.[1] Effective co-operation between land and air forces is regarded nowadays as a *sine qua non* of modern campaign planning. But even a superficial historical examination of the land/air interface reveals that this apparently happy state of joint affairs and mutual understanding between soldiers and airmen has not always been ever so. Inter-Service co-operative success in victory achieved in the latter stages of both the First and Second World Wars often depended on first learning the hard way on the harsh battlefield school of division, setback and defeat. More recent events in the Gulf and Balkans during the 1990s might tempt one to think that the land/air interface is becoming (or indeed has become) an outdated area of military-academic study.

Yet the land/air interface cuts both ways. It is simply not good enough for soldiers to complain about the lack of air support, and moan, as was often done when things went wrong during the early stages of the Second World War, about the 'Royal Absent Force'.[2] The British defeats culminating in Dunkirk, Crete and Singapore cannot be attributed to a particular Service; the Royal Air Force would be the wrong target in every case. And how many soldiers think of the need for land support? Air forces require assistance from land forces, particularly in signalling, logistics, and not least in military engineering however much senior army generals might view this as an undesirable dissipation of military effort. Occasionally, soldiers must fight for the air landing grounds, which in turn provide the basis for air cover over the sea. This was the case in Cyrenaica in the Mediterranean Theatre of Operations 1940-43, where culmination of forces on land can

---

1. Wing Commander J C Slessor, *Air Power and Armies* (London: Oxford University Press, 1936); Marshal of the Royal Air Force The Lord Tedder, *Air Power in War* (London: Hodder and Stoughton, 1947); Marshal of the Royal Air Force Sir John Slessor, *The Central Blue* (London: Cassell, 1956).
2. Richard Hallion, *Strike from the Sky*, p. 158.

THE LAND/AIR INTERFACE: AN HISTORICAL PERSPECTIVE

often be attributed to interdiction at sea, aided or effected by the application of air power. Above all, air power cannot be expected to work wonders, despite the 1999 headlines from the Balkans during the so-called air campaign against the Former Republic of Yugoslavia. An air force needs the appropriate resources, technology, people, intelligence and the time and space to train. As few would deny that there are practical limits in the extent to which air forces can be expected to look after their own ground-based air defence and the active protection of their air bases from land threats, no amount of air power can hold or dominate ground for any extensive period.

Further, in modern parlance, the litmus test of 'jointery' is not confined to the largely theoretical province of doctrine, teaching and joint professional military education. It should rather be applied in the 'real' world of wars, campaigns and major operations where organizations and commanders at all levels are put to the test. Only by looking behind the 'battles and headlines' can one isolate tactical or operational cause from strategic effect and derive the important and enduring lessons, if they are to be found at all.[3] And, as Tedder put it so aptly, "for our future security, we must look *forward from* the past and its lessons, not *back* to the past".[4] So in attempting to put the land/air interface into contemporary context, this chapter seeks answers to the following inter-related questions:

- What is intrinsically difficult about developing effective land/air co-operation?
- Why has promoting a state of mutual understanding and trust between the air and land commanders proved so difficult in practice?
- If appropriate land/air lessons have been learned in a particular theatre of war, why do we have to re-learn them in the same or in subsequent conflicts?
- Given that organizations and technologies change, what are the enduring lessons for the land/air interface?
- What needs to be done in order to improve land/air co-operation today and, critically, to guard against potential complacency?

---

3. I have borrowed the notion of looking behind the 'battles and headlines' from Tedder. Colin Gray makes a compelling argument for the need to study 'strategic effect' in his recently published *Modern Strategy* (Oxford: Oxford University Press, 1999) p. 17. He also denounces the notion of 'strategic air power' as a "hideous misnomer because it confuses capability with effect". The 'strategic effect of air power', however, "correctly distinguishes cause from consequence". Significantly, the latest edition of *British Air Power Doctrine* AP 3000, Third Edition (1999), carefully describes in Chapter 6 'The Strategic Effect of Air Power'.
4. Tedder, *Air Power in War* (London: Hodder and Stoughton, 1947); Marshal of the Royal Air Force Sir John Slessor, *The Central Blue* (London: Cassell, 1956) p. 25, italics in original.

THE LAND/AIR INTERFACE: AN HISTORICAL PERSPECTIVE

In considering these issues, the main object of this chapter is to present an historical perspective of the land/air interface in order to present some ensuring lessons for contemporary and future operations. For space considerations, it is restricted largely to an Anglo-American then NATO context. Unfortunately, important subjects such as air transport and airmobility have had to be left out. The common thread throughout this study is the development of joint command and control of air and land forces. In particular, an underlying theme is to discern where the points of friction lie and to establish what lubricants should be applied to ensure a greater chance of success when air and land forces are required to fight together in the 'joint battlespace' of the future.

POINTERS FROM THE FIRST AND SECOND WORLD WARS

The First World War and the Evolution of Inter-War Air Policy

The First World War provides an obvious starting point for the study of the land/air interface and, from an army perspective, to establish what an air force should provide in supporting the land battle. From the early days of air reconnaissance during 1914-1915, the potential (and the inherent costs) of close air support had become apparent during the battles of 1916-1917 on the Western Front. By 1918, the Germans, British and French had all developed procedures for employing aircraft to help secure military objectives, including the bombing of communications and supply centres and the low-level strafing of troops.[5] During the British counter-offensive at Amiens on 8 August 1918, the 'black day of the German Army', no less than 654 bombers and fighters out of a theoretical maximum of 1390 aircraft available in France took part.[6] However, nearly 100 aircraft of all types were lost or damaged beyond repair and some of the bombing results were disappointing. Yet it had been the German daylight attacks on London during the summer of 1917 that had convinced the British War Cabinet of the importance of large scale bombing. In the minds of the press, public and political leadership air power had become a dramatic and potentially decisive factor in winning (or losing) the war. In his first report to the War Cabinet, General Smuts had recommended the reorganization of the air defences of Great Britain; in his second report he went on to suggest the creation of sufficient offensive means, declaring that:

---

5. See P Dayell, 'The March Offensive' in *Air Power Review* Vol. 1, No. 2 (1998) for an account of the critical contribution of air power in the land battle during the final year of the First World War.
6. Figures taken from Slessor, Op Cit, p. 184 and 218. Slessor criticized this lack of concentration (only 47%) "in support of the decisive task" - what we would now describe as the operational main effort.

THE LAND/AIR INTERFACE: AN HISTORICAL PERSPECTIVE

'The day may not be far off when aerial operations with their devastation of enemy lands and destruction of industrial and populous centres on a vast scale may become the principal operations of war, to which the older forms of military and naval operations may become secondary and subordinate'.[7]

The most lasting result of Smuts's work was the formation of the Royal Air Force on 1 April 1918. After the First World War, however, the habit of air and land forces working together to achieve a common military objective quickly faded. The land/air interface broke down for several reasons: diverging Service policies and stringent economies across defence spending were the predominant factors. The RAF, under the firm grip of Chief of the Air Staff Lord Trenchard, did not see the primary role of the new Service as supporting the other two. In its British context, the theory and practice of the 'strategic' employment of air power was developed from the Independent Force of 1918, which Trenchard had commanded in France.[8] With our 20:20 hindsight at the beginning of the 21st Century, it is easy to see that a heavy bomber force *alone* could neither deter war, nor win one despite the irrepressible and exaggerated claims of air power enthusiasts.[9] Then as now there was no magic 'silver bullet' that provided a 'quick-fix' knockout weapon. Yet our views now are somewhat irrelevant for it is important to realise that, in the lead up to the Second World War, there was much pessimistic concern about the effects of enemy bombing and a corresponding optimistic faith in the British investment in 'strategic' bombing. Yet Trenchard also cut his strategic cloth to suit the perceived public mood: whilst air power, including defensive means, received its due financial priority, a 'continental-sized' army was a political non-starter for the entire inter-war period.[10] The long and bloody shadows of the Western Front remained: a deeply scarred Britain did not want to fight another costly war in Europe. Adequate preparation for high intensity war on land would have meant expensive re-equipment

---

7. Quoted by Tedder, *Air Power in War* (London: Hodder and Stoughton, 1947); Marshal of the Royal Air Force Sir John Slessor, *The Central Blue* (London: Cassell, 1956) p. 20-21.
8. Sir Llewellyn Woodward points out in his monumental *Great Britain and the War of 1914-1918* (London: Methuen, 1967) p. 375: the name "was not happily chosen, since at the very time when the Allies had attained to some unity of command on land it gave an impression that a large bombing force would act independently of the ground forces. Foch wanted in particular, to be assured that the 'Independent Force' should be at his disposition during the battle."
9. The most obvious proponent was Douhet, *Command of the Air.*
10. Richard Overy, *The Road to War* 2nd ed. (London: Penguin, 1999) p. 89. Overy makes clear, during the rearmament programme instituted in 1934 following the recommendations of the British Cabinet Defence Requirements Committee, the "army had to take third place, as it had throughout the 1920s. In 1935 military expenditure was a fifth higher than 1934, in 1936 two-thirds higher. Expenditure on the air force trebled across the same period." See also Brian Bond, *British Military Policy between the Wars* (Oxford: Clarendon, 1980).

which was hardly realistic in the face of the 'never again'. Thus in this policy and strategic context, 'tactical' air/land co-operation appeared to many an expensive luxury or a measure of last resort, despite the best efforts of individuals involved from both the Army and RAF at unit and school level.

Handley Page 0/400s of the Independent Air Force. In the inter-war years, the RAF saw the primary role of the new Service not as supporting the other two Services, but as providing strategic air power.

The operational value of any form of air power must be judged by its practical performance and hence overall strategic contribution to the war effort. Yet during the 1930s the jury was still out on how air forces should operate, and consequently views diverged over what types of aircraft should be produced. As a result, much heated discussion and debate took place in the Service ministries, the Committee for Imperial Defence (CID) in London and at the staff colleges. Not surprisingly, the experience of the Great War provided much of the teaching material during the inter-war period at the Army Staff College, Camberley and at the RAF Staff College, Andover. Each college possessed a member of the other Service on the Directing Staff (DS). Wing Commander J. C. Slessor, for example, served as the RAF DS at Camberley in the period 1931-34.[11] Slessor, like all airmen, stressed the inherent flexibility and responsiveness of air power. He also highlighted the need to achieve 'strategic concentration' (in other words avoid, almost at any cost, the 'penny-packeting' of scarce air resources) and, critically, to gain

---

11. The first RAF DS was appointed in 1925. Slessor, who followed Leigh-Mallory, was the fourth of seven RAF DS who served at Camberley before the Second World War.

and *maintain* air superiority in preference to providing direct assistance to the Army.[12] Slessor remarked:

> 'The struggle for air superiority is part and parcel of all air operations against a first-class enemy; and though much can be done by superior organization and equipment to provide for the physical and material factors before we go to war, the essential third factor-perhaps the most important of all-the moral factor, can only be secured by an instant and unremitting offensive directed against the primary object, whatever it happens to be at the time. 'Air superiority is only a means to an end.' But it happens that to go straight for the end is best, in fact the only sure, way of achieving the means.'[13]

In seeing air superiority as a 'means to an end', Slessor presaged Tedder's words after the Second World War: "Air superiority is, however, merely a means towards the end; it is the state in which the exercise of air power becomes possible".[14] By the exercise of air power Tedder (and Slessor before and after him) implied bombing against the enemy's means of military production or his lines of communication. All this was in preference to supporting *directly* the land battle. If the land battle had to be supported, then bombing attacks against points or areas of supply rather than against fighting troops were far more likely to be effective, as the results of air support during latter stages of the First World War had indicated. Many soldiers, however, failed to realise that air forces needed to defeat their *air* opponents before effective support could be given to ground forces. Air Vice-Marshal Coningham neatly summed up this point in 1943: "The Army has one battle to fight, the land battle. The Air [Force] has two. It has first of all to beat the enemy air, so that it may go into the land battle against the enemy land forces with the maximum possible hitting power."[15]

---

12. Tedder declared "Air warfare cannot be separated into little packets; it knows no boundaries on land and sea other than imposed by the radius of action of the aircraft; it is a unity and demands unity of command". Quoted in AP 3000 (2nd Ed.) p. iii.
13. Slessor, *Air Power in War* (London: Hodder and Stoughton, 1947); Marshal of the Royal Air Force Sir John Slessor, *The Central Blue* (London: Cassell, 1956) p. 10.
14. Tedder, *Air Power in War* (London: Hodder and Stoughton, 1947); Marshal of the Royal Air Force Sir John Slessor, *The Central Blue* (London: Cassell, 1956) p. 53.
15. Presentation to Eisenhower and other Allied senior officers at Tripoli on 16 February 1943. Quoted by John L Frisbee, "The Lessons of North Africa", *Air Force Magazine*, September 1990, p. 62.

THE LAND/AIR INTERFACE: AN HISTORICAL PERSPECTIVE

Yet this fundamental truth was not obvious in the inter-war years. Practical inter-Service co-operation in the 1920s and 1930s was hampered by the lack of a solid joint doctrinal foundation. The Army perspective, for example, was contained in publications such as *The Employment of Air Forces with the Army in the Field* (1932). The RAF had its own doctrine such as the Royal Air Force War Manual (Air Publication 1300) of which Part I - Operations, Chapter XI dealt with 'general policy governing the employment of air forces in support of the army'. A separate RAF Manual of Army Co-operation (Air Publication 1176) set out more detailed matters of procedure.

The existence of single-Service doctrine and the work conducted at the Army and RAF staff colleges, however, provides only a limited insight into the state of the land/air interface. In practice, the Army and RAF could not agree on how a field force should be supported by air power. This argument bedevilled inter-Service relations well into the Second World War. After the First World War, both the British Army and the Royal Air Force faced a massive reduction in numbers and were largely occupied operationally with imperial policing. Indeed, 'air control' in the 1920s provided the tangible *raison d'être* of the RAF at a time of increasing financial parsimony. Many of the leading airmen of the Second World War including Tedder, Coningham and Harris flew over Iraq.[16] But that was where the commonality of circumstance and task ended. For the RAF, the priority force planning and development tasks became the defence of Great Britain against enemy air attack and the creation of a heavy bomber force to forestall such an attack in the first place. Yet by their very nature these tasks were *strategic* in design. This forced the RAF to think at the higher levels of conflict in marked contrast to the Army's predominantly *tactical* pre-occupation with Empire. And neither the Army nor the RAF possessed the doctrine, force structure or an understanding of the *operational* level of command that provides the vital gearing between the strategic direction of war and its tactical execution.[17] As the Army turned its back on continental

---

16. Williamson Murray also makes this point in his essay 'Strategic Bombing' in Murray and Millett, Op Cit, p. 104. A more topical point is to consider whether those who have distinguished themselves in air operations over Iraq in the 1990s will become the future leaders of the RAF. For a good description of how 'air control' developed, including Trenchard's role, see Slessor, *The Central Blue*, p. 51-74.
17. The operational level was not adopted by the British Army until its brief mention in Army Field Manual *The Application of Force* (1985), and fuller treatment in *Design for Operations - British Military Doctrine* (1989). It was introduced into RAF doctrine in 1991 (AP 3000 First Edition, p. 3). However, the German Army Office had published 'Guidelines for the Conduct of the "operative" Air War' (*Richtlinien für die Führung des operativen Luftkrieges*) in 1926. For a description of what is meant by *'operative'* in this context and wider discussion of the doctrinal development of co-operation between the German Air Force and Army, see Michel Forget, 'French and German Army-Air Force Co-operation' in Horst Boog (ed.), *The Conduct of the Air War in the Second World War* (Oxford; Berg, 1992) p. 423-428.

warfare to get on with 'proper' soldiering - the familiar business of 'small wars' - the RAF prepared for war on a much larger scale notwithstanding its own contribution to imperial policing. This fundamental difference in professional outlook between the British Army and the RAF is significant for it defines loyalties even today. Broadly speaking, whilst the airman thinks first and foremost of his Service (in other words at a strategic level), the soldier identifies more naturally with his Regiment or Corps (or at the tactical level). The lack of a common approach to the planning and conduct of war at the strategic level was the source of much of the discord between the Services. Where the perceived threat was most acute, however, the Services did work better together. An often overlooked, yet largely successful land/air interface, was the defence of Great Britain against air attack. At the outbreak of the Second World War, the Anti-Aircraft Command of the Territorial Army included five anti-aircraft divisions (two more were forming). Its headquarters were at Stanmore alongside those of Fighter Command.[18] But what if any, then, was the basis of the operational land/air interface as Britain deployed, as in August 1914, an expeditionary force to France in September 1939?

Following the Second World War, in the after-glow of victory, Marshal of the Royal Air Force Lord Tedder wisely remarked in his 1947 Lees Knowles lectures that as a nation "we have a tendency to concentrate too much on our successes and our enemies' failures and consequently to draw our lessons too much from the final stages of war."[19] Tedder's eminently sensible point was reiterated in the official history of the campaign in France and Flanders 1939-1940 and subsequently picked up by David Fraser in his history of the British Army in the Second World War.[20] So it is to where things went wrong in the early stages of the War - rather to the later campaigns where matters were put right - that we should turn first for lessons.

---

18. For details, see Basil Collier, *The Defence of the United Kingdom* (London: HMSO, 1957) ch. iv and ch. v.
19. Slessor, *Air Power in War*, p. 25.
20. See *The History of the Second World War United Kingdom Military Series* (ed J R M Butler), L F Ellis, *The War in France and Flanders 1939-1940* (London: HMSO, 1953) p. xi, and David Fraser, *And We Shall Shock Them: The British Army in the Second World War* (London: Hodder & Stoughton, 1983).

THE LAND/AIR INTERFACE: AN HISTORICAL PERSPECTIVE

Joint Case Study 1 - Forward to Dunkirk

By 1939 the essential conceptual differences between the Army and the RAF lay in the command and control of air forces, and, as an intimately related issue, in the provision of 'close support' to the forward battle zone. In support of the land battle, the RAF regarded the interdiction of enemy reserves as the principal contribution of bomber aircraft, and further 'generally to create disorganisation and confusion behind the enemy front while the ground forces achieved their objectives.'[21] On 29 June 1939, the [Deputy] Director of Air Plans, Group Captain Slessor, despite having worked closely with the Army at Camberley, noted: "...when the soldier talks about co-operation between the Air Force and the Army he really means subordination of the Air Force to the Army".[22] So the provision of close support to land formations was to be the exception rather than the rule, and the Air Staff defined those exceptional circumstances in November 1939:

- In defence, in a critical situation when the overriding consideration was to stop a hostile breakthrough: to cover the withdrawal of our forward troops from untenable positions and to give time for the arrival of reserves. (The historical example quoted was the air action in support of Gough's battered Fifth Army in March 1918 during the German Michael offensive).
- In the pursuit of an already broken enemy: to turn a retreat into a rout, such as occurred after the battle of Megiddo in Palestine on 21 September 1918, when the Turkish Seventh and Eighth Armies were annihilated.
- On rare occasions in an attack on an highly organized defensive system when it might be justifiable to use aircraft 'temporarily' against such objectives as artillery areas and the movements of the enemy's immediate reserves, to make sure of breaking the crust of the defence for the initial break-in.[23]

So close air support could neither be planned nor relied on, except in the most dire or favourable circumstances. No wonder so many soldiers were uneasy, particularly as reports of German success, including the use of dive-bombers in the intimate support of armoured forces, began to circulate after the Spanish Civil War and especially after the

---

21. The Air Ministry, Air Publication 3235, *The Second World War 1939-1945 The Royal Air Force, Air Support* (London: Air Historical Branch, 1955) p. 11. Subsequent references are to 'Air Support'.
22. Quoted by Brian Bond, *British Military Policy between the Wars* (Oxford: Clarendon, 1980) p. 325.
23. *Air Support*, p. 10. The wording of this memorandum, and the use of historical examples, would appear to stem from Slessor's pre-war work. The RAF's associated doctrinal position was set out clearly in AP 1300 (Second Edition, February, 1940) Part I - Operations, Chapter XI, Paragraphs 45-46.

German conquest of Poland. Air defence against such threats, meanwhile, rested on whatever fighters the RAF could provide and on the limited ground-based anti-aircraft (AA) assets of the Army. In 1939, 'heavy' AA units were re-equipping with the underrated 3.7 inch gun (the equivalent of the famous German 88 mm dual-purpose weapon); 'light' units with the 40 mm Bofors.[24]

Military historians have rightly exploded the myth of Blitzkrieg as a fully thought-out integrated strategic concept but it was a bitter reality nonetheless for those on the 'receiving end'. The key to Blitzkrieg's success, moreover, lay not in the application of technology as is often thought, but rather in the largely opportunistic accelerating operational tempo that German forward commanders developed, a product of superior doctrine and training in peacetime and flexible command on operations.[25] Much has been written about the development of the German campaign plan for the defeat of France and her allies, particularly over the selection of the *Schwerpunkt* and consequent concentration of German armour and supporting air power in von Rundstedt's Army Group 'A'. Yet however good their theory and organization in comparison to their opponents, the Germans in *practice* concentrated their resources. After one week the Luftwaffe achieved 'clear superiority in the air and after a further week a degree of air supremacy that was but temporarily interrupted by enemy fighters'. Under these conditions, indirect support for the Army was concentrated on railways, roads, command posts and troop concentrations to cover exposed flanks, and direct support was ruthlessly concentrated on the operational main effort.[26]

Yet it remains a fact that the French high command did detect the German armoured thrust through the Ardennes towards Sedan by 11 May 1940, the second day of campaign, and began deploying strategic reserves to the threatened Sedan sector on 12 May 1940. However, the French were doomed by their relatively slow and inappropriate operational level decision making as much as by the poor tactical performance of their

---

24. The Army level (heavy) anti-aircraft Regiment typically had twenty-four 3.7 inch guns; the Light Anti-Aircraft Regiment to be found at both Army and Corps levels had up to 48 Bofors 40 mm guns. The BEF had three anti-aircraft brigades comprising a total of five heavy regiments and two and one third light regiments; in addition, each of the three corps had one light regiment. With the Advanced Air Striking Force was a brigade of two heavy regiments. Details from Ellis, *The War in France and Flanders* 1939-1940, p. 359-360, 367 and 371.
25. For example, J P Harris, 'The Myth of Blitzkrieg', *War in History* Volume 2, Number 3 (1995) p. 335-352, and J R Corum, *The Roots of Blitzkrieg: Hans von Seekt and German Military Reform* (Lawrence, Kan, 1997). For an authoritative German account, see Karl-Heinz Frieser, *Blitzkrieg-Legende: Der Westfeldzug 1940* (München: Oldenbourg, 1995) [Blitzkrieg Legends: The Campaign in the West 1940; Operations of the Second World War Volume 2 - Militärgeschlichtes Forschungsamt (MGFA)].
26. Hans Umbreit, 'German Victory in Western Europe' in (ed) MGFA, *Germany and the Second World War* (Oxford: Clarendon, 1991) p. 282-283.

THE LAND/AIR INTERFACE: AN HISTORICAL PERSPECTIVE

forces in the air and on land. Superior tempo, rather than better tanks, brought victory in the West to the Germans. Amongst many other failings in the Allied command set-up, the land/air interface failed to function effectively, at all levels of warfare, both in its joint and combined dimensions.[27]

Command and control of British air forces in France was over-complicated by the need to preserve the RAF's independence of army command, the desire to assist in the strategic bombing offensive from forward bases on the Continent and the concomitant requirement to co-operate with the French Air Force at the highest level. The RAF deployed two forces to France in 1939: the so-called 'Air Component'[28] of the British Expeditionary Force (thirteen squadrons of fighters and reconnaissance aircraft) and the ten light bomber and two fighter squadrons (later four) of the Advanced Air Striking Force (A.A.S.F.).[29] Initially these two elements were entirely separate and had different chains of command accordingly. The Air Component, commanded by Air Vice-Marshal C. H. B. Blunt, answered to Lord Gort. Air Vice-Marshal P. H. L. Playfair of the A.A.S.F, however, received orders directly from Bomber Command.[30] Co-operation and liaison with the French was effected at two levels: the British Chief of the Air Staff was represented at the headquarters of the Commander-in-Chief of the French Air Forces by Air Marshal A. S. Barratt, whilst Bomber Command was represented at the headquarters of the French First Air Army by Air Commodore F. P. Don.[31] As to support from the A.A.S.F, Lord Gort had received the following direction from Hore-Belisha, the Secretary of State for War:

> *'It is realised that you may require air co-operation beyond the resources of the Royal Air Force Component of the Field Force. Additional assistance may be necessary for the general protection of your Force against hostile air attack, for offensive action in furtherance of military operations, or to establish local air superiority at certain times. You should apply for such assistance when you require it to the Air Officer Commanding Advanced Air Striking Force'.*[32]

---

27. See Robert Doughty, *The Breaking Point: Sedan and the Fall of France* (Hamden, Conn.: Archon, 1990) p. 271-277 and Karl-Heinz Frieser, *Blitzkrieg-Legende: Der Westfeldzug 1940* (München: Oldenbourg, 1995) [Blitzkrieg Legends: The Campaign in the West 1940; Operations of the Second World War Volume 2 - Militärgeschlichtes Forschungsamt (MGFA)], p. 247-256.
28. The RAF referred to it, with some foundation, as the 'RAF Component'; see Denis Richards, *Royal Air Force 1939-1945 Volume I The Fight at Odds* (London: HMSO, 1953) p. 108-109.
29. See John Terraine, *The Right of the Line: The Royal Air Force in the European War, 1939-1945* (London: Hodder and Stoughton, 1985). [References in this chapter are taken from the 1997 Wordsworth paperback edition.]
30. Ludlow-Hewitt retired in April 1940 and was relieved by Portal.
31. J R M Butler, United Kingdom Military Series, *Grand Strategy Volume II September 1939 - June 1940* (London: HMSO, 1957) p. 153.
32. Quoted by Field Marshal The Viscount Montgomery, *Memoirs* (London: Collins, 1958) p. 53-54.

THE LAND/AIR INTERFACE: AN HISTORICAL PERSPECTIVE

The British Army, however, was not happy with this state of affairs and asked for 250 first-line bomber aircraft to come under its direct control, which was beyond the ability of the RAF to provide even if it had so agreed.[33] Eventually, following Cabinet-level intervention, a new structure was agreed between the Air Ministry and the War Office. Both the Air Component of the BEF and the A.A.S.F. were grouped together in the British Air Forces in France Command (B.A.F.F.) under Air Marshal Sir Arthur Barratt, who was appointed on 15 January 1940. The Official History describes the theory of this new arrangement as follows:

> 'The new Air Commander-in-Chief would decide in consultation with Gort how the British bomber squadrons in France should be used in support of the army; only when some major operation of a different character was in view, and with the sanction of the Cabinet, would these aircraft pass under the direct control of Bomber Command. It was judged that the ten squadrons of the Advanced Air Striking Force reinforced by the remaining six squadrons of medium bombers from the United Kingdom should provide sufficient support for the Army in many months to come'.[34]

Events would prove otherwise. In practice, B.A.F.F. proved to be largely administrative rather than operational in nature and the Air Component ostensibly remained under Lord Gort's operational control. Yet neither the Air Component nor the A.A.S.F. was what would later in the War be termed a 'composite force' of fighters and bombers. Whilst the BEF relied on the A.A.S.F. for bomber support, the A.A.S.F., with inadequate fighter resources, in turn relied on the French Air Force for fighter protection that could have been provided by the Air Component had the two RAF elements been fully resourced and integrated. The tragic unfolding of the campaign in France and Flanders demonstrated that support from other Services or allies could not be relied upon. In summary, the critical failings in the land/air interface in France and Flanders lay in the following areas:

- In the inadequate strength and flawed composition of the air forces involved.
- In the dissipation of bombing effort against strategic - largely economic - targets as opposed to more pressing operational level military objectives.
- In the completely inadequate means of calling for timely and concentrated tactical air support. Satisfactory air/ground tactical communications did not exist.

---

33. Fuller details of the Army's proposal are given by Terraine, p.121 [See AHB/II/117/5(A) p. 72-73].
34. Butler, United Kingdom Military Series, *Grand Strategy Volume II September 1939 - June 1940* (London: HMSO, 1957) p. 155.

THE LAND/AIR INTERFACE: AN HISTORICAL PERSPECTIVE

- In the lack of a laid down procedure for joint decision making and targeting at the operational level.

The absurdity of the system is that ultimately the only working land/air interface lay in Whitehall, not in a combined and joint theatre headquarters in France. As has been frequently recounted, army staff officers had to phone the War Office in order to call for bomber support. Lord Gort, as commander of the BEF, could not influence directly the prioritisation - and hence the apportionment - of Bomber Command aircraft, wherever they were based. Neither the communications nor sufficient air staff were available in BEF GHQ. This situation appeared less satisfactory than 1918 when Army commanders could call on the direct support of one or more Royal Flying Corps (and later RAF) brigades.

Fairey Battles of the A.A.S.F. The RAF made a gallant but largely ineffective contribution to stemming the German Blitzkrieg in May 1940.

From an Army viewpoint the price of an independent air force appeared too heavy to pay, and calls for an Army controlled air support arm intensified. But the RAF was making a gallant if largely ineffective contribution to stemming the movement of German armour, particularly in its brave attacks against Guderian's pontoon bridges over the Meuse at Sedan on 14 May 1940. Against a wall of German fighters and flak (200 guns alone protected the principal crossing site at Gaulier), this one action cost the

THE LAND/AIR INTERFACE: AN HISTORICAL PERSPECTIVE

A.A.S.F. over 50 per cent casualties.[35] Yet two weeks later during the most critical period of the embarkation of the BEF and considerable French forces at Dunkirk, the RAF, although largely unseen by the soldiers on the beaches, was beginning to win a physical and moral ascendancy over the German Air Force. The German official history concedes that the Luftwaffe, having 'suffered considerable losses from squadrons of highly effective Spitfires', 'lost its 'aura of invincibility', even though it claimed Dunkirk as one of its successes.'[36] The reason for this turn of events lay in the relative proximity of British bases and distance of German ones, despite the limited endurance of RAF fighters over the Channel. Although relatively few in numbers, the RAF achieved for limited periods a measure of air parity, albeit with further losses.[37] Whilst the air situation over Dunkirk was not good enough to prevent the loss of 13 destroyers and many other smaller craft to determined German air attacks, without RAF fighter protection the evacuation of over 330,000 men over a nine-day period would have been, in Gort's words, "well-nigh impossible".[38] Whilst the Luftwaffe's failure to anticipate the need for maritime attack may also have contributed to its relative lack of success against shipping at Dunkirk, the obscuration caused by the burning oil farms must have saved many an Allied life on the beaches and at sea. Lord Gort praised the RAF magnanimously, stating that the "B.E.F. owes a deep debt of gratitude to the Royal Air Force". However, Lieutenant General Sir Alan Brooke, commander of II Corps, remained less impressed by the air support he had seen from the start of the campaign - one can presume he spoke for many of the BEF:

'In the air we were provided with the Lysander, an army co-operation machine; it was entirely unsuited for its task and deficient of forward aerodromes. As regards fighter protection against bombers, I understand that the few machines we had were working in support of our bombers in forward missions. I practically never saw a fighter during the rest of my time in France'.[39]

---

35. See Terraine, *The Right of the Line: The Royal Air Force in the European War, 1939-1945* (London: Hodder and Stoughton, 1985) p 133-135.
36. Hans Umbreit, *The Right of the Line: The Royal Air Force in the European War, 1939-1945* (London: Hodder and Stoughton, 1985) p. 291 and 293.
37. Fighter Command lost 106 aircraft and 75 pilots over Dunkirk. Between 10 May and 20 June, the totals were 463 and 284 respectively. Figures taken from *Chester Wilmot, The Struggle for Europe* (London: Collins, 1952) p. 39. Ellis, *War in France and Flanders*, p. 246, states that over the 9-day evacuation period, total RAF losses were 177 aircraft destroyed and damaged.
38. Lord Gort's Second Despatch, 17 October 1941; Vice-Admiral Ramsay's Despatch, 17 July 1947; Ellis, *The War in France and Flanders*, p. 181-193, 212-235, 243-248; Richards, *The Fight at Odds*, p. 135-144.
39. From Arthur Bryant, *The Turn of the Tide* (London: Collins, 1957) p. 91.

THE LAND/AIR INTERFACE: AN HISTORICAL PERSPECTIVE

Despite the RAF's relative success at Dunkirk, the abiding impression was that the Luftwaffe had dominated the skies. Such was the strength of feeling of being let down by the RAF that for months afterwards, Dunkirk survivors physically assaulted those in light blue uniforms. This was, of course, grossly unfair to the RAF who had in fact destroyed 156 German aircraft, but had rather undermined its credibility by claiming 390.[40]

So what lessons were learned as a result of air and land operations in France and Flanders? A War Office committee under the chairmanship of General Sir W. H. Bartholomew studied the Campaign. The final report, whilst dwelling on a lot of lower level tactical detail, made several important recommendations on air power and inter-Service co-operation. The Army was particularly impressed by the effectiveness of German dive-bombers and the need for air superiority. The report concluded: 'Whilst being fully conscious of the magnificent effort of the R.A.F. in the face of great German numerical superiority, the Committee feels that urgent action is required to place co-operation between the two services on a better basis.' For the land/air interface, the Bartholomew Report stressed the German method of 'concentrating the maximum effort to assist achieving the immediate object in view', and noted particularly the 'outstanding value of air attack as "supporting fire" to cover the assault of armoured, and at times, infantry formations'. Not surprisingly, the report recommended:

> *'It is imperative to ensure forthwith that a system comparable to that of the Germans should be introduced into our Army and Air Force. Even the brigade group must be able to call up immediate support by wireless, a process which ought to be easier in the defence than in the attack'.*[41]

Meanwhile, the Air Ministry commissioned Air Chief Marshal Brooke-Popham to 'investigate war experiences 1939-40'.[42] Brooke-Popham's committee, working under very tight time pressures, considered operations in Norway, together with those in France and Flanders. Rather than looking at either campaign as a whole, it primarily dealt with air operations or tactical, technical and supply matters. Significantly, there was no Army representation on the committee, and that body did not interview anyone outside the RAF. Thus the vital subject of co-operation with the Army was noticeably absent from its proceedings and final report. In view of its limited scope, it is not particularly surprising that the report was not circulated outside RAF circles. A comparison of the Bartholomew and Brooke-Popham reports reveals little of common interest, except the

---

40. As recounted by Len Deighton, *Blitzkrieg* (London: Pimlico, 1996) p. 262.
41. The Bartholomew Committee Final Report, 1940, p. 3 and 11. [TDRC Index No 4396]
42. Air Council A.C.87(40) S.4982 dated 8 November 1940 minutes 'action taken'. [AHB IIH2/888/1]

mutual requirement for achieving air superiority over the enemy and the desirability of speeding up communications procedures in both the air and land environments.

Sixty years on, with the benefit of hindsight, the case need for a *joint* lessons-learned study immediately after Dunkirk - involving all three Services - would appear to be overwhelming. If not likely to be undertaken in the face of single-Service obstruction, conservatism and pride, the more pressing requirement to protect Britain from invasion dictated other staff priorities. As a junior partner in the Anglo-French alliance in terms of air and land forces fielded on the Continent, Britain could take little comfort from the disastrous campaign in France and Flanders. If the RAF and the Royal Navy emerged with some honour, for the British Army it was but one in the long catalogue of defeats. Among many other failings, the land/air interface appeared, notwithstanding some notable exceptions, fundamentally flawed. Yet this must be seen in strategic context: the German 'victory in the west' was based principally on the Allies' failure to prepare, plan, organize and train for modern war. Whilst a lack of funds and misguided political direction in the inter-war period on both sides of the Channel were the underlying causes of much misfortune, men in uniform must also share responsibility for inter-Service squabbling and the missed opportunities to develop and practise joint procedures. Learning the hard way is neither smart nor efficient - but it proved to be the only option available to Britain in 1940. As ever, improvisation rarely makes up for a lack of foresight, a matter modern planners ignore to their peril.

Joint Case Study 2 - Desert Triumph

The war in the Western Desert 1940-43 provided an essential practical laboratory in the development of British air and land operations. After early setbacks and limited resources, the necessity of defeating a highly skilled and determined opponent forced the pace of air/land co-operation. Much of the credit for improving battlefield air support in the Western Desert Air Force goes to Air Chief Marshal Sir Arthur Tedder and Air Marshal Sir Arthur Coningham. It is often forgotten that most of the essential work of improving communications, reorganizing staffs, collocating headquarters and ironing out effective joint procedures was completed before Lieutenant General Bernard Law Montgomery entered the theatre in August 1942.[43] Yet if the pioneering work of Tedder and Coningham on one hand and Wavell and Auchinleck on the other have received relatively little attention in comparison with Montgomery's later work, the fact remains that the RAF could not win the war in the desert on its own. After all, the 'Benghazi' stakes, that painful series of seesaw battles across Cyrenaica where every British

---

43. Richard Hallion, *Strike from the Sky*, p. 152-162.

offensive but the last was followed by retreat, demonstrated that the British Army had to learn to outfight the Germans and Italians decisively. Yet if the desert war turned on the key battles at El Alamein, the air/land clock had started much earlier.

Field Marshal Montgomery (right) and Air Marshal Coningham.
The effectiveness of the air/land interface in the Western Desert in 1943 was instrumental in the success of the campaign.

After his success at Second El Alamein, Montgomery endorsed with enthusiasm Coningham's air power lessons, publishing them under his own name in Some Notes on High Command in War in 1943. Perhaps the two key points Montgomery made were:

> 6. *The greatest asset of air power is its flexibility, and this enables it to be switched quickly from one objective to another in the theatre of operations. So long as this is realized, then the whole weight of the available air power can be used in selected areas in turn; this concentrated use of the air striking force is a battle winning factor of the first importance.*
> 7. *It follows that control of the available air power must be centralized, and command must be exercised through R.A.F. channels. Nothing could be more fatal to successful results than to dissipate the air resources into small packets placed under command of army formation commanders, with each packet working on its own plan. The soldier must not expect, or wish, to exercise direct command over air striking forces.*

THE LAND/AIR INTERFACE: AN HISTORICAL PERSPECTIVE

In the 'battle of the memoirs' after the Second World War, Montgomery's Chief of Staff, Major General Freddie de Guingand, was among the first to enter the fray. As Montgomery's 'Chief' in both the Eighth Army and 21st Army Group he was in a good position to comment on the effectiveness of the land/air interface. He singled out the Battle of Mareth, rather than either First or Second Alamein, as an example of where air and land operations had been integrated particularly well. Montgomery's initial frontal attack with 30 Corps (principally involving the 50th Division) on the German Mareth Line (20-23 March 1943) had not succeeded and the operational idea to get round this problem was largely inspired by de Guingand. The resulting plan was to reinforce the Freyberg's New Zealand Corps outflanking operation (a 'left-hook') already under way with Horrocks's 10 Corps, including the 1st Armoured Division, and to employ air power to devastating effect (see map).

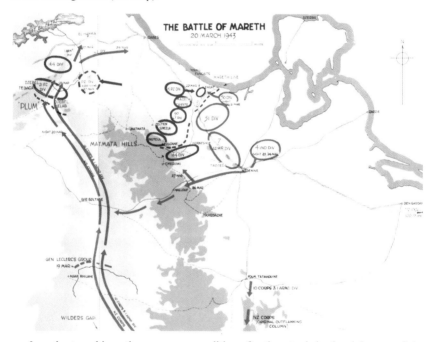

In order to achieve the necessary conditions for the attack in the right rear of the enemy, the Desert Air Force was required to 'blitz' the German forces held in depth guarding the 'Tebega Gap' (Objective Plum) 20 miles south-west of El Hamma (Objective Peach). In effect, tactical air power was being asked not only to complement artillery, adopting a well-tried German operational method, but also to convert an anticipated break-through into a break-out. De Guingand recounts:

THE LAND/AIR INTERFACE: AN HISTORICAL PERSPECTIVE

'The final air plan catered for a "crump" by forty light bombers on the narrow frontage of attack, to take place just before it commenced. Then, with five Spitfire squadrons as top cover, sixteen Kittybomber squadrons would operate over the battlefield for two and half hours, at an average density of two squadrons at a time. These using bomb and cannon would shoot up everything they saw. In addition a specially trained squadron of "tank busters" were to go for the enemy armour when located. In order to cause disorganisation to the enemy's rear areas, it was agreed to carry out night bombing raids during the previous two nights'.[44]

By this time, Broadhurst's Western Desert Air Force (now including a significant United States contribution) enjoyed air superiority and had the resources to accomplish this direct support task.[45] De Guingand was instrumental in convincing Broadhurst of the need for this type of integrated yet inherently risky low-level air attack, who in turn persuaded Montgomery of its practicality. The 'blitz' attack of the afternoon of 26 March 1943 was an outstanding success: joint action provided the necessary breakthrough at the Tebaga Gap which turned the German Mareth Line. However, the break-out to El Hamma, thence Gabes (Objective Grape) and on to the important airfields at Sfax, stalled in the face of a skilled German mobile defence. No envelopment was achieved: the tactical achievement could not be converted into a decisive operational success with strategic impact. Despite the substantial air support it was now receiving, rapid exploitation and pursuit operations were still not British Army strengths. In his sympathetic biography of de Guingand, General Sir Charles Richardson gives due credit to Broadhurst and the Desert Air Force in the battle. Its flexibility, responsiveness and performance was based on the growing mutual trust achieved between airmen and soldiers at command and senior staff level, thoughtful and timely preparation and close co-operation on and over the battlefield. Richardson notes:

'Broadhurst sent his squadron leaders on preliminary flights over the battle area to accustom themselves to the geography. An experienced RAF officer was sent up to go forward in an armoured car to control the 'cab-rank', and special arrangements were made in connection with

---

44. Major General Sir Francis De Guingand, *Operation Victory* (London: Hodder & Stoughton, 1947) p. 257-257.
45. The Western Desert Air Force was only a part of the overall air effort. It was subordinated to Coningham's Northwest African Tactical Air Force, which included No. 242 Group RAF, and the United States XII Air Support Command. Heavy support was provided by the Northwest African Strategic Air Force.

THE LAND/AIR INTERFACE: AN HISTORICAL PERSPECTIVE

landmarks and coloured smoke signals to show the position of our own troops. Broadhurst himself visited his squadrons to brief them in their critical role; he was received with immense enthusiasm'.[46]

In his memoirs, Montgomery heaped generous praise on the Desert Air Force, but included hints of the personality clashes later to come in the War:

'This blitz attack was the complete example of the close integration of land and air power up to that time. It should be noted that there were grave misgivings at the headquarters of the Tactical Air Forces; Coningham considered the risks were too great and an officer was sent over to try and stop the use of air power in this way. But the A.O.C. Desert Air Force (Harry Broadhurst) decided to accept the risks and refused to listen to the emissary. When it was all over and had been proved a great success with very small losses, he received many congratulations from Air Headquarters in Tunisia; and even from the Air Ministry!'[47]

How much matters had improved since the dark days of May-June 1940. At last the RAF was able to inflict real pain on formations of the German Army, throwing back in its face some of the 'Luftwaffe' treatment meted out on the BEF in France. The enduring lessons for the land/air interface were:

- The prior need for air superiority;
- A ready availability of sufficient and well-armed aircraft capable of ground attack.
- Carefully worked-up land/air procedures, including reliable ground/air communications and friend-from-foe recognition measures;
- Joint planning, collocation of headquarters and close co-operation at command and staff levels.
- The need for air and land commanders to know and trust each other.

As the British official history footnotes, no new technique had been used at Tebaga Gap, rather the 'novelty lay in the large-scale application, and the splendid co-ordination of detail between air force and army'[48] If de Guingand and Broadhurst were the men of

---

46. General Sir Charles Richardson, *Send For Freddie* (London: Kimber, 1987) p. 118-119.
47. Montgomery, *Memoirs*, p. 162-163.
48. Major General I.S.O. Playfair et al, History of the Second World War, *The Mediterranean and the Middle East* iv, p. 349-355.

THE LAND/AIR INTERFACE: AN HISTORICAL PERSPECTIVE

this particular match, Coningham's earlier role in forging the Desert Air Force as a potent battlefield support weapon and his cogent leadership of Northwest African Tactical Air Force in the closing stages of the Tunisian campaign should not be forgotten; nor must Tedder's strategic contribution as Commander-in-Chief, Mediterranean Allied Air Forces from February 1943. It was after all, for the increasingly successful land/air interface, more than the end of the beginning; it was rather the beginning of the end-game of the War for the Anglo-American partnership of arms.[49] The United States took stock of their experience in North Africa and formulated the lessons in Field Manual 100-20, 'Command and Employment of Air Power', published on 21 July 1943. The first priority for air forces was to gain and maintain air superiority, second was air interdiction, and third was close air support of ground forces. This remains the bed-rock of air power doctrine, nearly 60 years on.

Hurricane IID 'Tankbusters' of No 6 Squadron, Desert Air Force, 1942.

---

49. For details, see Richard Hallion, *Strike from the Sky*, p. 167-177; Stephen J McNamara, *Air Power's Gordian Knot* (Maxwell AFB: Air University Press, 1994) p. 11-22; Vincent Orange, 'Getting Together: Tedder, Coningham and Americans in the Desert and Tunisia, 1940-43' in Daniel R Mortensen, ed, *Airpower and Ground Armies: Essays on the Evolution of Anglo-American Air Doctrine, 1940-43* (Air University Press, Maxwell AFB, Alabama, 1998) p. 1-44.

THE LAND/AIR INTERFACE: AN HISTORICAL PERSPECTIVE

Joint Case Study 3 - Divisions in Normandy

In setting the strategic and operational level conditions for the invasion of Europe, air power provided the key. Without air superiority, the sea movements required during Operation Neptune, the assault phase (Operation Overlord) could never have been mounted. On land, once a successful lodgement on the Normandy coast had been made, air power would have to offset the predicted numerical advantage that the Germans defenders would enjoy in the race of the build up. Yet in order to achieve the necessary scale of air interdiction, disruption to the French rail network - known as the Transportation Plan - would have to commence three months before D-Day. Diversion of the necessary heavy bomber forces from attacking strategic targets in Germany was achieved, but not without protest from the 'bomber barons', Air Chief Marshal Harris of Bomber Command and Lieutenant General Carl Spaatz, commander of the US Strategic Air Forces in Europe (the Eighth and Fifteenth Air Forces). Once troops were ashore, the operational level air commanders pressed, as in North Africa, Sicily and mainland Italy, for the speedy capture of airfields (or sufficient space to build improvised strips) for tactical aircraft. Such intimate air support in previous theatres had often proved critical in disrupting the movement of German reserves and in beating off or destroying German armoured counter attacks, complementing the devastating power of Allied naval gunfire support demonstrated at Sicily, Salerno, Anzio and Normandy.

But as the British Second Army made slow progress towards capturing the Caen area in June and July (despite it being a D-Day objective), tensions mounted between air and land commanders. On the 'airfields' issue in particular, relations broke down between the Acting Ground Force commander, Montgomery, and the principal airmen: Air Marshal Tedder (Deputy Supreme Commander), Air Marshal Sir Trafford Leigh-Mallory (Commander-in-Chief Allied Expeditionary Air Force (AEAF)) and Air Marshal Sir Arthur Coningham (Commander Second Tactical Air Force (2 TAF), which supported 21st Army Group. Montgomery remained unrepentant at the time and after the War: to him the airfields were not 'all-important'. He wrote: "If we won the battle of Normandy, everything else would follow, airfields and all. I wasn't fighting to capture airfields; I was fighting to defeat Rommel in Normandy."[50] But the underlying problem was personal rather than operational: Montgomery no longer met Coningham regularly and did not regard him as an equal. Ironically it had been Montgomery who had pressed for the close integration of land and air commanders and their staffs in the Western Desert. After El Alamein he had written:

---

50. Field Marshal The Viscount Montgomery, *Memoirs* (London: Collins, 1958) p. 256-257. See Major L F Ellis, Victory in the West (London: HMSO, 1962) p. 353-356 for details of criticisms of Montgomery at SHAEF, largely inspired by Tedder.

THE LAND/AIR INTERFACE: AN HISTORICAL PERSPECTIVE

'When I took command, Army H.Q. was right forward, and Air H.Q. Western Desert was right back near the landing-grounds. The Army was fighting its battle and the R.A.F. its battle... Army H.Q. and Air H.Q. and the two staffs seem gradually to have drifted apart. I decided to remedy this at once and moved Army H.Q. back to Air H.Q. and brought the A.O.C. and his senior staff officers into my Mess. This was a good move, and from that moment we never looked back'.[51]

During the planning stage for Operation Overlord, the separation of headquarters in Southern England, and in the case of the Allied air forces, a surfeit of headquarters and layers of command, had thwarted close liaison and co-operation. Once the operation was underway, Montgomery had two air commanders to deal with. He consulted Leigh-Mallory over heavy bomber support and referred to Coningham for tactical air support. In practice, however, more often than not he dealt with Air Vice-Marshal Broadhurst, Commander of 83 Group which supported Second British Army. As Chester Wilmot observed, the 'honeymoon' between Montgomery and Coningham had ended long before the advance to Tripoli. By then Montgomery's predilection for operating forward in a small 'tactical' headquarters away from his Chief of Staff, who worked closely with the air staff at a joint Army/Air Main Headquarters, had become apparent.

Air Marshal Sir Trafford Leigh-Mallory (left) with Major General Pete Quesada, Normandy 1944.

---

51. Extract from Montgomery's diary notes entitled 'Review of the Situation in Eighth Army from 12 August to 23 October 1942', quoted by Stephen Brooks, ed, *Montgomery and the Eighth Army* (London: The Army Historical Records Society, 1991) p. 22-23. [Original: Imperial War Museum, Montgomery papers BLM 27/1]. But Richardson, *Send For Freddie* (London: Kimber, 1987) p. 89 notes, however, that the friendly relations between the AOC (Coningham) and Montgomery soon tailed off after the relocation of headquarters; Montgomery was rather economic on this point. See Vincent Orange, *Coningham* (London: Methuen, 1990) for another view.

THE LAND/AIR INTERFACE: AN HISTORICAL PERSPECTIVE

In his post-war despatch Coningham highlighted the problems he encountered as a result of the separation of Montgomery's headquarters. Whilst he berated the 'deliberate disassociation of C-in-C, 21 Army Group from his Main Headquarters', Coningham was quite clear on where he should locate himself and his staff:

> *'The Main Headquarters of Second Tactical Air Force and the Main Headquarters of 21 Army Group were always sited as close together as possible. I found it was not possible to conduct my business commanding the Second Tactical Air Force except by taking up my residence where it was located. The rapid decisions required in making the best use of the flexibility of air forces entailed my being close to my executive operational staff and in the centre of the communication network'.*[52]

Yet a fully joint force headquarters involving land and air commanders and their staffs was never formed for the campaign in Northwest Europe. Partly a result of different functions, the separation of headquarters in Southern Britain before D-Day continued thereafter during the campaign in Northwest Europe. Tedder, whilst Deputy Supreme Commander, had no dedicated air staff. Leigh-Mallory had little real power beyond what is described as 'co-ordinating authority' in modern NATO parlance. He appeared to soldiers and airmen alike as an unnecessary link in the chain of command above the Second Tactical Air Force and the United States Ninth Air Force. His mounting frustration at the lack of support from above and below is revealed by his diary entries for the immediate post D-Day period. On several occasions, strategic air power from either Bomber Command or, more typically, from Doolittle's Eighth Air Force, on which Leigh-Mallory had planned for support of the land battle, was withdrawn without consultation. Leigh-Mallory's terse diary entry for 29 June 1944 speaks volumes for the difficulties under which he operated:

> *'Today was the first day when it has been possible to use bombers and fighter bombers in daylight, for some considerable time, owing to the slight but definite improvement in the weather. I suppose, however, that it was for this reason that the American 8th Air Force, with all its fighter support, and two groups of the American 9th Air Force chose to go to Leipzig and bomb aircraft factories. This they did without reference to myself. I cannot but regard this as serious, for I wanted to attack without delay the big railway movement East of Paris. To do so today, I have had to take squadrons from the Tactical Air Force, though they are committed*

---

52. Coningham Despatch, p. 16-17.

THE LAND/AIR INTERFACE: AN HISTORICAL PERSPECTIVE

to a big programme of immediate support to the Army by bombing enemy movement in the area West and South-West of Paris. However, there it is. The Americans have gone off and I can do nothing about it'.[53]

So the effectiveness of the land/air interface, particularly in a coalition context, was undermined by organizational as well as by personality clashes. In retrospect, high level Allied and inter-Service relations were soured in Normandy by Anglo-American rivalry, friction between senior RAF officers and the inflated egos of Montgomery and Coningham. There are good grounds to suppose that Montgomery tended to regard the RAF as an 'auxiliary arm' and Coningham suffered from a 'junior service complex', like many other airmen. Richardson, on Montgomery's staff, described Coningham uncompromisingly as a 'fraternal *prima donna*'.[54] Yet it is a telling tribute to Montgomery's and Coningham's subordinates that tactical air support was made to work, and often spectacularly so. Much of this achievement in the British sector was based on the very successful working partnership between Broadhurst and de Guingand, as we have seen earlier. The wider roles of Coningham and Leigh-Mallory in organizing air power to support ground forces remain largely unrecognised, particularly in contrast to the weight of attention accorded to Montgomery both during and after the War. In action, however, the bravery and skill of the aircrew involved, including the famous Typhoon pilots, brought stunning results on the battlefield. For the German army in Normandy in general, and especially for those unlucky formations involved in the doomed Mortain counter attack (Operation Lüttich) or trapped in the Falaise Pocket, Allied tactical air power was devastating, both morally and physically. Although the amount of armour destroyed was disappointing, there can be no doubt as to the overall disruptive and attritional effect. Combined with the results of heavy 'strategic' bombing such as that which destroyed much of the Panzer Lehr Division on Operation Cobra, all types of air power reduced German operational and tactical freedom. It made a major contribution to Allied victory and to the German loss of France. Yet for the Germans, the institutional memory of the dangers in attempting to move and fight in a hostile air environment lingers on over 55 years later. Whereas the British Army on exercise undertakes road

---

53. Quoted by Bill Newton Dunn, *Big Wing* (Shrewsbury: Airlife, 1992) p. 146. Newton Dunn's sympathetic biography of Leigh-Mallory is uncritical and disappointingly weak on sources. For a critical examination of Leigh-Mallory's contribution to the campaign in Normandy, see Shaun Cowlam, 'Leigh-Mallory' RAF *Air Power Review* Vol. 2 No. 3, Autumn 1999, p. 76-90.
54. See Chester Wilmot, *The Struggle for Europe* (London: Collins, 1952) p. 339-340. For a more recent analysis of Montgomery's worsening relations with the airmen (and subsequently with Eisenhower), see Richard Lamb, *Montgomery in Europe 1943-45* (London: Buchan & Enright, 1987 [paperback edition]) p. 84; 114; 117-121.

marches with no air lookouts, the Bundeswehr typically still does.[55] Yet with modern stand-off weapons, any air lookout would be extremely luck ever to see an opponent in the sky.

Forward Air Controllers Squadron Leader Sutherland and Major Gray, Normandy 1944. For the German army in Normandy, Allied tactical air power was both morally and physically devastating.

LESSONS FROM AND SINCE THE SECOND WORLD WAR

Many of the hard-won lessons of land/air co-operation during the Second World War were incorporated in post-war structures and in associated doctrine and procedures. But a lot had to be re-learned the hard way in Korean and in Vietnam, thus repeating the pattern of forgotten lessons encountered in different theatres of the Second World War. In Korea, the newly formed United States Air Force (USAF) attempted to wage a strategic bomber offensive in the manner of the USAAF operations against Germany and Japan. Yet in a limited war, there are bound to be limits to strategic targeting, including

---

55. The practical test for this is to observe whether a vehicle cupola is open and manned and not covered by a camouflage net. In addition, the Germans still place greater emphasis today on all arms air defence, including employing gun calibres from 7.62 to 30 mm in this role. The British Army and Royal Air Force rely on missile defences alone beyond unit all arms air defence (AAAD) employing 5.56 and 7.62 mm automatic weapons, and exceptionally, 0.5 inch (12.7 mm) heavy machine guns.

THE LAND/AIR INTERFACE: AN HISTORICAL PERSPECTIVE

weapon choice. Meanwhile, it took time for soldiers on the ground and pilots in the air to learn and refine practical 'nuts and bolts' procedures against an enemy that offered no mass armoured target sets, that moved largely 'cross country' at night and was resupplied by bicycle rather than motor power. In Vietnam, as in Korea, air power could help set the conditions for military success at the tactical level, but rarely would provide decisive operational and strategic results within politically set targeting constraints. Underdogs fighting for national survival, however, do not play by the same 'rules', and would deny the existence of such.

Meanwhile, Cold War Allied practice, developed from close co-operation in the Mediterranean and Northwest Europe, became institutionalised in integrated NATO organizations and procedures. In the central region of Allied Command Europe, for example, both the northern and central groups of armies (NORTHAG and CENTAG) had affiliated tactical air forces (2 ATAF and 4 ATAF respectively). The most obvious manifestation of the land/air interface between NORTHAG and 2 ATAF was the joint headquarters (JHQ) located at Rheindahlen. Here the British commanders of the British Army of the Rhine (BAOR) and Royal Air Force Germany (RAF(G)) were double-hatted as NATO commanders. The British Army pamphlet *High Command* described the joint method of command in the following terms:

> *'The hub of the joint army group/tactical air force headquarters is the Joint Command Operations Centre. It is to this centre that all information flows, and from it go all orders and instructions to implement the directions of the army group and the commander of the tactical air force. Co-ordination of the operations of the land and air forces is brought about at a daily conference of the commanders, the commanders being represented by their Chiefs of Staff if they themselves are unable to attend'.*[56]

This situation which existed until the disbandment of NORTHAG, 2 ATAF, BAOR and RAF(G) in 1992 is one with which perhaps Montgomery and Coningham would have been comfortable. Direct descendants of 21st Army Group and 2 Tactical Air Force, the NORTHAG/2ATAF combination was arguably one of the most integrated joint and combined structures in NATO. Although untested by anything other than the Cold War, this joint system of command was practised nonetheless in countless exercises. Commanders and principal staff officers lived and worked together; differences were ironed out quietly and efficiently. There was, in other words, sufficient personal oil in the system to overcome the inevitable organizational frictional sand. Paradoxically, for

---

56. *High Command* (W.O. Code No. 9738, 1961) p. 28.

the United Kingdom's armed forces with the recent policy mantra of 'jointery', Army/RAF 'jointness' took a long step back with the break-up of the JHQ in Rheindahlen. Despite recent British initiatives such as the establishment of the UK Permanent Joint Headquarters, the Joint Services Command and Staff College, the Joint Doctrine and Concepts Centre and the 're-invention' of joint doctrine,[57] a more critical examination of such developments might indicate that practical substance of better inter-Service co-operation is a little less than that sometimes claimed. At the tactical level, for example, less joint land/air training (including critically Forward Air Controller (FAC) exercises) is carried out than in the 1980s, the numbers of RAF and Army officers serving in each others formations and units have been reduced, and there are no dedicated facilities for training in, or developing, land/air co-operation.

CONCLUSIONS

Applicability

In attempting to derive enduring principles of effective land/air co-operation, care must be taken to avoid taking tactical or operational lessons out of their historical context. Strategic circumstances change. Lessons from the Western Desert, directly applicable in the Gulf War, do not necessarily apply in the quite different conditions of the Balkans. Not all future campaigns will necessarily require the land/air interface to be exercised. For Western governments, if coercive air or missile power is seen as the weapon of first choice, close air support will probably be a weapon of last choice, given a reluctance to commit ground forces. Further, the greater the dispersion of enemy 'forces' on the modern battlefield, and the greater those forces are mixed up with the 'people', typically in urban environments, the *less* either close air support or air interdiction can be employed. The proximity of non-combatants and the risk of collateral damage may rule out a large number of otherwise inviting targets. Thus we might wish to condemn the 'traditional' battlefield with its carefully defined boundaries and neat fire support co-ordination lines as an object solely of historical study. However, we might live to regret writing off close air support prematurely. Had NATO needed to perform an 'opposed entry' operation in Kosovo, for example, the land component would have required ready close support from the air, and in large measure.

---

57. Joint structures and doctrines have been developed since the Second World War. See for example, Joint Service Publication (JSP) 1, Manual of Joint Warfare, Volume 1, 'Concept, Planning and Control of Limited War Operations' was published on 1 February 1964. The publishing authority was the Joint Warfare Committee.

THE LAND/AIR INTERFACE: AN HISTORICAL PERSPECTIVE

Resources, Time and Effects

The common denominator of success in land/air operations appears to be the provision of sufficient resources to mount all types of air operations in a given 'threat' environment. Otherwise direct air support to land forces may become the poor relation of efforts directed at gaining higher level 'strategic' effects. Thus a balanced campaign with integrated land/air operations requires sufficient air assets. Land forces wish to be freed from the threat of enemy air attack and free to manoeuvre without interference from enemy reserves. Therefore air superiority and air interdiction tasks are likely to remain the Joint Force Commander's priority until effort can be switched to the direct support of ground forces. Yet the greater the political reluctance to commit land forces to battle, the greater the overall investment in air power required. What is often overlooked is that the threat or actuality of ground operations typically produces the very conditions for the successful application of air power. In order to hurt the enemy effectively and to throttle his logistics, he must be forced to fight, move and resupply.[58] Further, *indirect* air action, however intensive, takes time to take effect, particularly against a largely static and hardened enemy who may simply reduce his need for logistics. Air operations in both World Wars, Korea, Vietnam, the Gulf and in the Balkans, all demonstrate that 'knock-out' blows seldom achieve their desired strategic effects, despite the enthusiastic encouragement from air power theorists. The irony of Kosovo is that far from achieving the publicized success, air power *under performed* because of the limitations placed on it.

Joint Command and Control

The entire notion of tactical air support to land forces is perhaps becoming outdated if one thinks in integrated campaign terms. Land forces, including long-range rocket and attack helicopter assets, may be required to support air forces, so the 'supporting' and 'supported' components may change during the course of a campaign. Thus the land/air interface, where air and land operations are closely co-ordinated, needs to be found at the appropriate level, where timely decisions on targeting and air apportionment can be made. This indicates the need for joint and fully integrated command at the operational level where campaigns are planned and executed. However, although current combined and joint doctrine states that this interaction should be achieved at the joint force level (normally in theatre), recent operations suggest that in practice the interface is moving

---

58. The wise words of Richard Hallion, *Strike from the Sky*, p. 264 bear repetition: "Air interdiction history indicates that, as a rule, air interdiction works best only when it is synchronized with ground maneuver warfare. Under those circumstances, an enemy is forced to maneuver across a battlefront while exposed to simultaneous air and ground threats."

up to the higher strategic and policy areas. Thus there is creeping danger of over-centralization of command at the higher level that threatens the required decentralization of control at the lower levels.[59] However it should be clear that even with modern information technology, tactical air support should not be run from capitals. The application of air power by remote control in a 'zero casualty' war is a dangerous myth.

Training and People

Whatever the doctrine or equipment involved in the land/air interface, people continue to play a key part in ensuring successful co-operation between air and land forces. The personal example given by alliance, coalition and component commanders and their principal staff officers in working together for a common joint cause will quickly set the tone throughout the force. In this connection, there is no place for *prima donnas* and *amour propre* in the land/air relationship. The creation of a co-operative attitude, as opposed to a competitive one, by senior commanders is crucial in setting the right atmosphere and example throughout their commands. No Service can afford discord either in peacetime or in wartime; ultimately military success in major operations, campaigns and wars depends on shared knowledge, mutual understanding and trust between the various components. Such a benign state of affairs rarely comes without hard work. In short, there is no substitute for joint training at the tactical and operational levels, and for the education of the senior figures (both in and out of uniform) who are likely to be involved in the strategic guidance, planning and execution of campaigns. To think or act otherwise is surely dangerously complacent. The land/air interface needs early investment in the right sort of people. It demands a continuous process of joint professional education and training, and the ruthless exploitation of training and operational opportunities in order to refine skills. So we forget the early days of the Second World War at our peril. Already some of the 'lessons identified' emerging out of the recent conflict in Kosovo hint at past land/air lessons learned being forgotten once again. This seems to be the way of things as lessons of the Second World War were re-learned in Korea and Vietnam. But when the 'wheels come off' the next time, there may not be the time to study, re-evaluate and learn how to put them back on again. In any final analysis, the practical effectiveness of the land/air interface is a sure indicator of the state of health of inter-Service co-operation, joint training and mutual understanding. Although it is tempting to highlight the many failures of doctrine, training, organization or personality, the fact remains that building and sustaining an effective land/air interface is difficult. Frictions abound, and the circumstances in which soldiers and airmen find themselves working together change from one campaign to the next: this is a 'given'.

---

59. Stephen J McNamara, *Air Power's Gordian Knot*, p. 151-154.

CHAPTER 8

AIR POWER AND EXPEDITIONARY WARFARE
Doctor Christina Goulter

IN THE NEW STRATEGIC ENVIRONMENT, the focus for both Great Britain and the US has shifted to operations in the littoral environment. There are a number of reasons for this. Threats to national interests posed by regional instability have led to a heightened emphasis on rapid reaction forces and expeditionary warfare, by which we mean operations launched from the sea. The USA and Britain have a large variety of global interests, and for both, protection of national interests overseas plays a prominent role in national security policy. Of course, the argument for expanded expeditionary forces was also a vital means for defence establishments, especially in the US and Britain, to peg defence budgets. In the years immediately following the break up of the Soviet Union, there was a very real threat of the Services being cut to cadre levels to satisfy calls for a 'peace dividend'. However, it has been relatively easy for the Services to sell the expeditionary warfare concept because of events in the Balkans and, more recently, in East Timor and Sierra Leone, which demonstrated that naval expeditionary forces are often the best, and sometimes the only, method of dealing with crises and projecting power ashore. It has also been predicted that the most likely source of instability in the new century will be found in the developing countries, which have rapidly expanding populations concentrated along the littoral.[1]

However, there is a very real danger that politicians see expeditionary warfare as a cheap alternative to the large standing forces of the Cold War, whereas the complexity of expeditionary warfare demands serious investment if it is to succeed. History is full of examples where expeditionary operations were mounted with insufficient weight, with disastrous consequences (Gallipoli and Dieppe are classic cases). Although the US and Britain are leading practitioners of expeditionary warfare, the challenges posed to expeditionary forces are far more numerous and potentially more serious than historically. So, although the universal principles of expeditionary warfare remain good for the future, the dangers posed to friendly forces should not be under-estimated.

---

1. *Challenges to Naval Expeditionary Warfare,* Office of Naval Intelligence, Washington DC, 1997, p. 19; USMC 'Sea Dragon' unclassified presentation, RN College, Greenwich, April 1997.

There was also a tendency in the early 1990s to argue that as certain capabilities were prominent during the Cold War, these could either be dispensed with or radically cut in the new strategic environment. Anti-submarine warfare was one such capability. But, as it will be demonstrated below, ASW is just as important in expeditionary warfare as in the Cold War.[2] Some systems or capabilities which were dominant during the Cold War are destined to play an even greater role in expeditionary warfare, none more so than air power. While air power has long been a key component of expeditionary warfare, the extent to which air power is a critical element has not always been appreciated. Air power's contribution can be assessed most easily if we consider the three main phases of expeditionary warfare: transit to the littoral; fighting from the sea; and the breakout from the beach-head. The challenges to expeditionary operations are numerous in all of these phases, and even the Americans admit that future expeditionary warfare will be difficult to prosecute.[3] However, air power increases the chances of success in two principal ways: first, by reducing the vulnerability of an amphibious force (both in transit and on land), and, second, by acting as a force multiplier. Further, air power must not be defined narrowly; land-based and carrier aviation are both essential and complementary in this environment.

The first challenge to expeditionary warfare is faced when forces are transiting to the littoral. After the collapse of the Former Soviet Union, there was a tendency for the navies on both sides of the Atlantic to de-emphasise blue water dominance in favour of littoral dominance, as blue water capability was seen to be too closely associated with the Cold War. In the US, this meant not only old battleships being offered up as sacrificial lambs, but also the US Navy's ASW capability being severely cut. The airborne component of ASW suffered particularly heavy cuts, with the P-3 force being cut in half (from 24 to 13 squadrons since 1989). The folly of such a radical cut was shown first during the Gulf War when the burden of ASW work fell on the RAF because the US lacked sufficient resources and currency in ASW training, especially in littoral waters against conventional submarines. During that war, the Coalition forces had the luxury of months to work up and bring assets into theatre using sealift. That sealift was essential to Coalition victory, and had preparation time been denied or had Iraq mounted vigorous submarine or surface operations against Coalition SLOCs, then the conflict would not have been won so quickly or decisively.[4]

---

2. C J M Goulter, 'The Royal Air Force and the Future of Maritime Aviation' in A Dorman, M Lawrence Smith and M Uttley, *The Changing Face of Maritime Power*, p. 150-166.
3. USMC White Paper, 1997, *From the Sea: the Naval Service for the 21st Century*, p. 6-7.
4. C J M Goulter, Op Cit, p. 151-157.

Blue water dominance has been enjoyed by the US and Britain since the middle of the Second World War, and this dominance has been taken for granted. But complacency is dangerous. A selection of 'countries of concern' to the US and Britain now possess conventional submarines, which are difficult to detect, and relatively cheap enhancements make these a serious threat. For example, the Iranians have purchased three Russian 'Kilo' class submarines, and the Iranians have already demonstrated their willingness and capability to interfere with international SLOCs. Between 1984 and 1988, they succeeded in restricting movement through the Straits of Hormuz, and 432 US Navy and international seamen died while attempting to keep oil flowing to the West.[5] As 20 per cent of the world's oil supplies have to pass through the Straits of Hormuz, Operation Earnest Will, as it was known, was of critical importance.[6] Meanwhile, China has embarked on a modernisation programme to upgrade its submarine fleet. The Chinese have also invested in 'Kilos', and have at least two in their naval order of battle. They are also continuing with further development of the 'Song' class of diesel submarine, which first appeared in 1994, and is capable of firing a submerged-launched anti-ship cruise missile.[7] Elsewhere in the world, over twenty countries now operate conventional submarines, many of them quiet diesel-electric types produced in the West, such as the Oberon, Daphne and Type 209 classes. All of these types have been enhanced by commercial off-the-shelf (COTS) hardware and software, especially sensors and C4I systems, and the countries purchasing or developing diesel submarines are also buying acoustic and wake-homing torpedoes.[8] These purchasing trends seem likely to continue, especially among the smaller and emerging states, which cannot afford to buy nuclear submarines. It can be argued, of course, that many of these nations lack the ethos and know-how to operate credible submarine forces, but the US and Britain cannot afford to be complacent and consider these acquisitions mere status symbols.

Among the more traditional 'countries of concern' to the West, a number are also forging ahead with SSN developments, which will pose an even greater threat to blue water transit of forces because of the nuclear submarine's increased endurance. For example, it is predicted that the Chinese will possess a handful of Type 093 SSN submarines by 2005. This type is considered to be comparable in performance to the second generation Russian nuclear designs, and the Chinese Navy is expected to deploy these well outside local waters. The Chinese are intent on extending their maritime influence hundreds of miles to the east, to the so-called 'second island chain'. This is

---

5. ONI, *Worldwide Maritime Challenges,* Washington DC, 1997, p. 26. See also p. 24, 27-28.
6. ONI, *Worldwide Submarine Challenges,* Washington DC, 1997, p. 30.
7. Ibid, p. 8, 20-21, 23.
8. Ibid, p. 5.

being done under the pretext of a perceived threat from long-range land-attack cruise missiles, but it is apparent that the Chinese are thinking increasingly about out-of-area operations, including ultimate possession of Taiwan and the Spratley Islands.[9]

In spite of such threats, the US Navy's ASW funding continues to decline, from $884 million in 1999 to $556 million by 2003.[10] Recent Fleet exercises show that the US Navy is less capable in ASW than it used to be, even in its traditional area of strength (ASW against nuclear powered submarines). There is little evidence that the Americans are redressing the balance, even when it is acknowledged by the US Navy's own assessments that conventional submarines will pose a serious threat to expeditionary warfare, especially in the littoral. For these reasons, Britain needs to be prepared to provide a substantial ASW effort in any Combined operations with the Americans, not only in the littoral, where a very high standard of ASW is required because of radar 'clutter' and congested waters, but also in open ocean. Both land-based and carrier aviation can contribute to this type of ASW. The enhanced Nimrod Maritime Patrol Aircraft (MPA) provides long-range surveillance, overt and covert, and the ability to destroy submarines using a variety of weapons, including homing torpedoes or mines. Carrier aviation, meanwhile, can provide close-in protection, in concert with on-board ASW assets, including ASW helicopters.

The Nimrod MRA4 will provide long-range surveillance, overt and covert, and the ability to destroy submarines using a variety of weapons.

---

9. ONI, *Worldwide Submarine Challenges*, Washington DC, 1997, p. 18, 21, 23.
10. *Defense News*, 23 August 1999, Vol. 14, No. 33, p. 10.

While the submarine is the principal threat to expeditionary forces *en route* to the littoral, those forces may also be challenged by nations who feel that their territorial waters are being infringed. This may be faced when expeditionary forces approach SLOC choke points in narrow seas, such as the Mediterranean, Red Sea or various straits in the Far East. Developments in surveillance technology mean that it is unlikely that an expeditionary force will be able to transit to a theatre of operations totally undetected and unchallenged. The ability to conduct surveillance from space is no longer the privilege of a few high-tech nations, and the proliferation of satellite technology means that space-derived imagery is relatively cheap. The expeditionary force entering a narrow sea may well find itself contesting command of the sea against a much weaker naval force, which has the upper hand because of its advantageous geo-strategic position. This is another reason why expeditionary forces require the protection of major naval units, especially carriers. A force in transit through narrow seas will be vulnerable to hostile surface action and land-based air, and the organic air assets of a carrier offer the most immediate defence against such threats. Organic air is particularly vital if the expeditionary forces lack forward basing. Since the end of the Cold War, fewer countries are prepared to host and support large Western forces, and financial pressure has also led to the withdrawal from many overseas bases. Even the US has cut its overseas bases from 115 at the height of the Cold War, to just twenty-seven in the mid-1990s.[11]

Even when expeditionary forces reach the littoral, those SLOCs will still need protection. An expeditionary force is only as good as its supply lines. The critical importance of maintaining SLOCs was seen most graphically during World War II. For D-Day to succeed, the Allies had to win the Battle of the Atlantic. D-Day, or indeed the Combined Bomber Offensive, was never going to happen unless this battle was won, and Britain came close to defeat in the war at sea in 1941 and 1942. The turning point is generally considered to be 1943, after the confluence of a number of critical factors, including the establishment of a Joint air and naval HQ at Liverpool, an intelligence breakthrough after nine months in the dark, the application of Operational Research techniques, the provision of Air-to-Surface (ASV) radar, and adequate supplies of aircraft and suitable ordnance. These were all force multipliers without which the battle could not have been won. Before these various factors were introduced, ASW in the Atlantic was little more than a 'needle in a haystack' exercise, and submarine detection, and occasionally a submarine kill, were more the result of aircrew persistence and courage. Air power's share of the U-boats killed throughout the war was at least 43%. In other words, air power played a decisive role in the Battle of the Atlantic. It could not have won the battle by itself, but nor could the battle be won without it. While we are

---

11. ONI, *Challenges to Naval Expeditionary Warfare*, Washington DC, 1997, p. 7. See also M Vego, *Naval Strategy and Operations in Narrow Seas* (Frank Cass, London, 1999).

unlikely to see ASW on this scale in the near future, this case is a salutary reminder that ASW is a complex business, requiring constant training and constant engagement. In the latter respect, it is akin to gaining air superiority; to have let up at any point in the war, even after the middle of 1943, would have led to defeat. This is why it is so important never to degrade ASW capability. The reason Britain came close to losing the Battle of the Atlantic in 1941 and 1942 was because ASW had been allowed to languish as a capability during the inter-war years, especially in the Royal Air Force, which was focused on building up a strategic bombing capability. But ASW's neglect was also due to over-confidence in ASDIC, the forerunner of SONAR. These were both classic early examples of faith in 'silver bullet' solutions, and, in the RAF's case, the dangers of defining air power too narrowly.[12]

RAF Liberator, 1943. Air power played a decisive role in the Battle of the Atlantic.

---

12. C J M Goulter, *A Forgotten Offensive: Royal Air Force Coastal Command's Anti-Shipping Campaign, 1940-1945* (Frank Cass, London, 1995), esp. Ch. 2-3; J Terraine, *The Right of the Line* (Sceptre, London, 1988) p. 456. See also J Terraine, *Business in Great Waters: the U-boat Wars* (Mandarin, London, 1989).

D-Day exercised a profound influence on amphibious doctrine after World War II, and two main lessons were taken on board: the vital importance of force protection, and security of SLOCs. In the months leading up to D-Day, one of the prime concerns for the planners was the threat of German interference, not only to the actual invasion fleet but the supply 'funnel' between Britain's south coast and Normandy. Three principal threats were identified: air, surface and sub-surface. The D-Day planners demanded Allied air superiority, and they spoke about building a fence either side of the 'funnel' to protect the invasion fleet and resupply operations from the predations of German air power. This was a total success; no Luftwaffe aircraft were able to penetrate the funnel area at any time from 6 June onwards. Next was the fear of German destroyer and torpedo boat activity. Again, air power played a decisive role in reducing this threat to an absolute minimum. Vigorous patrol work by RAF Coastal Command prevented any destroyers from entering the Channel from their main Bay of Biscay bases, and the anticipated E-boat challenge did not materialise, as they were compelled to limit their operations to night-time, and had to retreat further and further up the enemy coastline as the Allies started to overrun their bases. Nor did the sub-surface threat come to anything, again thanks largely to the ASW work of the RAF, the Fleet Air Arm and RN units in the Channel. On D-Day itself, no submarines were able even to enter the Channel area, and there was no subsequent U-boat interference in the 'funnel'. Of equal concern to the Allies was the one- or two-man submersible craft, five types of which were in production or under development by D-Day. These were designed to deliver torpedo attacks at close quarters but fortunately for the Allies, the Small Battle Units (SBUs), as they were known, did not become operational until a month after the invasion, when some found their way into the waters off Normandy. Although current adversaries are unlikely to invest in something akin to the SBU, the point here is that a determined enemy will use whatever means at his disposal to interrupt your operations.[13]

Force protection and SLOC security were also key features of the campaigns in the Pacific during World War II, but it was in this theatre that joint operations were perfected into what the author calls a 'Pacific Trinity' (land, sea and air), where each leg was entirely dependent on the other two. In today's language, we would speak of the three elements working together to create 'synergy'.[14] The nature of the island hopping campaign demanded force protection from warships and air assets *en route* to an objective, but land forces were required to secure island bases from which land-based air

---

13. C J M Goulter, *A Forgotten Offensive*, p. 215, 224-226.
14. Maritime Warfare Centre and HQ Royal Marines, *The United Kingdom Approach to Amphibious Operations*, April 1997, p. 21.

AIR POWER AND EXPEDITIONARY WARFARE

could operate and naval forces could use as secure anchorages. From their disastrous first amphibious operation at Guadalcanal between August 1942 and January 1943, the Americans learned that securing SLOCs and air superiority were vital prerequisites for amphibious operations.[15] The landings were hurriedly planned and executed, in an attempt to pre-empt a Japanese occupation and building of an airfield. The Americans failed to secure the SLOCs to the landing area, and no account was taken of the possibility of a Japanese aerial response. The Japanese reaction was swift, and naval and air forces were despatched immediately from their main island base at Rabaul. The strong naval force destroyed an Allied screening force off Savo Island, and the mere appearance of the Japanese bombers was sufficient to compel the US carriers' withdrawal. This left the Marines without essential supply lines and denied them air cover. It quickly became apparent to both sides that victory on land was not possible unless both sea and air superiority were achieved. In the following months, a number of naval actions occurred, the most fierce of which were in November 1942, and ultimate American victory was secured in large part due to the action of Marine Corps aviation, preventing the Japanese re-supply and reinforcement operations, so that by December, the Japanese forces on the island received only essential supplies by submarine. Later in 1943, the Japanese air base at Rabaul was hit repeatedly by Allied air attack, effectively eliminating the threat of enemy land-based air in the South-West Pacific. Coming on top of the American victory at Midway in June 1942, which decimated Japanese naval aviation, Allied air superiority in the Pacific had been won. This allowed the Americans to wage air attacks directly against the Japanese home islands, either bombing raids or blockading operations mounted from the Marianas. To reinforce the point about the inter-relatedness of land, sea and air, the Marianas had been secured by amphibious assault, covered by air, and it is not an exaggeration to say that without these islands the Americans could not have delivered the weight of aerial attack on Japan necessary for final victory. In the planning for an invasion of Japan, the Marianas were also going to be used as the major staging point for American forces.

What the Allies enjoyed in both the European and Pacific theatres by 1944 was air superiority, and this came to be considered the chief prerequisite for amphibious operations. In post-war amphibious doctrine, air superiority has always headed the list of the essential ingredients, especially in the assault phase of an operation.[16]

---

15. *The Oxford Companion to World War II*, I C B Dear and M R D Foot, eds, (Oxford University Press, 1995) p. 511-515.
16. *The United Kingdom Approach to Amphibious Operations*, p. 20.

AIR POWER AND EXPEDITIONARY WARFARE

This has been reaffirmed through the experience of amphibious forces since 1945, none more so than during the Falklands War in 1982.[17] Britain's lack of air superiority as the campaign opened had a major bearing on the conduct of the war. The loss of HMS *Sheffield* on 4 May to an Exocet launched from an Argentine Super Entendard showed that the British task force was deficient in both early warning radar and air defence. The threat of land-based air compelled the task force to position itself well east of the Total Exclusion Zone, thus limiting its ability to intercept Argentine vessels or aircraft *en route* to the Falklands. Land-based air again proved its utility when Argentine aircraft attacked the assault force in San Carlos on 22 May (D+1). The attacks came in a succession of waves, approaching from the east, and not the anticipated west, as the aircraft had been fitted with extra fuel tanks to enable them to make the longer journey. The focus first of their attention was the combat vessels, rather than the troops carriers, which were all concentrated in a small area. Five RN ships were hit, and HMS *Ardent* sank the next day. On 23 May, the Argentine air assault recommenced. In order to avoid the anticipated attacks by Exocets, smaller vessels of the Task Force moved closer in shore, but were hit by the slower Pucaras. Skyhawks, using 1,000 lb bombs, succeeded in sinking HMS *Antelope*. San Carlos Water quickly became known as 'Bomb Alley', and, at the end of D+2, all combat vessels and transports were ordered to leave the San Carlos area and remain clear during daylight hours. This slowed down the build up of the bridgehead. Both inside and outside the Sound, the attrition continued. Heavy air attacks occurred again on 25 May, sinking HMS *Coventry* and the *Atlantic Conveyor*, which was carrying key equipment (including three Chinook helicopters) and tons of supplies. In all, Britain lost five ships and twelve others were seriously damaged. However, the Argentines did not have everything their way, and, gradually, the air superiority pendulum swung in Britain's favour. By D+3 (24 May), the Argentines were starting to lose significant numbers of aircraft. On that day, they admitted to losing fifteen aircraft (but Britain claimed twenty-two, mainly to Sea Harrier action). Contrary to general expectation, the slower Sea Harriers were beating the faster Argentine Mirages in dogfights, in large part because the Harriers were more manoeuvrable and were equipped with Sidewinder missiles. But the Harriers' success can also be explained by the fact that the Mirages were compelled to fly at sub-sonic speeds in order to conserve fuel. By 26 May, the Argentine air offensive had lost momentum, having lost some of their best pilots. They admitted to losing fifty-five pilots during the campaign, although British claims put the number of Argentine aircraft shot down at more than 100.

---

17. See E O'Balance, 'The Falklands, 1982' in M Bartlett, ed, *Assault From the Sea: Essays on the History of Amphibious Warfare* (Naval Institute Press, Annapolis, 1983) p. 429-436; M Clapp and E Southby-Tailyour, *Amphibious Assault Falklands* (Orion, London, 1996), esp. Ch. 3-4.

AIR POWER AND EXPEDITIONARY WARFARE

'Bomb Alley'. Britain's lack of air superiority over the Falkland Islands threatened the build-up of the bridgehead at San Carlos.

The Falklands illustrated a number of important points about air operations in the littoral environment. It demonstrated just how important air superiority is, especially when forces afloat are concentrated in narrow waters. It demonstrated the utility of land-based air, which, in this case, compelled major naval units to stand off and smaller vessels to withdraw from inshore during daylight, thereby degrading the quick build up of a bridgehead. On the British side, land-based air, operating at the longest operational range ever attempted, played a critical air denial role by bombing Port Stanley airfield. But the war was also a clear demonstration of the utility of carrier-based aviation, as this succeeded ultimately in securing localised air superiority for Britain.

In the future, neither Britain nor the US can presume overwhelming superiority in the air, and the air threat in the littoral will continue to be a major problem. All of the principal countries of concern have aircraft technologies comparable to NATO specifications, or, if they do not as yet, are certainly embarking on vast modernisation programmes. For example, the Chinese air force was long dismissed as a collection of antique aircraft, but the PLAAF is modernising, with recent procurement of Su-27s and an agreement with Russia for licensed production of a Chinese Su-27 variant.[18] China has its own indigenous aircraft programmes developing at least six tactical aircraft at a time when most nations are finding it difficult to finance a single programme, and among

---

18. ONI, *Worldwide Challenges to Naval Strike Warfare*, p. 14-15, 18-19, 26-27.

the latest projects is an advanced fighter known as the XXJ, expected to come into service in 2015. This is likely to be a multi-role fighter with a reduced radar signature. Elsewhere, had events in East Timor escalated, then expeditionary forces would have faced F16s and an assortment of near competitor technologies. But even if an adversary cannot be classed as a strict peer, older technologies in determined hands can still inflict serious damage or, as a minimum, unwelcome friction. A good example of this was seen during the Kosovo campaign, where, although the Serbs lost 80% of their fighter force, they proved themselves determined and brave. Fighter pilots were prepared to fly at night with little or no ground control. Further, elements of their air defence system were based on 1950s-1960s technology, but still managed to see supposedly stealthy aircraft.

Whether or not an adversary possesses the latest technology, he will have one major advantage over an expeditionary force, especially if operations are being conducted offshore from a large land mass: that is the ability of land-based air to deliver a greater weight of attack, usually combined with a much greater rate of sortie generation. This will pose a major problem for an expeditionary force before it gets a foot ashore. While Britain's ASUW capability has been degraded by the disbandment of the two specialised maritime strike Tornado squadrons, many other nations, including some potential adversaries, continue to have dedicated anti-shipping squadrons. India, Russia and China are such countries, although the trend in all of these will probably be to acquire fighters with multi-role capabilities.[19]

Britain's decision to rely heavily on the stand-off ASUW weaponry in Maritime Patrol Aircraft may prove to be a serious mistake. In the highly congested waters of the littoral, occupied by allies, adversaries and neutrals, identification of vessels will be extremely difficult. Unless areas in the littoral are designated 'sink at sight', correct identification of friend and foe is essential, especially in a world where restrictive ROEs are the norm. In past wars, this has been less of an issue for Britain. In World War II, for example, Britain designated the area between Spain and the top of Norway as a 'sink at sight' zone, and the RAF's anti-shipping operations were, therefore, largely unrestricted.[20] However, in the current political environment, advocates of stand-off weapons are wrong to suggest that this is the only type of weapon needed. Political sensitivities demand attention to detail, and in the highly mobile littoral environment, 'Mark I eyeball' identification of targets is essential. This is particularly so when a number of 'countries of concern' have either developed or purchased fast attack craft. For example, the Chinese have sold their Houdong PTG fast attack craft to Iran.[21] Against such targets, weaving among friendly vessels, stand-off weapons are often worse

---

19. ONI, *Worldwide Challenges to Naval Strike Warfare*, p. 2, 4, 14-16, 18-19; ONI, *Challenges to Naval Expeditionary Warfare*, p. 22.
20. C J M Goulter, *A Forgotten Offensive*, esp. Ch. 4.
21. ONI, *Challenges to Naval Expeditionary Warfare*, p. 13.

than useless. Further, the ease with which fast attack craft are concealed and rapidly deployed demands a highly responsive ASUW capability. Many countries, including Russia, China, North Korea and Yugoslavia, have extensive underground naval facilities, excavated deep inside coastal rock formations.[22]

Expeditionary forces also need to be concerned about the quality and quantity of anti-ship cruise missiles now available around the world. Over seventy-five countries possess over 90 different types of anti-ship cruise missiles, and the proliferation continues, as cruise missiles are not considered strategic weapons and are, therefore, not covered by any arms limitation agreements. Competition for sales is particularly intense in the Middle East and Asian markets. China has been actively marketing C801 and C802 anti-ship missiles, and the latter were mounted on the Hudong fast attack craft sold to Iran. The Iraqi air force is known to possess the older C601 variant. Meanwhile, French exports of Exocet MM40s have guaranteed worldwide distribution, and the Italians, among others, have developed stealthy sub-sonic missiles such as the TESEO-3, which are extremely difficult to detect.[23]

Then there is the threat posed by the adversary's land-based weapon systems. Personnel may be threatened by the laser weapons starting to appear on the world market. The Chinese have offered for sale their ZM87 laser weapon, which can cause eye injuries at ranges up to 3 km and dazzle blindness to personnel up to 10 km. An expeditionary force's firepower is likely to be challenged by opposing weapons which have greater range, accuracy and lethality. The use of precision guided munitions (PGMs) is becoming widespread, with the semi-active laser (SAL) being the most common (such as the Russian Krasnopol 155 mm artillery round), and infra-red (IR), millimetre wave (MMW) and course corrected (CC) munitions are being developed. However, most troubling for expeditionary forces is the fact that much of the coastal artillery and other defensive systems currently available are mobile, and, therefore, less vulnerable to attack. The Gulf War demonstrated the frustrations of trying to find and target mobile Scud launchers, and, in the later stages of the air campaign, at least one third of the Coalition's air sorties were devoted to the Scud hunt.[24]

Most of the Theatre Ballistic Missiles (TBMs) currently available are Scuds or Scud derivatives, and have maximum ranges of up to 600kms. However, the Chinese, in particular, continue to develop TBMs, using data obtained from their exercise firings around Taiwan in March 1996. It is predicted that, in the future, TBMs will have separating payloads, containing sub-munitions and possibly chemical, biological or

---

22. ONI, *Worldwide Challenges to Naval Strike Warfare*, p. 24.
23. Ibid, p. 12-13.
24. Ibid, p. 14-15; R Hallion, *Storm Over Iraq: Air Power and the Gulf War* (Airlife, 1992) p. 179, 180-185.

nuclear warheads. Even the threat of TBM use may be sufficient to halt an expeditionary force before it lands or advances inland.[25]

In facing such a variety of lethal challenges even before a lodgement ashore is secured, an expeditionary force must consider very carefully how it can reduce its vulnerability. We have concentrated heavily on the air power contribution, but there are other elements which work synergistically with air power, acting as force multipliers or enablers. One of the most important is deception. One of the finest examples of strategic deception performed in support of an expeditionary force was Operation Fortitude, which aimed at persuading Hitler and the German General Staff that the Normandy landings in June 1944 were merely a feint to cover the real attack, further north, in the Pas de Calais. The deception plan had a number of key elements, chief of which was convincing the Germans of the existence of a First US Army Group, under Patton. This was successfully achieved by spoof signals' transmissions, dummy invasion craft in eastern ports, careful manipulation of double agents, and a diversionary air operation. The air contribution had two main facets. First, bombing of coastal batteries was concentrated in the area around Calais, so that for every ton of bombs dropped on coastal batteries west of Le Havre, two tons were dropped north of it. Meanwhile, the largest proportion of the 2nd Tactical Air Force was concentrated in Kent, which gave the Germans the impression that the shorter-range aircraft of this force were being placed as close as possible to the operational area, ie just opposite Calais. The whole Operation Fortitude plan was a total success; the Germans kept the Fifteenth Army in the Pas de Calais until well after D-Day, so that the invasion force had one and not two Armies opposing the landing. Without this relief, the breakout from the beaches would have been immeasurably more difficult, if not impossible. Thus, as we have demonstrated, air power played a critical role not only in securing SLOCs for D-Day, providing protection *en route* to the littoral, but also in misleading the enemy and adding to the element of surprise.[26]

The D-Day deception plan was part of a general operation to shape the littoral battlespace. Other shaping operations occurred in the months leading up to the invasion, and, again, air power played a vital role. A prime concern for the planners was the extent to which the Germans could reinforce quickly the Normandy area. Therefore, from March, Bomber Command and the US Eighth Air Force attacked the French rail network for a radius of 150 miles from the Normandy beaches. The Transportation Plan, as it was known, succeeded in isolating the battlefield by causing widespread paralysis in the French rail system, compelling the Germans to rely increasingly on already congested

---

25. ONI, *Challenges to Naval Expeditionary Warfare*, p. 16-17.
26. J Terraine, *Right of the Line*, p. 625; R Hesketh, *Fortitude: The D-Day Deception Campaign* (St Ermin's Press, 1999) p. 121; M Howard, *Strategic Deception in the Second World War* (Norton, London, 1995) Ch. 6. See also Joint Doctrine Pamphlet 2/98, *Deception*.

roads. In the days immediately prior to the invasion, bombers and fighter-bombers were also directed against coastal radar stations and gun batteries the length of the Atlantic Wall. Not all of these were successfully hit, some remaining almost completely intact (especially in the American sector at Omaha beach, and was a major factor in the much higher casualty rate in this sector compared with the other beaches).[27]

The importance of getting battlefield preparation absolutely right was also demonstrated in the Pacific at the same time. In the battle for Saipan, in particular, the failure of the pre-landing bombardment to soften up the opposition led to some 4,000 Marine casualties within the space of forty-eight hours. However, the capture of Tinian, three miles away, a month later was made possible by an intensive air and naval bombardment, which allowed the Marines to subdue the island within twelve days. The operation to take Tinian was regarded by the US Marine Corps as the finest example of amphibious warfare to date.[28]

These historical examples show the versatility of air power's contribution to shaping operations, and, in the modern context, air power will be called upon to perform similar work. Historical examples also help us in our understanding of air power's role once an expeditionary force is ashore, in the third phase of an expeditionary operation. Again, using the Normandy case, air power played an essential role in the consolidation and breakout from the landing area. Montgomery had planned for the British contingent to punch at least forty miles inland on the first day, securing a line between Caen, Falaise, Argentan and Granville. However, the advance soon stalled because of the fierce resistance from the German defenders, and Montgomery's plan began to unravel. To maintain a high operational tempo, he needed air support, but to have that air support, he needed to secure enough ground on day one to permit the building of airfields. When he failed to push far enough inland, tactical air support had to fly all the way from bases in southern England, thereby preventing the immediacy of response required of tactical air. Deteriorating weather in the weeks following D-Day also meant that the British and American tactical air forces could not provide all the desired support. Montgomery's position was exacerbated by the loss of a substantial amount of artillery and other equipment when storms hit the Channel during the second week, especially on 19 June. This proved crippling when Montgomery attempted to reduce Caen, which remained in German hands until well into July. This denied the Allies access to the plain to the south, ideal both for armoured warfare and for the construction of airfields. Montgomery was compelled to call in heavy bomber support, acting as flying artillery. What the subsequent bombing operations around Caen demonstrated was that bombing can have an important morale effect on enemy troops, but that bombing needs to be performed

---

27. J Terraine, *Right of the Line*, p. 625.
28. *Oxford Companion to World War II*, p. 718, 974-975, 1109.

precisely in this role if it is to be of use. In this case, bombing stopped short of taking out German defences just outside Caen, and a British tank advance was decimated on 18 July. The solution was to provide tactical air support, to mop up those parts of enemy defence which had not been knocked out, but this was lacking on the day because of a breakdown in communications between the British tank crews and tactical air assets in the area. The breakdown in communications was caused by the loss of the single communications car provided.[29]

The Normandy case illustrated, among other things, the close relationship between land operations and the provision of airfields, and how important quick provision of airfields is to maintaining a high operational tempo. To get a footprint ashore is essential if air power is to offer an effective weight of delivery in support of follow-on operations. This is critical when establishing a traditional beach-head is not possible for reasons of terrain or high threat. In the current environment, and that predicted for the immediate future, the challenges to manoeuvre dominance are many and varied. Unlike the Cold War period, when NATO forces had the luxury of training in a relatively narrow selection of geographical areas, the modern expeditionary force must now contemplate operating in every conceivable terrain, from northern Europe, southern Europe, Africa, the Far East to Oceania. The expanded training burden that this fact places on expeditionary forces today is just one of the many reasons politicians are wrong to view this capability as a much cheaper option than Cold War forces. It is just one of the many reasons why expeditionary warfare requires serious investment.

Regardless of which part of the world an expeditionary force goes to, it will find that an adversary will have identified and obstructed the best landing beaches. Next, an adversary will try to deny an expeditionary force its air support. Control of the air will be challenged by both shipborne and land-based Surface-to-Air Missiles (SAMs), including Stinger man-portable varieties. Many potential adversaries will possess integrated air defence systems, and many of the radar, optical and thermal target detection and tracking sensors currently available are affordable, even to developing countries. The latest generation French Crotale is widely employed as it can be retrofitted into older SAM systems. It can be housed in a single vehicle and, therefore, can be easily concealed. China is one of the countries that both uses and sells versions of the Crotale system. Computer enhancements mean that many integrated air defence systems among developing countries have comparable performance to those in the West, and so the US and Britain can no longer presume that their forces possess massive technological superiority.[30]

---

29. J Terraine, *Right of the Line*, p. 616f; I Gooderson, *Air Power at the Battlefront: Allied Close Air Support in Europe, 1943-45* (Frank Cass, London, 1998) p. 144-145; V Orange, *Coningham* (Methuen, London, 1990) p. 198-199.
30. ONI, *Worldwide Challenges to Naval Strike Warfare*, p. 17.

There is a very real need for serious investment in Suppression of Enemy Air Defence (SEAD) assets, especially in the current political climate. Losses to our own forces are becoming less and less acceptable to a public who expects perfect wars. If Britain has the US as an expeditionary partner, then the US will provide the necessary SEAD assets. However, if Britain has to operate alone or in tandem with allies other than the US, force protection becomes a serious question. Every 'strike package' launched in the Kosovo campaign, for example, required SEAD assets, provided largely by the US. This campaign highlighted the growing complexity of eliminating surface-to-air threats as the enemy air defences become more capable, and this capability is sobering. SAM sites are becoming less reliant on active tracking, and now make use of passive optical technology. So, this is compelling the US to invest in detection systems which do not rely on emissions to pin-point sites. Because of the high cost of SEAD technology, Britain may have to be content with her dependence on the US.

Even in the field of information dominance, the US and Britain's lead has been diminished as the proliferation of space users continues and satellite imagery is available commercially. Current NATO standard communications are vulnerable to foreign signals intelligence operations, and are the targets of jamming and information warfare. The US and Britain still enjoy a substantial lead in computer technology over most other nations, but this also makes them more vulnerable in many areas because of a dependence on computer systems. This is particularly so for the US, whose military, governmental and commercial interests would be seriously threatened by a concerted information warfare campaign by an enemy. The Pentagon has admitted that computer hackers gained entry to sensitive defence material at the time of the Kosovo conflict. But, most seriously for both the US and Britain, the increasing dependence on computers for ground control and data distribution means vulnerability to cyber war. Unlike most military threats, where there is usually time to prepare for an attack, countering computer assaults requires instantaneous responses. For this reason, the US Defence Department has just established a Joint Task Force for Computer Defence. In Britain, similar counter-measures are being developed, hastened by reports early in 1999 that hackers had hijacked a British military communications satellite.[31]

The dangers of over-dependence on electronic communications and methods of obtaining intelligence have been amply demonstrated a number of times within the last twenty years. One such case was the expeditionary operation mounted by the US against Grenada in 1983. The invasion was triggered by the Grenadan Peoples' Revolutionary Army (PRA) coup against the established government, and the US feared the spread of Cuban backed revolutions in the Caribbean. The Americans were overly reliant on

---

31. *Defense News*, 9 August 1999, Vol. 14, No. 31, p. 6, 14-16. See also ONI, *Challenges to Naval Expeditionary Warfare*, p. 25; USMC, *From the Sea*, p. 9.

satellite imagery for their intelligence on the PRA and supporting militia groups, which gave only a partial and out-of-date picture. Uncertainty about the size, location and intentions of opposing forces meant that the US was compelled to apply a sledgehammer rather than a rapier, and this was seen most graphically in the way air power was used. Heavy air bombardments against suspected militia sites were used in a number of instances where an infantry unit could have achieved the objective with little or no cost to itself, and civilian casualties would have been avoided.[32]

Timely, all-source intelligence, particularly humint, is of even greater importance to the success of expeditionary operations when forces venture into the urban environment. Out-of-date intelligence can have major political ramifications, especially when the media spotlight is present, as the bombing of the Chinese Embassy during the recent Kosovo conflict demonstrated. The Urban Warrior concept is key to the US Marine Corps vision of expeditionary warfare, but is less of a feature for Britain, as the size of her forces historically has precluded urban engagement. Nevertheless, urban warfare is likely to be an increasing feature of operations in the future, given the nature of Peace Support Operations (PSOs) and similar interventions. The urban environment is a high threat environment, in which targets and weapons systems are easily concealed. Leaving aside the sophisticated integrated air defence systems which have been used by the West's foes within the last decade, even unsophisticated enemies can wreak havoc against NATO quality forces with man-portable SAMs and small arms fire, as the Americans found to their cost in Somalia. For this reason, expeditionary forces entering the urban environment may have to make increasing use of UAVs and, if data links are sufficiently secure, UCAVs. Having said this, there are dangers in taking the man out of the cockpit completely in limited wars or intervention scenarios, as the political constraints often demand 'on the scene' last minute judgements. The resolution of photographs taken by UAVs during the Kosovo conflict was often poor, because the UAVs were compelled to fly above 8,000 feet to avoid the worst of the ground-based anti-aircraft fire, and clear identification of targets was not always possible.[33]

So, in the face of these multiple threats and varied challenges, the US and Britain can meet most calls on their expeditionary forces, but, as even the US admits, only barely so.[34] The more lethal battlespace will place a greater premium on C4ISR, precision, stealth, mobility and high operational tempo, and the US and Britain must make optimal use of those assets or capabilities in which they have a comparative advantage. Currently, the US and Britain together have a comparative advantage in C4ISR, and this assists dominant manoeuvre across the full range of operations. Joint forces can be

---

32. Joint Chiefs of Staff, *Joint Military Operations Historical Collection* (Washington DC, July 1997) Ch. III, Operation *Urgent Fury*.
33. Kosovo Conference, Joint Services Command and Staff College, January 2000.
34. Chairman of the Joint Chiefs of Staff paper, *Joint Vision 2010*, p. 14, 20-27.

synchronised from dispersed locations, and this connectivity leads to a higher operational tempo, forcing the adversary always to be reactive. However, in spite of the information superiority possessed by the two leading NATO members, this cannot be taken for granted. Both the US and Britain have yet to achieve a fully integrated battlefield picture capability, especially in relation to missile threats. For expeditionary forces to be secure and free to manoeuvre, there needs to be a Joint Integrated Air Picture (IAP), and much more work needs to be done in integrating the multiple Service sensors and processing systems.

In expeditionary warfare of the future, Britain and the US, as the most likely alliance partners, will also need to address the problem of alliance targeting. The Kosovo campaign underlined the fact that NATO was incapable of doing most targeting on an alliance basis. There were delays in the decision-making cycle when Coalition members referred back to their respective governments for approval on specific targets. In expeditionary warfare, timely target clearance is essential for maintaining a high operational tempo, and a high operational tempo is critical in the consolidation phase of an expeditionary operation. Britain also found that its closest ally was launching long-range attacks from Continental USA without consultation with Britain. On a number of occasions, British aircrews would be tasked to hit a specific target, only to find on arrival over the target that it had already been visited by USAF aircraft. Understandably, the British crews felt incensed that they had been put in harm's way unnecessarily. This is reminiscent of the situation in World War II where the Combined Bomber Offensive was combined only in name, because the RAF and the USAAF undertook very little combined planning and there was very little sharing of target intelligence, especially early on.[35]

Targeting for effect demands not only good intelligence but also correct feedback on operational performance. As events in Kosovo showed, NATO analysts seriously underestimated Serbian resolve and resourcefulness, and were not prepared for the scale of deception. Claims for success against Serbian armour, in particular, were inflated as a result of faulty Battle Damage Assessment (BDA).[36]

The US and Britain currently enjoy a comparative advantage in precision weapons, and their utility is now a familiar argument (providing greater assurance of delivering the desired effect, lessening the risk to one's own forces, and minimising collateral damage). Suffice it to say that they are an ideal weapon in a high threat environment where repeated sorties against a target would be too dangerous for expeditionary aircraft. However, precision must not be regarded as a 'silver bullet' solution to all operational challenges. In many respects, the Gulf War did NATO partners few favours, because the

---

35. Kosovo Conference, January 2000; C Webster and N Frankland, *The Strategic Air Offensive Against Germany, 1939-1945* (HMSO, London, 1961) p. 302-303.
36. Kosovo Conference, January 2000.

expectation afterwards was that all conflicts could now be waged relatively cheaply by using precision weapons. Again, as Kosovo showed, targeting for effect demands that what you hit precisely must be important to the adversary. A trap that many commentators, especially Americans, fell into after the Gulf War was to think that because precision is achievable, any precision attack is furthering the national objectives in a conflict. Further, because current air-delivered precision technology is heavily weather-dependent, there are operational limitations, especially when there are fears over collateral damage. But even when technological advances permit all-weather precision, it would be wrong to dispense with 'dumb' bombs entirely. It makes little sense to attack some military objectives with expensive PGMs when unguided munitions are more than sufficient. In Kosovo, Serbian tanks were hit with PGMs almost exclusively, which proved a very expensive way of doing business. A10s would have been just as effective, if not more so, in this role. Also, there may be scenarios where a psychological effect on the enemy is demanded, and a concentrated massed munitions attack may be called for. The use of B52s against Republican Guard positions during the Gulf War is one such example.[37]

Stealth is another technology in which the US places great faith, and has a definite place. F117s contributed less than 10% of the total sorties in the Gulf War, in high threat environments such as Baghdad, without loss.[38] But, again, this led to the public's perception that stealth aircraft are both entirely invisible and invincible, which the loss of an F117 in the Kosovo campaign should have dispelled. A determined enemy will negate the effects of stealth by working out the stealth aircraft's flight corridors and then apply concentrated AAA.

However, the benefits of using long range land-based aircraft such as the B2, or air-to-air refuelled (AAR) aircraft, should not be underestimated. Such aircraft offer an immediacy of response and weight of delivery which may be required if forward basing is problematic, or before other land-based aircraft can come into theatre to provide effective bombloads. The finest example of this in expeditionary warfare was in the Falklands Conflict in 1982, when the Vulcan was used to bomb the airfield at Port Stanley. These raids were the longest point-to-point bombing attacks to date, and although the Port Stanley airfield was not put out of commission entirely, the psychological impact of the raids on the Argentines was considerable. They demonstrated that the RAF had the range and the resolve to mount operations against mainland Argentina if it chose to do so. The Argentines responded by pulling back their Mirage squadron and redeployed it to cover potential targets on the mainland. Thereafter, the Royal Navy's Sea Harriers enjoyed air superiority, or at least reasonable air freedom, over the Falklands.[39]

---

37. R Hallion, *Storm Over Iraq: Air Power and the Gulf War* (Airlife, 1992) p. 154; Kosovo Conference.
38. Ibid, p. 248-250; Kosovo Conference.
39. E O'Balance, 'The Falklands, 1982' in M Bartlett, ed, *Assault From the Sea: Essays on the History of Amphibious Warfare* (Naval Institute Press, Annapolis, 1983).

There may also be overfly restrictions which prevent other land-based aircraft from participating in an operation. The US faced such a problem during Operation El Dorado Canyon in 1986, and F111s based in Britain were compelled to 'dog-leg' around France, which denied overfly passage in order to bomb Gaddafi's HQ and other installations in Libya.

The speed of response and range of land-based air also allow for the quick insertion of troops and equipment, either by parachute or onto temporary airfields or land strips. Any nation engaging in expeditionary operations requires a substantial airlift capability, and Britain's recent prevarication over the leasing of four C17s from the US seemed to underline the government's lack of understanding of the type of investment needed to perform this type of warfare.[40] Follow-on operations in the littoral cannot be supported entirely by sealift, and the importance of timely air resupply has been demonstrated in historical examples too numerous to list here, but a few examples will suffice: resupply of Wingate's Chindits and the British Army in Burma during World War II; air resupply of Allied forces in China over the Himilayas 'hump' from India; and air resupply of various firebases during both the French Indochina war and Vietnam, especially Na San in 1952-53 and Khe Sanh in 1968. Airlift is essential in low intensity conflicts and PSO-style operations, where humanitarian aid often demands quick supply of isolated areas. In short, this capability is so key it should be non-negotiable.

Airlift is just one of the areas where there have been questions over Britain's capability and ability to contribute to a Joint and Combined expeditionary operation. As to what Britain can contribute or add to a Combined venture is a particularly fair question, especially in relation to what is now known as Joint Force Harrier (JFH), formerly Joint Force 2000.

---

40. *Defense News*, 16 August 1999, p. 3, 20.

AIR POWER AND EXPEDITIONARY WARFARE

Joint Force Harrier.

The 1998 Strategic Defence Review identified the need for a rapidly deployable offensive air capability to meet the demands of expeditionary warfare. As originally conceived, JF2000 was to integrate the Royal Navy's FA2 Sea Harrier and the RAF's GR7 Harrier forces. The initiative aimed to build on the success achieved by the RAF and the Royal Navy in previous joint operations, such as the Gulf crisis of 1997-98, when HMS *Invincible* and HMS *Illustrious* embarked joint air groups, using the FA2s for Air Defence of the Task Group, and GR7s for offensive air support against ground targets. This represents a revolutionary concept. Although there were voices in the wilderness in the past proposing joint RAF/RN enterprises such as this, the disputes over ownership of land- and carrier-based air ran too deep up to the end of the Cold War for anything to be done. The RAF had an ingrained distrust of the Navy, dating back to the First World War, when the Navy made its first bid to control shore-based maritime air assets, and at least four other serious attempts after that meant that the RAF's relationship with the Navy was dominated by the ownership issue. As a result, maritime aviation stagnated in the inter-war period, succeeded in the Second World War only because victory depended upon it, and was then allowed to languish again, even when the Cold War demanded a certain level of investment in ASW.[41]

---

41. Discussion with former Team Leader, JF 2000 Study Team, Jan 1999; 'Joint Harrier Force', *Air Forces*, May 2000, p. 4.

Since the JF2000 decision was announced, a number of organisational advances have been made. JFH now comes under the aegis of the reconfigured Strike Command, under the command of an RN 2-Star and an RAF Air Commodore, and the groundwork is being done for the eventual location of JFH at RAF Cottesmore from 2003. However, beyond this, there appears to have been very little wider discussion of how exactly JFH will be utilised in modern conflicts, and where it fits in a Combined expeditionary effort. In view of the many and varied threats and challenges to expeditionary warfare discussed above, there is a very real question as to JFH's effectiveness across the full spectrum of conflict. The JFH concept has considerable strengths, but also significant weaknesses, which suggest that it may not be suited to high intensity conflicts, unless part of a Combined Task Force with the Americans.

The obvious strengths of the JFH concept are very appealing. The embarked aircraft offer the usual air power characteristics of speed of response, ubiquity and flexibility etc, but these characteristics are enhanced by the mobility and flexibility provided by floating platforms. As discussed above, host nation support, over-fly permission and terrain suitable for land basing cannot always be guaranteed, and so the aircraft carrier offers a self-contained airfield. In theatre, the carrier can choose to engage the littoral closely or at distance, depending on the operational requirements or threat posed, and can loiter for months. Therefore, JFH will be able to exploit sea access to almost all littoral areas.

However, these considerable strengths must be balanced against a selection of weaknesses which affect the ability of such a force to project power ashore, especially given the weight and nature of the current equipment. The FA2 has a loiter capability of a mere 90 minutes and a radius of action of only about 100 nm in a Defensive Counter-Air (DCA) role, and a similar radius in an anti-shipping role.[42] Meanwhile, the GR7 cannot launch with an optimum bombload (more than one Laser Guided Bomb). The GR7 has no 'stealth' capability, and so cannot be used during a first night's operations in a high threat environment, nor can British carriers mount SEAD or EW operations, because of their limited fixed-wing carrying capacity. For the same reason, any air-to-air refuelling of the Harriers will have to be done by bringing tanking assets from outside. In short, JFH's aircraft will be extremely vulnerable in the high intensity environment.

Some of these weaknesses could be overcome if the Harrier force can deploy rapidly onto land bases, especially if sufficient logistics support can be brought into theatre. However, land basing itself has drawbacks. To enable an airfield to generate and recover air missions, a number of factors need to be considered. First is operations support, which includes force protection and C2 facilities. Second is logistics, including fuel and

---

42. *Jane's Defence Weekly 1997-98*, p. 507. See also N Meadows, 'To Sea or Not To Sea: That is the Question', *Air Power Review*, Vol 3 No 1, p. 82 - 106.

storage. Not least is administration, including the management of personnel, equipment and accommodation. Temporary land bases are vulnerable to determined attack by adversaries, particularly using asymmetric forms of attack. In short, JFH will require a support infrastructure of considerable size, which some may argue outweighs the advantages which a force of that size can bring to bear.

In its current form, JFH is most suited to peace support or peacekeeping operations, in which threats to the force are less than in a high intensity conflict. However, the Future Aircraft Carrier (FAC) and the Future Carrier-Borne Aircraft (FCBA) may permit a greater contribution to high intensity conflict. As the Americans found in Vietnam, only the larger carriers were capable of providing the type of force protection and sortie generation required in higher intensity warfare.[43] But, as both the FAC and the FCBA are not expected to be in service until at least 2012, the vulnerability of Britain's carriers will be a major constraint on operations.

The Future Aircraft Carrier is not expected to be in service until at least 2012.

---

43. D Wragg, *Carrier Combat* (Sutton Publishing, 1997) p. 243-247.

AIR POWER AND EXPEDITIONARY WARFARE

One consolation is that, by this time, the RAF and RN teams should be working together seamlessly. Team building and mutual understanding are not built up overnight. As any Joint enterprises in the past have shown, mere co-location of Service components is never enough for effective Jointery. The relationship between a ship and its squadrons has to be measured in years, rather than months. The fact that FA2s and GR7s worked well during Operation Bolton in early 1998 was due to an exceptional set of circumstances. HMS *Illustrious* expended a great deal of effort to accommodate and acclimatise the GR7 crews, but this was made possible only because the ship was already fully worked up, and there was sufficient time before entry into the Theatre of operations.[44] The ship was entirely dedicated to the GR7 work up, and was not involved in any other tasking or training. Such a focus can rarely be relied upon, especially if rapid deployment is demanded. An important factor was the near-perfect weather during the work up period, which allowed intensive training of the GR7 crews. As with any Jointery, regular training together will enable JFH to operate effectively when it is called upon.

With the passing of the battleship, the carrier remains an important way of exercising influence and projecting power. As an instrument of diplomacy, it is the most visible form of sea power and is, therefore, likely to remain in the inventories of the US and British navies for some time. Future carriers will doubtless be very capable, providing the air defence bubble over whatever littoral areas are chosen in expeditionary operations. But certainly for the foreseeable future, they cannot be regarded as a substitute for land-based air. The limited range and payload of shipborne aircraft means that land-based air will always have a role in littoral warfare. So, the two forms of aviation should be viewed as complementary, and certainly not competing assets in the nation's arsenal.

One advantage that Britain has over potential adversaries is that she, along with the US, is a world leader in Joint Operations Doctrine. Britain has had a codified Allied Joint Operations Doctrine since 1994, and it can be argued that Britain has been well practised in Joint operations since the middle of the Second World War.[45] As far as air power's contribution to expeditionary warfare is concerned, Britain has worked hard to develop a concept of Joint Air Operations and Airspace Control. The most important element of this is the Joint Force Air Component Commander (JFACC), who ensures a unity of air effort to meet all the air requirements within a given operation. By being responsible for the planning, co-ordination and tasking of air missions, the JFACC not only ensures that there

---

44. Joint Force 2000 Implementation Team Statement (unclass), Oct 1999; discussion with former JF2000 Team Leader, Jan 1999.
45. Allied Joint Publication 1 (AJP-1), *Allied Joint Operations Doctrine*, 1994.

is the most efficient use of a nation's or an alliance's air assets, but also that there is a seamless air contribution to an entire operation. This seamlessness is vitally important in the expeditionary context because this allows high operational tempo, and high operational tempo is one of the key factors enabling a smaller expeditionary force to succeed against a larger adversary by keeping him off balance. Thus, it can be said that air power, especially in the littoral context, is a force multiplier, along with intelligence and deception.

In an unstable world, expeditionary forces are likely to be called upon increasingly to deploy rapidly either to prevent the escalation of a crisis or to act as the spearhead for follow-on forces. As it has been demonstrated, expeditionary warfare is an immensely complex business, requiring high levels of investment and training if forces are to be in a position to deploy rapidly with effect. Air power is just one element of an expeditionary operation, but, as we have seen above, because air power plays a vital role in all three phases of expeditionary warfare (transit to the littoral, fighting from the sea, and breakout), any nation that practices expeditionary warfare cannot afford to cut specific capabilities (such as ASW or ASUW). In an uncertain world, which is increasingly dangerous, flexibility comes from having a full spectrum of capabilities, unless you are very certain of your alliance partners and their ability to assist you. In Britain's case, she has had to act alone in expeditionary warfare before (in the Falklands), and has been the chief player most recently in Sierra Leone. Financial realities mean that Britain will remain dependent on the US for provision of capabilities such as SEAD, but the Services need to guard against being too proud of their ability to do conflicts and other interventions on the cheap.

AIR POWER AND EXPEDITIONARY WARFARE

CHAPTER 9

RETHINKING THE CONCEPTUAL FRAMEWORK
Professor Tony Mason

IN THE LAST DECADE of the Century, air power has been used to great effect by western Coalitions in the Gulf War of 1990-91, in the later stages of the Bosnian conflict of 1995 and in the Kosovo Crisis in 1999. Not only have their circumstances been very different from those of the preceding period of confrontation between East and West, they have been very different from each other.

The collective difference between the circumstances of the 1990s and those of preceding periods stimulates the re-evaluation of several underlying concepts of air power which evolved during eighty years of air operations. The differences between the events of the 1990s themselves induce great caution in projecting conceptual frameworks or paradigms with validity for air power into the next Century. Nonetheless, alongside the differences in the circumstances of the 1990s, there have been significant similarities in achievements. From the similarities, a paradigm may be constructed which more clearly indicates, and explains, the overall contribution of western air power to contemporary defence and security policies.

At present, and for the foreseeable future, the full potential of modern air power can only be exercised by the United States. The new paradigm, however, is equally relevant to a state less well endowed than the US, or to a Coalition of states which did not include the USA.

THE INHERITANCE

Air power is a product of the 20th Century: a Century in which military evolution has been dominated by three wars which engulfed the globe. The first two were fought to bloody conclusions in 1914-18 and 1939-1945. The Cold War mercifully ended virtually bloodless after fifty years, with the collapse of the Soviet Union and its satellites. All three were fought with the instruments of the industrial age.

In the struggles of World War I and World War II, and in sustaining deterrence in the Cold War, attacks on civilian infrastructure and populations were widely accepted as unfortunate but inevitable, when national will, government control, national resources and armed forces were inextricably harnessed to total warfare. At the same time, images of Guernica, Coventry, Dresden and Hiroshima never disappeared, at least from media memory. Underlying all was a residual, albeit minority and controversial, unease at the legal and moral justification for air attacks which inflicted heavy civilian casualties. Such casualties, even in the well remarked instances, were far less than those endured in the ravaging of civilian populations by contending armies. Such comparisons, however, had little apparent effect on entrenched critics of air power.

Militarily, the 20th Century ended with the Gulf War of 1990-91. In Operation Desert Storm, the technology of the information age made its first dramatic impact in a conflict fought for limited objectives in one small geographical region. The technology was further refined in the unfamiliar surroundings of two very different wars in the Balkans. Air warfare throughout the last decade of the century, except in Chechnya, was conditioned by limited political objectives and the promise of precision munitions.

In the later stages of World War II, the United States came to possess the largest air forces in the world. There was not yet, however, a noticeable difference in the technology of aircraft, weapons and other systems from those of the United Kingdom, except for the possession of the atomic bomb. In the NATO years, the technology gap between the US and its allies progressively widened. Its dimensions, however, lay largely unrevealed because of the absence of alliance or coalition warfare and periods of long operational stagnation in the shadow of nuclear confrontation. In 1991, Operation Desert Storm revealed the real extent of United States' dominance in the air. There were now two kinds of air power: that wielded by the US, and the capacity of the rest. The distinction was no longer simply one of scale. The United States had crossed the threshold of the information age in air warfare, marked by stealth, precision guided munitions (PGM), information systems, and command, control and communications (C3).

Meanwhile, the Russian Federation rapidly became a spent military force, with little prospect of conventional arms regeneration in the foreseeable future. With one or two honourable exceptions, the United States' allies and putative coalition partners gave higher priority to consuming their post- Cold War peace dividends than to modernizing or restructuring their armed forces to meet new technological and international realities.

Together, these factors changed the nature of air power and its environment. As a result, concepts which evolved in a century of operations require scrutiny to ensure their continued validity.

GLOBAL WAR

'Global War', the environment in which air power matured, was defined in the Royal Air Force Manual of Operations, AP 1300, published in March 1957, as 'The unrestricted conflict between the USSR and its allies on the one side and the USA and its allies on the other. As the concept of global war envisages war without restrictions of any kind, it is unnecessary to qualify the term global war in any way. Throughout this manual it is, therefore, assumed that the kiloton and megaton nuclear weapons would be used from the outset.'[1]

Had a later Manual of Operations been published before 1989, the assumption of the use of nuclear weapons "from the outset" may have been dropped but not the nuclear dominance of strategy. In several fundamental respects, the 'Global War' envisaged in AP 1300 resembled World War I and Wolrd War II with the addition of nuclear weapons. For the major participants, national survival was at stake.

In World Wars I and II, national resources were harnessed and focused on the war effort. In Global War, similar conditions were expected but in a shorter time scale. In all three cases, 'victory' entailed, or would have entailed, the capitulation and submission of the enemy. There were no limits to resources allocated, no limits to casualties inflicted or endured and, with the exception of chemical warfare in World War II, no limits to the weaponry employed. On all sides the media was incorporated, with little or no demur, in support of national policy and to the favourable presentation of national operations.

In all three wars, the focus of the participants was on Central Europe, even after confrontation spread across the globe. The prize was territory. Strategies were ultimately directed at the occupation of territory by armies. Decision would be reached by the destruction of the enemy's capacity to resist by battle. The symbol of that resistance, despite attacks by air power and submarine warfare on a state's economic and political infrastructure, remained the enemy's deployed ground forces. Had deterrence failed, Central Europe would have become a nuclear battlefield.

The 1957 Manual defined 'Cold War' as simply 'the continuing world wide struggle between Communism and the Free World, waged by all means short of armed conflict.'[2] The Cold War was the Global War which was never fought. Other conflicts, described as 'Limited War' were defined by their relationship to Global War. 'The reasons which limit any particular conflict may be many and varied; but in the background will inevitably be the fear of the war becoming global in scope, and thus laying open the homelands of the Great Powers to nuclear devastation.'[3]

---

1. *Royal Air Force Manual of Operations* (Air Ministry: London, March 1957) ch. 1, para 5.
2. Ibid, para 7.
3. Ibid.

RETHINKING THE CONCEPTUAL FRAMEWORK

An RAF Phantom intercepts a Soviet Bear over the North Sea.
The Cold War was the Global War that was never fought.

Such a definition was perhaps a little simplistic. Nevertheless, the circumspection of the US in Korea and Vietnam, fears about Yugoslavia after Tito, and the tension induced by conflict in the Middle East in the 1960s and 1970s may be compared with the comparatively relaxed approaches of the great powers to the Gulf and the Balkans in the 1990s, when international confrontation had dissolved.

The end of the Cold War has restored traditional sources of conflict to international relations. Interests have replaced survival in the foreign and defence policies of the western powers and friends. All our foreseeable scenarios are of limited war and limited commitment. All our armed forces have to readjust to these new circumstances, but for air power, they are especially significant.

WARS OF THE NEW ERA

The Gulf War

The transition from three global wars was made in the Gulf in 1991. Here, the concepts of the Cold War met the realities of the new era. Coalition political and military objectives, to restore the independence of Kuwait and to expel Iraqi forces from its territory, were agreed by all Coalition members and empowered by the UN Security Council.

Seldom have circumstances combined so favourably for one side in a conflict. Command and control of Coalition forces, under US leadership, was unified and unambiguously directed. Iraq enjoyed little international support or sympathy. Saddam Hussein was strategically blinkered. His armed forces were stifled by Soviet doctrine and practice. His air force was heavily outnumbered and technologically inferior. His ground forces were deployed in open, largely uninhabited territory. His lines of reinforcement were highly vulnerable to air attack. The Coalition could exploit its massive supremacy in the air by attacking from the South, West and North. The Coalition air forces were well trained and well led. Coalition information dominance was overwhelming. Only his air defences presented a serious threat to the Coalition. His surface-to-surface missiles would threaten the unity of the alliance, by tempting independent Israeli retribution. Iraq's weapons of mass destruction would remain inert.

After Saddam Hussein was content to consolidate his position in Kuwait, in August 1990, and took no action to impede Coalition forces massing in the Gulf area, the Coalition determined the tempo of the confrontation. Poor weather slowed down the air campaign but had no influence on its outcome at the end of February 1991. Considerable synergy was achieved between air, land and naval forces.

It is likely that most of the significant facts about the Gulf War are now in the public domain. The impact of air power was greater than all but the most confident of believers could have imagined. Iraq, and its Soviet training mentors, were taken completely by surprise by the sustained intensity of the Coalition air attacks, sharpened in concentration by the combination of stealth and PGM. Iraqi air defences were neutralized, command and control almost decapitated and deployed ground forces cut off, demoralised and degraded. After forty-three days of incessant Coalition air attacks, Iraq's ground forces were expelled from Kuwait, not in 'the mother of all battles', but in a heavily one-sided four- day engagement. The war, as the present author later wrote, "marked the apotheosis of 20th Century air power."[4]

There was, naturally, widespread jubilation among air power enthusiasts about such an outcome. From the outset, however, there were extensive grounds for caution about projecting the air campaign of Desert Storm as a model for the future application of air power. The unusual combination of favourable circumstances which enabled the domination of air power in the Gulf War was not repeated in the remainder of that decade and is unlikely to re-occur in the next.

---

4. *The Air War in the Gulf,* Survival Vol. XXXIII, No 3, May/June 1991, p. 225.

RETHINKING THE CONCEPTUAL FRAMEWORK

Bosnia

In the Bosnian conflict, from 1992-1995, the circumstances were very different. For three years, the United Nations' humanitarian objectives co-existed uneasily with the need to coerce the combatants, and especially the Serbs, to agree to a peaceful resolution of the disputes. There was no consensus among potential Coalition members about either political objectives or the role and nature of military force. The humanitarian origins of the Bosnian intervention discouraged the early employment of combat aircraft. Command, control and authorisation of air power were convoluted and constrained by the duplication of UN and NATO structures. Rules of engagement, designed to reduce friendly and hostile force casualties, inhibited pre-emptive air attack and delayed retribution. Such factors aggravated the inherent difficulties for air power when combatants were frequently in close contact with civilians in either built-up areas or countryside which provided plenty of natural cover. Typical European weather produced some degree of cloud cover in the region for a large majority of the time.

In 1995 however, UN army and civilian units were withdrawn from vulnerable positions in Serb controlled territory. In the same period, Croatian and Bosnian Muslim ground forces increased their pressure on Bosnia Serb positions, while large scale NATO ground force deployments into the region began. For the first time in the conflict, joint force synergy could be achieved. After fourteen days of suffering intensive air attacks, the Bosnian Serbs accepted the Dayton Peace Accords.

Kosovo

In the third situation, in Kosovo in 1999, several of the features of the Bosnia conflict re-appeared. The topographical and climatic environment was very similar. While stopping Serbian persecution of ethnic Kosovars was widely supported within NATO, there was little agreement on the means to be adopted. The crisis unfolded, however, in a very different way from its predecessors.

Political and military objectives were defined, but without the clarity of those in the Gulf. NATO sought to persuade President Milosevic to put an immediate and verifiable end to violence, to withdraw all his troops from Kosovo, to agree to the deployment in Kosovo of an international force, to allow all refugees to return, and to accept an interim political solution.

Supreme Allied Commander Europe, General Wesley Clark, announced that "The military mission is to attack Yugoslav military and security forces and associated facilities with sufficient effect to degrade its capacity to continue repression of the civilian population and to deter its further military actions against his own people. We aim to put its military at risk. We are going to systematically and progressively disrupt, degrade, devastate and ultimately destroy those forces and support unless President Milosevic complies with the demands of the international community."[5]

After 78 days, only the 'objective of an interim political solution' remained outstanding. No NATO combat casualties had been suffered and in approximately 35,000 sorties, unintended Yugoslavian civilian casualties probably numbered less than 1,000. Yet, from the first days of the conflict, at the end of March 1999, there were rumbles of criticism of NATO's strategy, of the employment of air power and even of air power itself.

On 23 March, Pentagon spokesman Kenneth Bacon, in a Press briefing, announced, "We have plans for a swift and severe air campaign. This will be painful for the Serbs. We hope that, relatively quickly, ... the Serbs will realise that they have made a mistake."[6] But the initial weight of air attacks on Yugoslavia was, compared to that of the Gulf War, relatively light. In the first week, an average of 48 air strikes sorties a day were flown.[7] In Desert Storm, the overall daily rate was approximately 1,300. To a certain extent, the sortie rates reflected the numbers of combat aircraft deployed to the Balkan theatre compared to the Gulf: approximately 400 as opposed to 2,600.

However, not only was the weight of attack much less, but the targets attacked in 1999 were very different from those of 1991. In the Gulf, the well known opening 'parallel' attacks on air defence, political, infrastructure and other military targets were subsequently enshrined in official United States Air Force Doctrine: '.... aerospace power is usually employed to greatest effect in parallel, asymmetric operations. This includes precision strikes against surface forces, information attack against command and control systems, or precision strikes against infrastructure and centers of gravity.'[8] In the early days of the Kosovo conflict on the other hand, various air defence and military targets were attacked, including munitions factories and deployed Serbian forces in Kosovo. No attacks were made on political or other targets in Belgrade.

Reports of disagreements between NATO members about targeting began to reach the media by the beginning of April.[9] The official NATO position was defined by a Deputy Chief of the UK Defence Staff in the second week of the conflict: "NATO's plan had never envisaged beginning the air campaign with a massive application of air bombardment. This was not the start of a war where we were determined to win as quickly and as harshly as possible to overwhelm his entire military forces."[10]

---

5. NATO Briefing, Brussels, 25 March 1999.
6. Pentagon Briefing, Washington DC, 23 March 1999.
7. Daily Telegraph 2 April, 1999.
8. Air Force Doctrine Document 2, "Organisation and Employment of Aerospace Power", USAF, 28 September 1998, p. 6-7.
9. Daily Telegraph 1 April, 1999.
10. Air Marshal Sir John Day, Deputy Chief of Defence Staff UK, Press Briefing, 3 April 1999 as reported in the New York Times 4 April 1999.

The difference between NATO's position, summarised by Air Marshal Day, and the inclinations of many senior USAF airmen, was most succinctly illustrated by Lieutenant General Michael Short, Joint Forces Air Component Commander, in his statement to the Senate Armed Services Committee on 21 October 1999: "I believe the way to stop ethnic cleansing was to go to the heart of the leadership, and put a dagger in that heart as rapidly and decisively as possible .... I'd have turned the lights out on the first night. I'd have dropped the bridges across the Danube. I'd have hit five or six political and military Headquarters in downtown Belgrade ......"[11]

In interviews during the war, General Short had expressed similar opinions, raising the spectre of 'gradualism', the USAF memory of the air war in Vietnam. "Airmen," he said, "would like to have gone after that target set (Serbian leadership) on the first night and sent a clear signal that we were taking the gloves off from the very beginning, that we were not going to try a little bit of this and see how you like it and try a little bit of that and see how you like it."[12]

In Operation Allied Force, senior US airmen believed that NATO's air power should have been directed against the Serbian leadership from the outset.

---

11. Washington Post 22 October 1999 p. 14.
12. New York Times 13 May 1999

The 'gradualism' was well documented. On 31 March, General Clark requested an expanded range of targets.[13] On 2 April, targets in Belgrade were attacked, apparently for the first time. In the following week additional British and US combat aircraft were deployed into theatre before General Clark requested an additional 300 on 12 April.[14] On 6 April, oil targets were struck for the first time; on 8 April a warning of attacks on TV antennae and 'facilities' was given.[15] On 21 April, NATO spokesman Jamie Shea announced that "any aspect of Milosevic's power structure is a target."[16] On 23 April, Milosevic's official residence and a TV station were destroyed. On 2 May, the electricity grid was put out of action by carbon fibre sub-munitions. Meanwhile, attacks on deployed Serbian forces in Kosovo were also intensified, facilitated by improved weather and an increase from 120 to 550 strike aircraft.[17] On 27 May, NATO reported that 308 strike sorties had been flown, including 50 against Belgrade and 74 defence suppression.[18]

Near its conclusion, the air campaign was summarised by USAF Chief of Staff, General Michael Ryan. He observed, "The campaign did not begin the way that America would normally apply air power - massively striking at strategic centres of gravity that support Milosevic and his oppressive regime. A month into the campaign, it became apparent that a constrained, phased approach was not effective. NATO broadened the campaign to achieve strategic effects. The result is that Serbia's air force is essentially useless and its air defences are dangerous but ineffective. Military armament production is destroyed. Military supply areas are under siege. Oil refinement(sic) has ceased and petroleum storage is being systematically destroyed. Electricity is sporadic, at best. Major transportation routes are cut. NATO aircraft are attacking with impunity throughout the country. With the continued build up of aircraft and better weather, the attacks are intensifying and the effects are mounting."[19] In a post-war interview, the General added, "Air power could not stop the door to door thuggery and ethic cleansing that were going on directly. The only way you were going to be able to do that was by taking it to the heart of the matter - in this case, Belgrade."[20]

---

13. The Guardian 1 April 1999.
14. Daily Telegraph 13 April 1999.
15. Daily Telegraph 9 April 1999.
16. The Guardian 22 April 1999.
17. Air Force Magazine August 1999 p. 62.
18. The Guardian 28 May 1999.
19. Washington Post 4 June 1999.
20. Air Force Magazine, August 1999 p. 23.

By this time, there were widespread reports of anti-war sentiments within Yugoslavia and increased expectations of peace talks.[21] Nonetheless, the alliance's reliance upon air power as the only military instrument came under widespread fire. The general antithesis was that the contribution of ground forces would inevitably be required because air power had never won a war on its own.[22] Arguments ranged from the simplistic, 'In Vietnam, for example, the Air Force dropped some six million tons of bombs, almost triple the tonnage dropped in World War Two, without breaking the Vietnamese will to resist,'[23] through the more debatable, 'The challenge of just using air power is that you leave it in the hands of your adversary to decide when he's been punished enough. So the initiative will remain with President Milosevic',[24] to the well founded, 'Not having ground troops in place in the region not only permitted Milosevic to accelerate his ethnic cleansing, but precluded him from having to arrange Serbian defensive forces differently, to protect both northern and southern borders.'[25]

A rather diffident estimation of the contribution by the Kosovan Liberation Army to the final result came from US army sources: "What you have, in effect, was the KLA acting as a surrogate ground force. It was a confirmation, of sorts, of our joint doctrine, which calls for using air and ground forces together."[26] Others attributed Milosevic's capitulation to the assembly of the NATO Implementation Force in Macedonia, the dispatch of Apache helicopters to the theatre, and the threat of a ground invasion.

It was left to one of the most trenchant and inveterate British critics of air power to refute the pretenders to air power's achievements. John Keegan wrote, "After the war ..... there will be no grounds for debate or dispute. Aircraft and pilot-less weapons have been the only weapons employed. The outcome is, therefore, a victory for air power and air power alone".[27] In case any of his readers had missed the point, he followed up, two days later, "Already some of the critics of the war are indulging in ungracious revisionism, suggesting that we have not witnessed a strategic revolution and that Milosevic was humbled by the threat to deploy ground troops or by the processes of traditional diplomacy, in this case exercised - we should be grateful for their skills - by the Russians and the Finns. All to be said to that is that diplomacy had not worked before 24 March when the bombing started, while the deployment of a large ground force, though clearly

---

21. Eg Daily Telegraph 21 and 26 May, The Guardian 2 June 1999.
22. See Alan Stephens, 'Kosovo or the Future of War', *Air Power Studies Centre Paper* 77, p. 2-8, for a selective list of notable critics.
23. Colonel Harry Summers USA (retd), Washington Times 12 May 1999.
24. General Colin Powell USA (retd), in Press interview at Blackstock, Virginia, 3 April 1999.
25. Major General Charles Link USAF (retd), National Journal 8 May 1999.
26. An 'Army General', Washington Post 22 June 1999.
27. John Keegan, Daily Telegraph 4 June 1999.

a growing threat, would still have taken weeks to accomplish at the moment Milosevic caved in. The revisionists are wrong. This was a victory through air power."[28]

A similar sentiment was more circumspectly expressed by General Clark to the US Senate: "The Victory over Yugoslavia was the result of a variety of factors, but the indispensable condition for all the other factors was the success of the air campaign itself.....Everything else hinged on that." [29]

The conversion of a heretic is always a source of rejoicing, as long as it is accompanied by a broadening of the mind and not simply the replacement of one form of myopia by another. In fact, some earlier criticism of the air operations by John Keegan and others was accurately directed, if insecurely based.

THE ALLIANCE CONTEXT

The initial air attacks were light. Even had overwhelming force been available, the Alliance would have been reluctant to use it. After many months of prevarication and clear evidence of oppression in Kosovo by Milosevic's forces, some doubts remained about the legitimacy, purpose and extent of the use of force. At the outset of the conflict, British MOD media briefing notes included the comment, "Phased air operations (will be) conducted by Allied aircraft and UK and US cruise missile attacks. Phases could include a demonstration element, but, if no compliance, would extend progressively to military strikes throughout the FRY. The operations would be 'controlled, minimal and proportionate.' A possible NATO peace implementation force of 36,000 troops was being considered."[30]

There was no provision for an opposed Alliance ground force invasion because the members could not agree to mount one. As US Defence Secretary Cohen explained to the Senate Armed Services Committee, "Let me say that the reason that we have gone forward as we have with an air campaign is that there was not a consensus within the NATO alliance to do anything but this. There was a year - nearly a year, let me say three quarters of a year - spent dealing with the NATO allies in terms of taking collective action".[31] Six weeks later, nothing had changed, "The President said he would not take any option off the table, but it's clear to me that there would need to be a consensus. There is not a consensus for a major ground effort."[32]

---

28. John Keegan, Daily Telegraph 6 June 1999.
29. Quoted in John A Tirpak, "The NATO Way of War", *Air Force Magazine*, December 1999.
30. UK MOD Media Contributors' Briefing, 23 March 1999.
31. US Secretary of Defense William S Cohen, before Senate Armed Services Committee, 15 April 1999.
32. US Secretary of Defense William S Cohen, Department of Defense Briefing, Washington DC, 28 May 1999.

After the conflict, the British Chief of the Defence Staff described the frustrations and tensions within the Alliance during "the most complex political and military operation (I have) experienced in 40 years in the army .... It was an enormously complicated thing, with NATO's 19 member nations - each with its own political view and varying public opinion - having to agree by consensus ..... There were those who felt that the alliance would fall apart .... In the end, the ability of the alliance to remain united was pretty remarkable."[33]

The conflict began with a desire to end persecution in Kosovo. It ultimately threatened the existence of the NATO alliance itself. This was the overall context of the application of air power in the Kosovo crisis. It exposed air power adherents who have sometimes appeared to believe that military operations should not be constrained by political circumstances. Colonel John Warden predictably observed, "The way the air war has been designed suggests it was a very bureaucratised, compartmentalised and not very competent approach. The target list has clearly not been designed to have a systematic impact on the Serb forces.....This is very unprofessional on the part of the various political authorities."[34]

Colonel Phillip Meilinger offered a refreshingly direct and perceptive alternative view: "This air war is different than any we have ever fought. There is a feeling of frustration among the Air Force about the way it's going, but I say, 'Tough. Grow up. That's life.' We aren't in charge. The politicians are in charge because there are other larger considerations."[35] Colonel Meilinger was in good company. "No major proposal required for war," wrote Clausewitz, "can be worked out in ignorance of political factors; and when people talk, as they often do, about harmful political influence on the management of war, they are not really saying what they mean. Their quarrel should be with the policy itself."[36]

Nor were the larger considerations restricted to allies' political sensitivities. Italian and other European bases were essential for the prosecution of the air campaign. Allied airspace was used for several kinds of mission from multiple directions. Greek support was required for access to NATO's ground forces in Macedonia. Other than the USA, twelve NATO members contributed over 40% of NATO's bombing missions and 30% of the total.[37]

---

33. General Sir Charles Guthrie UK Chief of the Defence Staff, The Guardian 15 June 1999.
34. Colonel John Warden USAF (retd), Washington Post 16 May 1999.
35. Colonel Philip Meilinger, USAF, ibid.
36. Clausewitz, *On War*, Book Eight, Chapter Six, Howard and Paret, eds (Princeton 1976) p. 608.
37. "Washington Watch", Air Force Association, 10 June 1999 p. 1.

The operational penalties of the 'larger considerations' were identified by General Klaus Naumann, in the middle of the war, as he handed over his duties as Chairman of NATO's Military Committee: "Quite frankly and honestly, we did not succeed in our initial attempts to coerce Milosovic through air strikes to accept our demands, nor did we succeed in preventing Yugoslavia pursuing a campaign of ethnic separation and expulsion ....We need to find a way to reconcile the conditions of a coalition war with the principles of military operations, such as surprise and overwhelming force."[38]

From the outset, air power was the only military instrument available to NATO, and it was applied in the only way possible. The alternatives were not a replay of Instant Thunder from the Gulf or Rolling Thunder from Vietnam. The circumstances of this coalition war dictated that there were no alternatives at all. It was not "the condition of coalition war" *per se* which precluded "surprise and overwhelming force", as alleged by General Naumann, but one coalition which was not prepared to risk heavy casualties and costs either in pursuit of humanitarian objectives or to forestall a wider Balkan crisis. Just eight years previously, in very different circumstances in the Gulf, a coalition had required sensitive control and management, but surprise and overwhelming force had not been compromised.

The true extent of the success of the Kosovo action may be measured against two theoretical alternatives. The first would have entailed no military action against Milosevic at all. There is no evidence to suggest that ethnic cleansing of Kosovo would have been halted by diplomacy or by any other pressure and there remained a serious risk of an expanding Balkan war. The second alternative was of an opposed invasion by NATO ground forces at some unspecified later date. Assuming that sufficient troops could have been mustered, then transported and supplied over mountainous territory in winter, it is likely that Kosovo would have become a battleground of World War II proportions: all in a humanitarian cause. In comparison, the casualties and damage inflicted by NATO aircraft in Belgrade and elsewhere were small indeed.

GRADUALISM AND RESPONSIVENESS

Air power, like any other kind of military force, must be focused on, and subordinate to, a political objective defined by political leaders. Limited objectives imply limits on the military force applied. If a political objective falls short of destruction or overthrow of a government, or occupation of territory, or destruction of economic infrastructure or total annihilation of armed services, coercive military force will be limited. In Kosovo, there was for a time a mismatch between the level of force required to coerce Milosevic and

---

38. General Klaus Naumann, NATO Briefing, 4 May 1999, Daily Telegraph 5 May 1999.

the willingness of NATO to apply it. That is not a weakness of air power but of a political judgement about the use of armed force itself.

Nevertheless, the accusations of 'gradualism' in Kosovo, laid in many quarters against NATO planning staff, are well founded. Similarly, a widely held belief in the USAF that gradualism significantly weakened the US bombing campaign in Vietnam can be strongly argued. Undoubtedly, the pauses in the bombing campaign in Vietnam to allow diplomatic exchanges were exploited by the North Vietnamese to repair damage and reinforce defences. Prohibition of attacks on North Vietnamese airfields is difficult to understand.

A problem arises, however, if 'gradualism' as a principle is considered to be incompatible with the effective use of air power. Air power exponents consistently and justifiably uphold flexibility as its primary characteristic. It can be applied swiftly in different ways, against different targets, in different directions and over different distances. It is that flexibility which arguably makes air power even more suited to limited warfare than it was to the previous era of global, unlimited conflict. In a period of hesitant and unpredictable political commitment, the apparent weakness of air power - that it cannot sustain a presence - becomes a desirable attribute.

From a distance, air power can threaten, it can be applied, it can disengage. It can concentrate and it can select. It can be devastating on a large scale or it can, as in Iraq in 1981 or Libya in 1986, apply precise and limited force. Allied to such flexibility is speed, increasingly accelerated by the acquisition of relevant and timely information. The aggregate of those attributes is versatility and responsiveness, which enable air power to be swiftly coupled with a wide range of diplomatic activities and political decisions. Under these circumstances, gradualism becomes a significant and flexible option for the application of air power, not inferior to the high intensity 'parallel, asymmetric' operations incorporated in USAF doctrine.

If, however, air power is to be applied in cadence with diplomatic and other pressures, it becomes essential to ensure that the target state or entity is not allowed to take advantage of pauses in the cadence. In Vietnam the weakness lay not in an attempt to coordinate bombing and diplomacy, but in failing to prevent North Vietnam from exploiting the pauses and in the erroneous allocation of sanctuaries to its airforce. The problem was not the principle of gradualism, but the failure in practice to harness air power tightly to the diplomatic process. By contrast, in the later stages of the conflict in Bosnia, a combination of clearly drawn 'lines in the sand' and the close association of diplomatic pressure with the threatened destruction of Bosnian Serb war stocks, swiftly brought the conflict to an end without any need to 'go downtown Belgrade'.

The virtues of intensive parallel air attack have been credibly argued, and in Desert Storm powerfully demonstrated. But only in the opening hours of the highly favourable circumstances of the Gulf War has air power been used in the manner described by General Ryan. Such intensity will not always be possible, desirable or acceptable. If air power can indeed only be used effectively with overwhelming force, it is difficult to envisage its frequent application in a sensitive and complex political environment. The USA, even without the constraints of an entangling alliance, may not always see highly intensive 'parallel, asymmetric' attacks as a productive military instrument.

Conversely, if air power is flexibly applied in concert with diplomacy, it can finally enter the Clausewitzian lexicon. Moreover, air power will not be just one of 'the other means' which, in war, is added to 'political intercourse'[39] but increasingly will become 'the means' of first choice.

SHAPING THE ENVIRONMENT

Over the decade, air power's effectiveness in the very different environments of the Gulf, Bosnia and Kosovo has been based on a versatility hitherto only available in doctrine and theory. It has contributed to the resolution of conflict in three ways: by shaping an environment, by providing support to surface forces and by operating distinctly. These three contributions of air power are not new, nor are the roles which they include, but such a classification highlights its inherent versatility, put at risk by undue concentration on overwhelming parallel attack. By placing air operations in a different conceptual framework, air power's complete potential may be more easily recognised, explained and understood in a post-global war environment. Such a conceptual framework sits well in joint service or multi-national operations, and is relevant to many levels of engagement, from low level peace support to traditional large scale conflict.

Perhaps the most emphatic use of air power to shape an environment before the Gulf War occurred when allied air forces isolated and weakened German defences in Normandy prior to the invasion in June 1944. Now, the combination of information dominance, precision attack and effective control offers much greater strength. In the Gulf and in Bosnia in 1995, air power shaped an environment for surface forces to exploit, and denied an opponent the opportunity to fight on his terms. In the Gulf, the 'mother of all battles' disintegrated into large scale demoralisation and defeat. In Bosnia, conventional operations were inhibited and threats of partisan-style opposition were stifled by the severing of Bosnian Serb communications and destruction of war stocks.

Aerial preparation will exploit air power's reach, speed, penetration and concentration. Versatility can be exploited to attack political leadership, command and control and war stocks. The opponent's war-fighting capacity can be reduced by air attacks which deny him opportunities for concentration, manoeuvre, momentum and

---

39. Clausewitz, *On War*, Book Eight, Chapter Six, Howard and Paret, eds (Princeton 1976) p. 605

reinforcement. Air power used in this mode will, as in the Gulf, make the ensuing task of surface forces easier and cheaper, with reduced casualty risks and requiring smaller numbers for a given objective. This is an attractive proposition to politicians and one readily understood by tax-payers.

However, for air power to be employed for its maximum effectiveness in the 'Preparation' mode, it should be incorporated in a joint service plan from the outset, with surface movement coordinated with air operations rather than vice-versa. In Bosnia, without such coordination, surface force deployment actually inhibited air operations for many months, creating hostages rather than synergy.

The overall contribution of air power in shaping the environment is to determine the extent and nature of the battle-space. It now extends Theatre-wide beyond the reach of ground or littoral forces. It is no longer the space above and behind an enlarged, old fashioned battlefield. Traditional battlefield fronts, lines, edges, depths and formations will become increasingly rare. Potential opponents will note the vulnerability to air power of conventionally deployed armies. As in the Balkans, 'expeditionary' governments will be reluctant to expose their own ground forces in large numbers to unpredictable opposition on hostile territory. Under these circumstances there are opportunities to create new joint service synergies by the exploitation of air power by ground forces.

SUPPORT

Traditionally, the synergy of joint service operations has been most obvious in direct air support of surface forces engaged in a traditional ground force engagement. It was effective in the Gulf War; much less so at first in Bosnia, for well rehearsed reasons of conflicting objectives, unrealistic constraints and convoluted command and control. In Kosovo, except for attacks on Serbian forces deployed against the KLA in the closing stages of the conflict, close air support of any kind was not required.

The Kosovo experience suggested that difficulties long associated with direct air support may increase if the traditional battlefield is replaced by less definable, more fluid engagements. Discrimination between friendly and hostile ground forces in close contact has always been difficult, even with good visibility, definable 'front lines' and local air control. In theory, precision attack capability reduces these problems. Ground forces however, when threatened by air attack, have quickly learned the value of proximity to non-combatants, rapid movement, small numbers and concealment. In Kosovo, the Serbs never had to confront an invading NATO force, but even had they done so, there is no guarantee that they would have obligingly taken up formal defence positions. The lessons of the Gulf War have been studied by many countries.

RETHINKING THE CONCEPTUAL FRAMEWORK

That said, while direct fire support may in some circumstances be problematical, protecting friendly forces from air attack, inhibiting hostile manoeuvre, concentration and reconnaissance and providing tactical airlift and re-supply will remain significant air power contributions to deployed surface forces. Airborne surveillance and PGM availability offer the Joint Force Commander far more options than his predecessors. Deeper vision, earlier warning and swifter communication will enable him to deploy both his ground and supporting air assets far more effectively. Hopefully, such roles will have been largely discharged in an earlier phase of aerial preparation of the battle-space. In both preparation and direct support, the roles are likely to have been carried out by similar aircraft or UAVs, with similar weapons and systems.

DISTINCT OPERATIONS

In Kosovo, air power was NATO's sole military instrument. In traditional language, it was 'independent' of activity by naval or ground forces. Unfortunately, the term 'independent' has associations which may impede, rather than enhance, air power's versatility in the post-Global War age.

The British decision in 1917 to create an independent Royal Air Force flowed directly from the failure of the two existing air services, the Royal Flying Corps and the Royal Naval Air Service, to provide adequately for the nation's home defence. At a most critical period of the war, the previous separation of the flying services was widely perceived to have generated wasteful duplication of procurement, training, infrastructure and operations to the detriment of activities not directly associated with the immediate needs of the Army and the Royal Navy.

The Second Smuts Report of 17th August 1917 established the Royal Air Force. It explained how, unlike artillery for example, "Air Service .... can be used as an independent means of war operations far from, and independently of, both Army and Navy ....The day may not be far off when aerial operations, with their devastation of enemy lands and destruction of industrial and populous centres on a vast scale, may become the principal operations of war ...."[40]

Such a capability for air power lay far into the future, but up to that point Smuts's comments were visionary and positive. Unfortunately, the sentence concluded with the words "to which the older forms of military and naval operations may become secondary and subordinate." By implication, air operations in support of armies and navies were also 'secondary' and 'subordinate'. First for the Royal Air Force, and later for the USAF, 'independent operations' became synonymous with 'independence'.

---

40. Appendix II to Cabinet Minutes (WC 233) 24th August 1917. See the present writer's *Air Power, A Centennial Appraisal* (Brassey's 1994) p. 20-27, for a more detailed appraisal of the Smuts Report.

RETHINKING THE CONCEPTUAL FRAMEWORK

In an age of coalitions and joint service components in expeditionary forces, there is a need to distinguish, carefully and publicly, between the need for an independent armed service whose professional raison d'etre is the military exploitation of air and space, and the misunderstanding that such independence depends upon a requirement for 'independent' operations.

There are good grounds, therefore, to replace 'independent' by 'distinct' to describe air operations which are not accompanied by, or related to, surface or maritime action. The Oxford Dictionary definition of 'distinct' is most appropriate: 'Different in kind, unmistakable, positive.' Thereby, the mind-set, which instinctively associates 'independence' with 'independent' action, can be broken. Consequently, 'support' or 'preparation' operations become 'complementary', and not 'subordinate' to action by armies or navies.

In the past, 'distinct' operations have ranged from the Strategic Bomber Offensive against Germany, with its considerable influence not just on the German war effort but on surface operations elsewhere, to the pre-emptive Israeli attack on Osirak in 1981, or the punitive US attack on Libya in 1986.

In some respects, air power in Kosovo was a victim of its earlier success in the Gulf and Bosnia. It is difficult to exaggerate the impact of PGMs on air power in the last decade of the Century. Their operational cost effectiveness has been widely documented. They reduce the number of aircraft and weapons required to achieve a particular kill or destruction probability. That reduction may be taken back through numbers of air crew, numbers of ground crew, amount of infrastructure and support staff, fuel, logistics and, indeed, to all aspects of force size, shape and costs. But their well publicised impact in the Gulf War also coincided with a reassertion of humanitarian values in warfare, and with the unprecedented, international exposure by the media of war's individual tragedies and brutalities. In these circumstances, the PGM has been welcomed as the harbinger of sanitised, bloodless conflict. Ironically, the technology which, more than any other, has realised the promise of air power, is now stimulating a further level of expectation from believers which is likely to be at least as difficult to fulfil as its predecessor.

In Bosnia, the impact of air power was delayed by lack of UN consensus and political determination. Consequently, the Bosnian Serbs were not inhibited from escalation nor coerced to serious negotiations until operation Deliberate Force was launched in August 1995. The Kosovo experience reinforces the requirement in limited war, whether in coalition or not, to apply force commensurate with the objectives to be achieved and with considerations of post conflict reconstruction and rehabilitation. Dropping the Danube bridges may or may not have delivered a message to President Milosevic but the attacks certainly blocked one of Europe's most important trade arteries and damaged the economies of several countries dependent upon it.

Modern air power can attack strengths or weaknesses beyond the reach, capacity and responsiveness of friendly surface and naval forces. In the previous era, 'strategic bombing' was a blunt instrument. Now, in distinct operations, PGMs have transformed the bludgeon into a rapier which, on many occasions, may be wielded directly in support of policy with a fraction of the resources previously required. It may be brandished for deterrence or coercion. It may be inserted or withdrawn in cadence with diplomatic and other coordinated pressures. Distinct, direct air action can be taken at all levels, from response to state-inspired terrorism to specific strikes in large scale conflicts. Its targets may range from the centre of government to an isolated and otherwise inaccessible terrorist training base.

An air force which is known to have a long reach, with or without flight refuelling, can directly influence policy by its very existence. An increase in alert states and augmentation of front line personnel are the modern equivalent of Mahan's 'fleet in being', except that diplomacy may now be supported without the expense of surface deployment. Deterrence by air power is as relevant to peace inducement as it is to major nuclear or conventional confrontation, provided it is accompanied by a manifest determination to use it, if necessary.

Tornado F3s refuelling from a VC10. An air force which is known to have a long reach can directly influence policy by its very existence.

Nor are distinct operations associated solely with combat. Perhaps the most influential uses of air power in the entire Cold War period were the Berlin airlift, which determined the political shape of Europe, and strategic reconnaissance, which continuously informed western political and strategic decisions. In activities such as disaster relief, the monitoring of treaties and the early identification of crises, contributions may now be less spectacular, but they are still powerful projectors of the national or cooperative interest.

COMMAND OF THE AIR

Within an overall conceptual framework, the oldest and most enduring air power concept, 'command of the air', also requires re-examination in the light of recent experience. At Chicago in 1893, Major Fullerton observed that "command of the air would be an essential prerequisite for all land and air warfare."[41] In 1911, in the first article on air power in the Journal of the Royal United Services Institute, Captain C J Burke of the British Army Air Battalion wrote: "As aeroplanes employed on (such) reconnaissance duties will encounter hostile aeroplanes with a similar mission to themselves, ...one must be prepared for a struggle between hostile aeroplanes, similar in its object to the struggle between the independent cavalries of two hostile armies".[42] In that same year however, the first battle damage sustained by aircraft came from Turkish troops firing on Italian aircraft over Tripoli. From the outset, command of the air would also be challenged from the ground.

Opinions about how to achieve 'command of the air' would vary, but all would focus on combat between aircraft. Trenchard believed in the offensive, against enemy aircraft on the ground and over their own lines.[43] Churchill also envisaged 'real mastery of the air' in 1918 by exploiting an expected allied numerical superiority of aircraft.[44]

In World War I, 'Archie' (anti-aircraft guns) exacted a heavy toll on allied aircraft, but it was the fighter pilots who passed into legend, which was reinforced in World War Two. 'Command of the air' came to denote a degree of control which allowed one side to operate with little or no enemy interference in a theatre of war while denying the

---

41. Cited in A F Hurley, in the Appendix "Additional Insights" to *Billy Mitchell, Crusader for Air Power* (Indiana: University Press, Bloomington 1975) p. 142.
42. Captain C J Burke, "Aeroplanes of Today and Their Use in War", *Journal of the Royal United Services Institute*, May 1911, p. 626.
43. Eg RFC HQ memo, 22 September 1916, cited by present author in *Readings in Air Power* (Bracknell 1980) p. 171.
44. W S Churchill, "Munitions Possibilities of 1918", Memorandum 21 October 1917, cited in Emme, *The Impact of Air Power* (Van Nostrand 1959) p. 40.

opponent similar opportunities. The diminutives, "favourable air situation" and "air superiority" suggested limitations of time or space on "command". In each case, however, the concept denoted a relationship between aircraft. Despite the lethality of German surface-to-air defences in North West Europe, for example, command of the air continued to be measured by defeating the enemy air force, either in the air or on the ground.

In 1960, the shooting down of Gary Powers's U2 near Sverdlovsk focused attention on the impact of the guided surface-to-air missile (SAM). Western responses were to switch to low-level offensive operations and to accelerate the acquisition of defence suppression measures. In South East Asia, the strength of the North Vietnamese air defences stimulated the creation of the USAF's Wild Weasel role. It was estimated that surface-to-air defences accounted for 85% of all USAF losses during the Vietnam War, including 637 shot down over North Vietnam.[45] In 1973, the Israeli Air Force was surprised and seriously wounded by the coordinated medium and low-level air defences deployed by Egypt and Syria at the outset of the October War.

Heavy aircrew losses in the two World Wars were accepted by grieving populations as a sacrifice justified by the immensity of the cause. In the nuclear shadows of the Cold War, potential casualties were seldom mentioned, but their scale may be assumed. But as protection of interests replaced national survival, the sacrifice in war of human lives was re-evaluated in western democracies. When protection of interests was itself followed by more nebulous humanitarian motivation, sensitivity to casualties would begin to shape operational behaviour.

By the time of the Gulf War in 1990-91, the attitude of the USA to casualties was no longer that of World Wars One and Two. Memories of losses in Korea and later in Vietnam were to influence political and military considerations about casualties in a conflict which, initially at least, did not receive unqualified public support in the USA.

Among many relevant comments was General Horner's on the 7th February 1991, when he "stressed that American support at home for the war depended in large measure on the ability to operate 'with less than anticipated' losses of human lives among Coalition airmen, soldiers, sailors and Marines".[46] In Washington, Congressman Lee Hamilton, Democratic Chairman of the House of Representatives sub-committee on European and Middle Eastern affairs, warned, "Saddam Hussein does not need to win the war; he doesn't need to win the battles. All he needs to do is keep this war going and

---

45. Directorate of Management Analysis, USAF Management Summary: Southeast Asia Review, 30 June 1973, quoted in Keaney and Cohen, *Revolution in Warfare?* (Naval Institute Press 1995) p. 52.
46. Quoted by Keaney and Cohen from the Checkmate Historian's File, *Chain of Command*, Op Cit, p. 53.

to create casualties. If he does that over a period of time, then you are going to see an erosion of support for the war. That is a worst case scenario."[47]

In one sense, the lessons had been learned by the time of the Gulf War. The massive attacks on Iraq's air defence network and destruction of those IQAF aircraft foolhardy enough to attempt opposition led General Schwarzkof to declare after three days that Coalition air superiority had been achieved.

This was not strictly accurate. Control of the air had been established only against Iraqi aircraft and only above the range of low-level air defences. It was estimated that 16,000 SAM and 7,000 anti-aircraft guns were deployed throughout Iraq and occupied Kuwait.[48] Destruction of the integrated air defence system degraded the effectiveness of medium- and high-level SAM, but the sheer volume of mobile and hand-held SAM, plus AA guns, restrained low-level Coalition attacks until the end of the war. Throughout Desert Storm, most Coalition sorties took place above 10,000 feet except for attacks by A10 aircraft on Iraqi forces deployed near to the Kuwait-Saudi Arabian border.[49]

Nonetheless, fighter pilots' preoccupation with other fighter pilots died hard. Eight years later, General Horner wrote, "AAA and SAMs were dangerous, but the most lethal threat to our attack was the enemy's interceptor aircraft". He then allocated four pages of careful analysis to explain how easily, in the event, that threat had been overcome.[50]

The Coalition was, however, so superior in aircraft numbers and quality, in weapons, in aircrew skills, in electronic warfare, in strategy, in tactics, in training and in leadership, and Iraqi ground forces so vulnerable, that conceding the lower air space to Iraqi air defences had little or no impact on the outcome of the Gulf War. The overall loss rate of Coalition aircraft was approximately one fixed-wing aircraft in 1800 sorties. At most, only one aircraft was lost to Iraqi fighters, in a 33-to-1 exchange, but 32 out of 38 Coalition losses were attributed to Iraq's surface-to-air defences.

Circumstances were different in the two Balkan conflicts, when national interests among Coalition members became mixed with humanitarian considerations. As the first Balkan crisis unfolded in Bosnia between 1992 and 1995, disagreements over the use of air power were aggravated by the priorities afforded to force protection by air and ground force commanders. In June 1995, a single F16 was shot down by an SA 6 missile. The pilot was recovered safely but the USAF commander readjusted his combat patrol routes away from hostile SAM range. In this same conflict, a British Defence Secretary asserted that, "our primary responsibility as the United Kingdom is obviously the safety

---

47. Cited in Philip M Taylor, *War and the Media, Propaganda and Persuasion in the Gulf War* (Manchester 1992) p. 26.
48. Richard P Hallion, *Storm over Iraq* (Smithsonian 1992) p. 147.
49. Clancy/Horner, *Every man a Tiger* (Putnam 1991) p. 479-482.
50. Ibid, p. 554-558.

of our own forces (ground troops)."[51] Such well-publicised Coalition sensitivity to casualties relayed encouraging messages to the Bosnian Serbs but still did not affect the final impact of air power.

In the Kosovo crisis of 1999, there were insufficient aircraft to launch parallel attacks on air defences and deployed forces powerful enough to induce shock or paralysis. Priority was, in the traditional manner, given to achieving control of the air, while attacks on deployed Serbian forces were made from medium level for reasons of force protection. Moreover, there is strong circumstantial evidence to suggest that Coalition concern about friendly casualties was even more acute than during the Bosnian crisis. NATO Commander General Wesley Clark was reported as issuing a 'no loss of aircraft' restriction in November 1998.[52] Lieutenant General Short subsequently denied receiving such an order, but acknowledged that "zero losses were a major goal."[53]

Now, however, the operational circumstances were very different. In the Gulf War, Iraqi armour and other ground forces had been largely deployed in open terrain well away from civilian settlements. There had been no crescendo of persecution in Kuwait. In 1999, the world watched as Serbian repression accelerated in Kosovo, apparently impervious to NATO air power. Serbian forces were mobile and mingled with the population they were persecuting. General purpose unguided munitions could only be used when there was no risk of collateral damage or civilian casualties. The biggest single technological advantage possessed by NATO lay in its PGM, which also promised maximum target discrimination. But targets were frequently obscured by low cloud and bad weather. Even in clear skies, with considerable care, distinguishing between military and civilian vehicles in convoys from medium altitude proved difficult.

Yugoslavia was reported to have fifteen MiG 29s and forty-seven MiG 21s at the outbreak of the Kosovo crisis. Of these, fourteen and twenty-four respectively were destroyed. By contrast, the US Department of Defence subsequently reported that NATO aircrew observed almost 700 firings of various SAMs.[54] Even then, it appears that the air defence operators, well aware of their vulnerability to counter-attack from anti-radiation missiles, were reluctant to maintain illumination or guidance for any length of time. As a result, in the words of General Ryan, Serbia's air defences remained "dangerous but ineffective". Not surprisingly, one of the earliest 'lessons' to be drawn by the USAF from the air campaign in Kosovo was the shortage of dedicated SEAD aircraft

---

51. UK Secretary of State for Defence, Malcolm Riffkind, Press Conference Transcript, London 14 January 1993.
52. Washington Post 30 May 1999.
53. "Washington Watch", Air Force Association, 10 June 1999, p. 5.
54. Air Force Magazine August 1999, p. 61.

and electronic warfare systems.[55] General Ryan observed, "To do any kind of military activity, whether that's air or ground, we absolutely must have air superiority."[56]

Handfuls of MiGs and Sukhois, a few advanced western aircraft and weapons inherited by unfriendly governments, even a handful of obsolescent Galebs could make life unpleasant for civilians or unprotected ground forces. Indeed, no expeditionary force, and especially one drawn only from European air forces, could afford to ignore any air-to-air threat. But the prospect of any opponent in the foreseeable future offering a serious challenge in the air to a western operation by a coalition led by the US using air power as its primary instrument is very remote.

On the other hand, the proliferation and evolution of SAM continue unabated. Systems such as the S300 series, SA14, SA16, SA18, Stingers, Rolands and other widely circulating western missiles supplement residual Cold War stocks. They are cheap and readily available for countries and factions who have the political will, but not the military capacity, to challenge the US and friends in the air. Their function is not to secure military victory, but to inhibit air power effectiveness and to threaten unacceptable levels of casualties. So far in this decade, they have been more successful than they have been given credit for.

Tornado GR1 with ALARM. Air-to-air superiority over hostile aircraft remains imperative, but SEAD should be given equal priority.

---

55. Interview in Air Force Magazine, ibid, p. 23.
56. Interview in Air Force Magazine, p. 25.

RETHINKING THE CONCEPTUAL FRAMEWORK

Superiority over hostile aircraft remains imperative, but the conflicts in this decade have demonstrated that defence suppression should be given as much priority in procurement, planning, and training as other more traditional offensive operations. Otherwise, while we may still be able to deny an opponent opportunities to use his air power, we may not be able to exploit our own. Command of the air has, since the days of Captain Burke, been a means to an end, not an end in itself. Moreover, superiority is no longer required simply to operate, but now to operate with minimal or no casualties. That innovation, if sustained, has considerable implications for the effectiveness of air power. In the dynamic operational environment of Kosovo, because there were insufficient assets to achieve air superiority and to inhibit Serbian ground forces at the same time, the latter retained the initiative for several weeks. On this occasion, giving priority to gaining such a degree of air superiority weakened, rather than enhanced, air operations elsewhere. When, in addition, concern about aircrew casualties inhibited the use of PGMs below medium level, the total impact on air operations of modern surface to air defences could be clearly seen.

In sum, if air power is to fully exploit its versatility across the spectrum of 21st Century conflict, the fundamental concept of command of the air is now even more important. Political sensitivity to casualties suggests that it continues to be given the highest priority. If the prospect of single-figure casualties should ever become a deterrent to the use of air power, the instrument of choice will be neutralized. Without air power, the *opposition* will be freed to determine the conditions of the battle-space. These are good grounds for re-emphasising the fundamental concept of command of the air and, after almost a century, for elevating defence suppression to the same priority as the fighter aircraft.

THE OBSOLESCENCE OF STRATEGIC AND TACTICAL DISTINCTION

Finally, while command of the air is still an essential and meaningful concept, the equally venerable distinction between the expressions 'strategic' and 'tactical' to identify different kinds of operations is no longer quite so helpful. It may indeed be argued that the distinction has frequently inhibited the most effective application of air power and, in the new international environment, has lost its utility altogether. The distinction originated in World War One to distinguish between direct attacks on an enemy's heartland and direct support of surface forces.[57] After World War II the concept was formally identified in the United States' Strategic Bombing Survey.

---

57. Eg John Terraine, *The Right of The Line* (Sceptre 1988) p. 9.

RETHINKING THE CONCEPTUAL FRAMEWORK

Subsequently, strategic air power became synonymous with long-range nuclear attack on the USSR, the role allocated to Strategic Air Command. Tactical air power was used in Theatres such as Korea or Europe. Strategic air operations were defined in the USAF as attacks 'designed to disrupt an enemy nation to the extent that its will and capability to resist are broken'. Such operations 'are conducted directly against the nation itself rather than its deployed armed forces.'[58] In contrast, theater or tactical operations were conducted in a confined geographical area with the objective of destroying or neutralising the enemy's military forces.[59] The distinction persisted to absurdity with the advent of tactical nuclear weapons deployed by both sides in Europe.

In 1999, General Horner contributed a typically rumbustuous critique of the terms in his reflections on the Gulf War. 'More recently', he wrote, '"strategic" has come to mean nuclear strikes against the Soviet Union, or other powerful enemies, and "tactical" all other forms of warfare... I don't understand tactical or strategic. The words have become meaningless and dysfunctional. In fact, in modern military speech, they are more often used to divide people and frustrate efforts than to illuminate and facilitate.'[60] As General Homer's comments imply, there are more reasons to re-evaluate the concepts of strategic and tactical air power than mere pedantry or fashionable revisionism.

Strategic effect, in the sense of bringing pressure to bear on an opponent's decision-making process, remains a primary task of offensive air power. Now, however, it can be achieved by tactical F117s as well as by B2s. Within the theatre battle-space, any air attack which has a direct impact on that decision-making process justifies the appellation strategic. It could be against the Iraqi Republican Guard, Bosnian Serb war stocks or oil refineries in Yugoslavia. In Kosovo it could have been to inflict unacceptable losses among Serbian ground forces or unacceptable damage to the infrastructure of the state. The accurate identification of the most productive and accessible pressure point to achieve strategic effect becomes an even more important precursor to operations.

When the confines of a theatre of operations are commensurate with the boundaries of the conflict as a whole, General Horner's criticism is thoroughly well founded. The terms strategic and tactical have little further to contribute to the understanding of air power's contemporary versatility. They may be confidently subsumed in the more helpful categorisation of roles which prepare an operational environment for surface force exploitation, or directly support surface forces or contribute distinctly to coercive diplomacy.

---

58. USAF Manual 1-8, "Strategic Air Operations", 1 May 1954, p. 2 and 6, cited in Clodfelter, *The Limits of War* (Free Press/MacMillan 1989) p. 28 and 29.
59. USAF Manual 1-7 March 1954, cited Clodfelter, ibid, p. 30.
60. Clancy/Horner, *Every man a Tiger* (Putnam 1991) p. 15.

BEYOND THE MILLENNIUM

Technology has transported air power from the industrial to the information age. For those states which may choose air power as their preferred military instrument, survival has been replaced as a primary security concern by the protection and projection of interests, tinged with hesitant humanitarian aspirations. A great deal of positive revision of air power doctrine has already taken place in the last decade to ensure that intellectual mastery of air power's new environment is sustained.

There is, however, a danger that the malign shadow of Douhet will be cast over the next millennium. There can be no single template for the successful application of air power. The versatility of air power application is as wide as the spectrum of conflict itself and the range of political objectives being pursued. There is now the need and opportunity to revisit some well worn ideas and construct a conceptual paradigm appropriate to many different scenarios, in which air power can sustain coercive diplomacy and become a primary instrument reinforcing the ongoing political dialogue. Thereby, it may sometimes act distinctly and directly, with overwhelming strength or more gradually, against an opponent's will to resist. On other occasions it may shape an environment for others to exploit. Elsewhere, it may protect and enhance other forces. These are contributions which can be made nationally or in coalitions, whatever the size and capacity of air forces. Provided air power is released from its strands of dogmatic inheritance, it can cross the millennium as a most versatile, effective, comprehensible and politically attractive military option.

BIOGRAPHIES

PROFESSOR M CLARKE

Professor Michael Clarke is the Director of the Centre for Defence Studies at King's College London. He has previously been a teacher of international politics at the Universities of Aberystwyth, Manchester and Newcastle upon Tyne, and has also taught at the University of New Brunswick, and the Open University. He has been a Guest Fellow at the Brookings Institution, Washington, DC, and a Fellow in Foreign Policy Studies at the Royal Institute of International Affairs in London. He is presently a specialist Advisor to the House of Commons Defence Committee.

DOCTOR D GATES

Doctor David Gates was recently the Deputy Director of The Centre for Defence and International Security Studies at Lancaster University, having previously been the MoD Lecturer in Defence Studies at Aberdeen University. One of the relatively few academics who specialise in both military history and contemporary strategic studies, he holds a doctorate from Oxford University, is a Fellow of the Royal Historical Society, and has held Visiting Fellowships at the Miltärgeschichtliches, Gonville and Caius College and The Centre of International Studies, Cambridge University. His numerous books and other publications include several pieces on air power topics.

WING COMMANDER D J CADDICK

Wing Commander David Caddick joined the Royal Air Force Regiment in 1979 and has served in a wide variety of posts in the United Kingdom and overseas. These include operational deployments to Northern Ireland, command of the Queen's Colour Squadron of the Royal Air Force and staff appointments in the MOD, Headquarters Strike Command and the Permanent Joint Headquarters.

He holds a BA(Hons) in International Relations and Geography from North Staffordshire Polytechnic, a Master of Letters in Strategic Studies from the University of Aberdeen and a Master of Arts with distinction in Defence Studies from King's College London. He is also a graduate of the Joint Services Advanced Command and Staff Course. He was the winner of the 1998 Bertrand Stewart Prize Essay competition and the 1999 Sir Michael Howard Prize from Kings College.

He has previously had work published in various Regimental Journals, the British Army Review and Air Power Review.

BIOGRAPHIES

PROFESSOR P A G SABIN

Philip Sabin is Professor of Strategic Studies at the Department of War Studies, King's College London. He serves as Director of Defence Education within the War Studies Group, and has played a leading role in King's College's growing involvement with the British Staff Colleges, culminating in its assumption of full responsibility for academic support at the new Joint Services Command and Staff College at Watchfield in 2000. Professor Sabin has published widely on modern defence issues, including in the previous two volumes produced by this workshop. At the other chronological extreme, he also teaches and researches extensively on Greek and Roman warfare!

SIR TIMOTHY GARDEN

Tim Garden read Physics at Oxford and joined the RAF in 1963. His opeational flying tours have included both tactical and strategic bombers, a period as a flying instructor, and a tour commanding a helicopter base. In mid career he took a Cambridge International Relations degree before becoming Director of Defence Studies for the RAF. His many Whitehall appointments included a period on the Air Force Board as Assistant Chief of the Air Staff and then as the Assistant Chief of the Defence Staff responsible for planning the defence programme. He was Commandant of the Royal College of Defence Studies, and then Director of the Royal Institute of International Affairs at Chatham House until mid 1998. He was a member of the UK government panel of experts for the strategic defence review. He has written for many years on foreign and security policy issues, and is the Defence Editor of The Source.

BIOGRAPHIES

AIR COMMODORE S W PEACH

Stuart Peach joined the Royal Air Force in 1977. A graduate of the universities of Sheffield and Cambridge, the Royal Air Force Staff College and the UK Higher Command and Staff Course, he has lectured and written widely on air power and related subjects. He is the author of the current edition of AP3000, British Air Power Doctrine. He was Director of Defence Studies (Royal Air Force) from 1997 to 1999, the creator and first Managing Chairman of the Royal Air Force Air Power Review and editor of Perspectives on Air Power. He has completed six operational tours, four in the Middle East and two in the Balkans and has held operational command appointments in every RAF rank from Flight Lieutenant to Air Commodore. He is a qualified weapons instructor and electronic warfare instructor and has 20 years fast jet flying experience with a total of 2750 flying hours. At the time of publication, he is serving as Commandant Air Warfare Centre, Air Officer for Doctrine and Collective Training, Headquarters Strike Command and UK Director of the Defence Electronic Warfare Centre, RAF Waddington.

BRIGADIER R A M S MELVIN

Brigadier Mungo Melvin was born in 1955 and commissioned into the Royal Engineers in 1975. He has seen regimental service and staff employment in the United Kingdom, Germany, the Balkans, the Middle East, Africa and Central America. On promotion to Colonel in 1997 he was appointed Colonel Defence Studies and Director of the British Army's Strategic and Combat Studies Institute (SCSI). Having completed the Higher Command and Staff Course at the Joint Services Command and Staff College in 1998 he became the course's Deputy Director, and the United Kingdom's facilitator on the SHAPE HILEX programme. Brigadier Melvin wrote the British Army's doctrine on command in 1994 and edited the SCSI series of Occasional Papers during 1997-98. He has contributed to a wide variety of military and academic studies, including the forthcoming Oxford Companion to Military History and the Fitzroy Dearborn Reader's Guide to Military History. He is currently involved in two further military historical projects.

BIOGRAPHIES

DOCTOR C GOULTER

Christina Goulter took first-class honours in History at the University of Canterbury, New Zealand, and was awarded a PhD at King's College, University of London in 1993. She worked for two years as a historian in the Ministry of Defence, Air Historical Branch (RAF) before becoming the Associate Visiting Professor of Strategy at the United States Naval War College, Newport, Rhode Island. In 1997 she became a Senior Lecturer at the United Kingdom Joint Services Command and Staff College.

AIR VICE-MARSHAL PROFESSOR R A MASON

Air Vice-Marshal Professor Tony Mason is Director of the Centre for Studies in Security and Diplomacy at the University of Birmingham. He retired from the Royal Air Force in 1989 where his last appointment was Air Secretary. He is a graduate of the USAF Air War College and of the Royal Air Force Staff College. For over 20 years Air Vice-Marshal Mason has published and spoken worldwide to universities and military colleges on air power in warfare and international security. His 12 books include 'Air Power in the Nuclear Age' (with Sir Michael Armitage), 'War in the Third Dimension', 'Air Power: A Centennial Appraisal' and 'The Aerospace Revolution: Revised Roles and Technology'. In recent years he has contributed to studies for the Royal Air Force, United States Air Force, German, Australian, New Zealand, Netherlands, Norwegian, Swedish, Indian, South Korean and Thai Air Forces. Since the Gulf War, AVM Mason has been a frequent analyst for the BBC, ITN, CNN and other media on air related international security issues.